CHINA: A LITERARY COMPANION

CHINA
A Literary Companion

A.C. Grayling
and
Susan Whitfield

JOHN MURRAY

© A.C. Grayling and Susan Whitfield 1994

First published in 1994
by John Murray (Publishers) Ltd.,
50 Albemarle Street, London W1X 4BD

The moral right of the authors has been asserted

A catalogue record for this book is available
from the British Library

ISBN 0-7195-5353-9

Typeset in 12½/12½pt Bembo by Colset Private Ltd, Singapore
Printed and bound in Great Britain by
Biddles Limited, Guildford and King's Lynn

To our nieces
Gemma
Catherine and Toni

CONTENTS

ILLUSTRATIONS

The authors and publishers would like to thank Alastair Morrison for his kind permission to reproduce Plates 1, 2, 4 and 9, all photographs by Hedda Morrison; and the Central Party Literature Publishing House, Beijing, for Plate 8.

PREFACE

Books can be co-written in various ways. This one is the result of a simple division of responsibilities: A.C. Grayling wrote the Introduction and Chapters 1, 2, 5, 6 and 10, and Susan Whitfield wrote Chapters 3, 4, 7, 8 and 9.

Among those who helped in various ways we particularly thank Catherine Baber, Robert Bickers, Elizabeth Cotton, Frances Wood, and our excellent editor, Gail Pirkis. Our Chinese friends, who over the years have taught us about their country and culture, and have helped us to enjoy both, are too numerous to thank individually; but we cannot resist picking out three who, in their different ways, have been special to us: Xu Youyu, Qiu Renzong and Zhang Jinyan. Over a decade ago Zhang first dined with us in our flat in Peking's Youyi Bingguan, and reminisced about his days as a pupil of William Empson at Peking University; and the next morning sent a thank-you note in beautiful English verse. Since then we have been entirely in his debt.

ACG
SW
London, 1994

Note on Chinese
Names

Chinese names are now romanized according to the 'pinyin'
system developed by the Chinese Communist government.
People writing before this system was introduced, and some
since, use many different forms. Therefore different versions
of the same name appear in text and quotations. For the sake
of consistency we use the pinyin system throughout the text
except for certain places commonly known in an older form
of romanization, such as Peking (in pinyin, Beijing), Canton
(Guangzhou) and the Yangtse River (Yangzi). We have also
retained Kuomintang (instead of Guomindang) and Chiang
Kaishek. We have, however, used 'Dao' and 'Daoism' instead
of the older 'Tao' and 'Taoism', because these latter prompt
mispronunciation by Western readers (as does 'toufu' for
'doufu').

In a few cases where we have introduced a quotation containing a name that occurs nowhere else, we have used the
form in which it appears. If the name recurs elsewhere in the
text we have used pinyin.

A list of the most commonly occurring names and some
of their equivalents found in the quotations cited is given
below:

Pinyin	*Equivalent(s)*
Beijing	Peking, Pekin
Daodejing	Tao-te-ching
Daoist	Taoist, Tauist
Fujian	Fuh-kien

Guangdong	Kwantung, Kuantung
Guanyin	Kuan-yin
Guizi	Kwei-tzu
Hangzhou	Hangchow, Hangchou
Henan	Honan
Huangpo (river)	Whangpoo
Jiangsu	Kiangsu
Jiayuguan	Kaiyükwan
Kangxi	K'ang-Hsi
Laozi	Lao-tze
Li Hongchang	Li Hung Chang
Liulichang	Liu Li Chang
Lu Xun	Lu Hsun
Mao Zedong	Mao Tse-tung
Qianlong	Ch'ien-Lung
Qianmen	Ch'ien men
renao	je-nao
Sichuan	Ssu-Ch'uan
Sima Qian	Szuma Chien, Ssuma Ch'ien
Suzhou	Suchow, Soochow
Xian	Sian (Sianfu)
Yanan	Yenan
Yangzi (river)	Yangtse, Yangtze
Yongle (emperor)	Yung Lo
Yuan Shikai	Yuan Shih-K'ai
Zhejiang	Che-kiang
Zhengzhou	Cheng-chow

INTRODUCTION

Confucius said, 'To approach a task from the wrong
end can lead to nothing but trouble.'

Confucius, *The Analects* 2.16

No country in the world, now or at any time in the past,
has been able to compete with China for sheer volume,
whether in the size of its population or in the length of its
continuous history. These factors combine to explain its
cultural distinctiveness and richness. Simple Western ideas
of historical progress do not comfortably fit its complexities.
Passing through China's countryside today one sees peasants
and their buffalo working the fields just as they have done
for thousands of years. Yet well before 1000 BC the Chinese
had an advanced bronze-making industry; by the fourth century BC they were casting iron, by the second century BC
making paper, and by the sixth century AD porcelain. By the
seventh century they had invented printing, and by the tenth
they were making gunpowder and firearms. Their textile
industry was so advanced that already in the third century BC
they were exporting silk to Rome.

These technological precocities were not, however, accompanied by the development of systematic science, nor did
they result in what Westerners call 'modernization'. Historical
circumstances for most of the millennium since the end of
the Tang (618–907) and Song (960–1279) dynasties – two of
China's most splendid periods – were such that, to the cursory
eye, China's institutions seemed to ossify, so that when the
revolution of 1911 ended the last of China's imperial dynasties,
it was as if until then nothing had changed in the funda-
mentals of state and society, particularly during the Ming
(1368–1644) and Qing (1644–1911) periods. But after 1911

change was dramatic; and especially so since the foundation of the People's Republic of China in 1949. As a result of rapid industrialization China is now one of the world's largest economies.

But institutional ossification – real or apparent – before the twentieth century by no means entailed cultural ossification. Here matters were far otherwise. Poetry, theatre, music and opera, sprawling episodic novels, painting, calligraphy, the plastic arts, and – for good measure – several rich traditions of philosophy, have flourished throughout, because the Chinese honour such things and enjoy them when they can. And given the human and historical voluminousness of China, there is much indeed to celebrate in these respects.

China might now be a developing industrial giant, but its past everywhere remains. One's train passes from the crowded station of a huge industrial city into timeless farmlands; one's ship threads its way into a busy port, where traditional fishing sampans risk being swamped by oil tankers and freighters. City streets might be choked by factory pollution and traffic, but around the next corner there is a quiet temple with curved eaves and meditative, self-enclosed courtyards, guarded by statues of fearsome demons.

The past is vividly present in China, conferring upon the country and its peoples their distinctive character. One's enjoyment of everything Chinese is enhanced by having some sense of the history which, in its rich distillations, produced this thronging and ebullient culture: so here, by way of preparation for the chapters that follow, is a thumbnail sketch of its most recent few thousand years.

China's history emerges from the mists of legend in the Shang dynasty (c. 1700–c. 1100 BC) in the region of its mightiest stream, the Yellow River (Huang He). Western historians for a time thought that Chinese claims about their history in these remote epochs were merely a rehearsal of myths, but archaeology has given them substance. Palace-dwelling, chariot-driving rulers, who might also have been shamans, presided over great cities whose suburbs were divided by occupation – in one suburb bronze-casting; in another, the manufacture of pottery; in a third, the carving of bone and jade. Shang nobles buried their dead in enormous subterranean graves stocked with food and wine, chariots and implements of the hunt, and human sacrifices to attend them in their *post mortem* state.

The Shang were overthrown by the Zhou (*c.* 1100–221 BC), a warrior group from the western marches of the Shang world. The Zhou adopted many Shang practices and crafts. At first their capital was situated in the Wei valley, but pressure from encroaching nomadic tribes forced them to move their capital east to Luoyang in 771 BC. This event divides the Zhou into two periods, the Western Zhou (*c.* 1100–771 BC) and the Eastern Zhou (771–221 BC). During the latter period central control progressively decayed until the Zhou world consisted of a plurality of states chronically at war among themselves. The later Eastern Zhou is accordingly labelled the Warring States period. The earlier Eastern Zhou is more poetically known as the Spring and Autumn period, after historical annals of that name recording events in the Kingdom of Lu.

Culture flourished under the Zhou despite the uncertainty of the times: historical records were kept, crafts advanced, texts were inscribed on bamboo and silk as well as bronze. Iron-working began during the sixth century BC, and before long agricultural tools were being manufactured for widespread use. Improvements in agriculture led to population growth, and therefore expansion of cities and trade. With these developments came a growing administrative class of scholar-officials, of whom Confucius (*c.* 551–479 BC) is the most notable example.

One of the combatant states in the late Zhou was the Qin. It had an able and ambitious ruler, who by a rapid succession of conquests united all the warring states under his rule, earning for himself the title First Emperor of China. His capital was Chang'an (close to present-day Xian), and near it he built the vast tomb with the famous terracotta army which is one of China's wonders. He also built – or, more accurately, extended and unified – the Great Wall. He was a harsh ruler, executing scholars who disagreed with him and burning their books; and although his reign was short it left a vivid unifying mark on China, as representing a new direction in its history.

The First Emperor bequeathed his domain to an untalented son, who was quickly unseated by uprisings in various parts of the empire. In 206 BC one of the rebel leaders, Liu Bang, emerged supreme and established a new dynasty, the Han (206 BC–AD 220), which proved to be one of China's Golden Ages.

The Han dynasty divides into two periods, the Western Han with its capital at Chang'an (206 BC–AD 25), and the Eastern Han, so named to mark another eastward relocation of the capital to Luoyang (AD 25–220). Han emperors looked back to the Confucian tradition which the Qin had attempted to quash, and after the establishment of an imperial university in 124 BC, many leading positions in the burgeoning civil service were taken by men steeped in the Confucian classics. The empire expanded westwards and northwards and for a long period flourished; in the census of AD 2 the population numbered 60 million, with several cities containing up to a million inhabitants each. Agriculture and technology, crafts and arts advanced, and a great civilization prospered within the empire's boundaries.

In the Eastern Han, however, familiar patterns of decay at length began to appear. In enlarging their estates rich nobles turned peasants off their traditional lands, fomenting discontent. Expensive wars against border barbarians caused higher taxes, increasing discontent. Corruption and complacency infected the ruling classes, contumacy the ruled classes. Peasant uprisings – the usual vehicle of national change in China – increased in frequency, and for several centuries after the fall in 220 of the Eastern Han there was a long interval of disunion. Disaffection with what seemed to be failed Confucian notions of social order made room for Daoism and Buddhism to flourish, the former an ancient native Chinese philosophy, the latter a recent import from India.

The adventurous anarchy of the time has been immortalized in *The Romance of the Three Kingdoms* by the fourteenth-century novelist Luo Guanzhong, who tells stirring tales of cunning generals, clever stratagems and heroic feats of arms. Just as in the Qin, turbulent China was reunited by a severe, single-minded and short-lived dynasty, the Sui (581–618), which restored discipline and paved the way for another

Golden Age, perhaps the most golden of them all in China's history: the Tang dynasty (618–907).

The Tang was a time of high achievement both in literature and in the techniques of imperial administration. By means of a land distribution programme in which each able-bodied man was entitled to the tenancy of a small farm, and by a return to the Han system of staffing the upper echelons of the civil service by competitive examination, the Tang laid the basis for a flourishing economy and efficient government. Lively international trade along the Silk Road increased China's wealth; her capital, Chang'an, was a rich, cosmopolitan city extending far beyond the surviving Ming walls of present-day Xian.

For two centuries the empire prospered. China's network of canals grew, facilitating trade and the distribution of agricultural produce. Printing was invented, Chinese poetry found its two greatest voices in Li Bai and Du Fu, and wealthy aristocrats cultivated enjoyment of elegant porcelain tea-sets, silk garments, silver and gold tableware, and paintings. China's cultural hegemony of the eastern world was unquestioned, and left its mark ever afterwards on neighbours like Korea and Japan.

But after military reverses against Arab forces at the western end of the Silk Road, and a nearly successful rebellion led by a famous general called An Lushan, decay set in once again. The economy began to founder, and as the dynasty entered its final years it mounted a brief but intense persecution of Buddhism, dispossessing wealthy monasteries and nunneries and forcing their inmates back to secular life.

The disintegration of the Tang was complete by 907, and it left China in fragments for half a century. The period is known as the Five Dynasties and Ten Kingdoms (907–60) after the petty states which sprang up as central control dissipated. The Five Dynasties in the north of China were chronically at war among themselves, but the Ten Kingdoms in the south were more peaceable. It was a soldier of one of the Five Dynasties who at length asserted control and reunified the empire, thereby founding the Song dynasty (960–1279), a third Golden Age.

The Song dynasty was less outward looking than the Tang

had been. There were fewer foreigners in its capital or barter-
ing along its roads and canals, although for almost the only
time in its history China sent trade missions by sea to other
countries. But the Song was a time of renaissance in both
philosophical and artistic matters. A major revival of Confucian thought gave the Song its ideological foundation, and
scholarship in mathematics, cartography, astronomy and historical studies advanced apace. Artists working in bronze and
jade revived antique designs. Women became more closeted,
losing not only the *décolletée* fashions in dress but also the personal freedom of their Tang grandmothers. Foot-binding was
introduced, among the aristocracy at first but soon among all
except peasant girls, whose families needed them whole for
labour in the fields.

As with some earlier dynasties, the Song divides into two
periods, the Northern Song and the Southern Song. In the
former (960–1127) the capital stood at Kaifeng on the Yellow
River. But the growing danger from powerful northern
nomad groups forced the court to transfer to Hangzhou in
1127, thus beginning the Southern Song (1127–1279). This
period ended when the ferocious and effective Mongol armies
of Genghis Khan swept across the Great Wall in 1279. The
Mongols established their own dynasty, the Yuan (1279–
1368), with their capital in what was then the far north of
China, at Peking.

China's culture was barely influenced by these Mongol
invaders – the Chinese are absorbers, and their character and
culture are far too robust to be deflected from their own
growth by alien rulers. Theatre and the Chinese novel made
their appearance in the Yuan, and it is in this period that
Marco Polo's alleged visit took place.

The Chinese were not, however, tranquil under the Mongols; there were many uprisings, and eventually a Chinese
rebel from Anhui province, Zhu Yuanzhang, succeeded in
ejecting them and establishing a new Chinese dynasty, the
Ming (1368–1644). The Ming modelled itself on the Han,
Tang and Song dynasties, except in the matter of its capital, which it built in the heart of Peking – the glorious
Forbidden City. Ming times saw a huge extension of book-
printing and a concomitant diffusion of learning, and develop-

ment of the blue-and-white glazing characteristic of Ming porcelain. Literature flourished, and the Great Wall received the brick facing which those stretches today seen by tourists still display.

But, in the all too familiar way, the dynasty eventually grew effete. Mongol raiders, internal uprisings and Japanese pirates sapped its military and economic strength, and at length the emperors, trapped in the coils of a corrupt bureaucracy of self-serving eunuchs in the Forbidden City, lost control. In the resulting anarchy Manchus from the north descended on Peking and captured it – and with it the empire. Thus began the last of China's imperial dynasties, the Qing (1644–1911).

The Qing ruled China but did not change it. They preserved a caste distinction between Manchus and Chinese, and forced the latter to adopt, as a visible display of loyalty, the 'queue' or pigtail. Manchus did not intermarry with Chinese, and did not adopt the practice of foot-binding. They were a tiny minority in a vast Chinese population, but by astute control of the military and administrative structures they managed to keep themselves in power until their failure to modernize caused their demise. When Western powers started to help themselves to parts of China in pursuit of trade, the Qing dynasty was unable to resist, and within a century it had collapsed.

In earlier Qing times China had able rulers like the Kangxi and Qianlong emperors, although it was the great expense of the latter's military campaigns which caused the country's eventual decline. Perhaps the most notorious member of the dynasty was its penultimate ruler, the Dowager Empress Cixi, whose death in 1908 marked the effective end of imperial China. Regarded as a harsh and intransigent woman, Cixi's refusal to modernize China is blamed for the difficulties the country experienced in the face of foreign intervention and aggression.

Between 1911 and the foundation of the Communist People's Republic in 1949 China was wracked by civil war and a bloody Japanese occupation. To these more recent events, and to the story of Communist China since 1949, the final chapter (Chapter 10) is devoted.

For citizens of Renaissance Europe, China was a distant region of marvels, fascinating because of its rich and complicated strangeness. But increasing contacts between Europe and China changed the picture. China became all the rage in eighteenth-century Europe, prompting fashions in diet, hairstyles, dress, the decorative arts, garden design and even architecture. There was lively if patchy humanistic interest in China's history and thought. And it did not take long for more practical minds to see that these literary and fashionable tastes related to what was potentially a huge market. In 1792 and 1816 the British government sent embassies to Peking, the first under Lord Macartney, the second under Lord Amherst, with the aim of opening China to trade.

In their wake, and with the aid of gunboat diplomacy, followed merchants, missionaries and civil servants. The relationship of the West to China changed from admiration to more familiar, less elevated kinds of interest – the accumulation of commercial profits and religious converts. Many Chinese naturally objected to colonial exploitation of their country, and hostility grew; a celebrated symptom was the Boxer Rebellion of 1900, in which an attempt (secretly sanctioned by Cixi, then reigning as regent) was made to kill or eject all foreigners – a special resentment being felt towards the swarms of missionaries, of dozens of different denominations, infesting the country. It is amazing now to contemplate the fact that to protect its traders and missionaries, the West patrolled China's rivers with gunboats and its territory with troops.

But despite the generally unwholesome character of the West's presence in China, especially in the nineteenth and early twentieth centuries, and the racist contempt displayed by many Westerners towards the Chinese, there were others who cherished an appreciation for China's culture and the immense charm of its people. 'If China had not been there,' wrote Lord Dunsany, expressing these more discriminating sentiments, 'this land of dragons, peach-trees, peonies and plum blossoms, with its ages and ages of culture, slowly storing its dreams in green jade, is just the land that poets would have invented.' As the following pages testify, he is right.

1

POINTS OF ENTRY: PEKING AND SHANGHAI

> When Confucius arrives in a country, he invariably
> gets to know about its government. Does he seek
> this information, or is it given him?
>
> Confucius gets it through being cordial, good,
> respectful, temperate and deferential. The way Con-
> fucius seeks it is, perhaps, different from the way
> other men seek it.
>
> Confucius, *The Analects*, 1.10

For some, Peking was love at first sight. Harold Acton arrived
in 1932 from Japan, which he had found uncongenial. It was
a love prepared; Acton had been longing for years to visit
China, and was already an enthusiastic student of its history
and art. He likened his response to Peking to Gibbon's feelings
on first entering Rome: 'several days of intoxication were lost
or enjoyed,' Gibbon had written, 'before I could descend to
a cool and minute examination.' Acton quotes him, and then
describes his first encounter with the Forbidden City:

> Neither Versailles, nor the Pitti, nor any aggregation of
> palaces I had seen or imagined, with the exception of
> the Vatican, had the magnificence of this extensive city
> of open courtyards and pavilions. Within our time no
> handiwork of man has achieved such a dignified and
> spacious harmony of buildings. The proportion of every
> courtyard in relation to the surrounding pavilions seemed
> to me perfect. For once the sky was part of the archi-

tectural design. The sweeping curves of the golden roofs held the blue sky like jewelled chalices. Massive though the buildings were – half shimmering roof, half pillared portico and marble balustrade – they had an aerial lightness and grace. Instead of clamping them down to earth, the roofs helped them to soar. Thus the whole plan had an aspiring spiritual quality. Huge ramparts, of a colour that varied with the time of day from pale rose to deep coral, separated it from the outside world.[1]

Like all for whom love was the natural response to China, Acton was charmed by its people and immediately romanticized them:

> Outside the palace I found myself the bone of contention between a horde of rickshaw coolies who had sprung forward madly at the sight of me, an obvious stranger, and hemmed me in on all sides, yelling wild Indian warwhoops and fiercely trying to jolt each other out of the way. It was painful to be the centre of such competitive commotion. These shouting, straining bodies appeared to range from nine to ninety years of age. All these eyes pleaded with me to enter their rickshaws and I could but close mine and step into the nearest, whereupon the others withdrew laughing and joking. In spite of their poverty they managed to inject excitement and humour into life. Their forward plunge had been like the casting of dice; but as soon as the dice were thrown they resigned themselves, and my rickshaw set off among cheers at a happy trot.
>
> I could never get accustomed to the plight of these human beasts of burden, so many of whose ribs were visible through their torn sweat-soaked jackets. Yet their cheerfulness was as striking as their poverty. To counteract the latter, nature seemed to have helped them to find everything a subject of entertainment. They were always ready to smile. No education had disenchanted them; and perhaps the world was more beautiful in their eyes than in mine.[2]

Longer acquaintance tends to rub the bloom off early delight, but Acton's affection did not diminish throughout his years of residence in China. The protagonist of his novel *Peonies and Ponies*, Philip Flower, woken early by the sound of pigs being slaughtered in the nearby market at Longfu Temple, speaks for him in announcing that it is supremely good to be alive in a Peking dawn:

> The old watchmen with rattle and gong were still doddering on their rounds. Click-click, plong-plong, at regular intervals, reverberations indispensable to some folks' slumber: the sharply defined rhythms assured the dreamers on their *k'angs* that they could safely dream on. Philip gazed up at the rectangle of sky that belonged to him, and was as near as *Homo Sapiens* could be to purring. The scent of the lilacs flattered his nostrils. He half-expected a phoenix to swoop down on his *wu-t'ung* tree – the only tree whereon a phoenix will deign to alight – and Philip was proud to possess one. He was astonished to be alive. We do not realize, he thought, what a miracle life is. He made a resolve to rise with the dawn in future, if only to listen to the murmurs of the slowly wakening city and dabble in dew.[3]

Philip's – Acton's – delight was a product of his inhabiting one of the world's great sites both of imagination and history, where Coleridge's Kublai Khan had planted his gardens, and where the last millennium of China's imperial history played itself out in magnificence and disaster. Nowhere is like Peking: it is more than a place, it is a personality, an actor in a historic drama.

Peking is an invaders' city. China's great domestic dynasties, the Qin, Han, Tang and their successors, built their capitals at Xian and Luoyang in China's traditional heartland of the Yellow River plain. But when barbarians invaded from the north, none more successfully than the Mongols, they established a capital closer to their roots, on the margin of the steppes where they could feel the raw winds and smell the dust of home. Displaying a fine sense of irony, they raised their capital just inside the Great Wall which their victims had originally and futilely built to keep them out.

The only Han Chinese dynasty to accept Peking as its capital was the Ming, but they were its chief beautifiers. Their pigtail-wearing Qing or 'Tartar' successors were yet more northern invaders, this time from Manchuria. The Qing found Peking a congenial location for the same reasons as the Mongols before them: proximity to home, familiar weather. But by the time of their arrival Peking was a splendid capital, boasting at its centre the world's most exotic royal demesne: the Forbidden City.

A thirteenth-century traveller to Peking – so he claimed – was Marco Polo, whose visit took place when the 'Great Khan', Kublai son of Genghis, was on the throne. Kublai learned from an astrologer that the existing city, then called Khan-balik, would rebel; so, Polo tells us, he built a new city directly alongside and called it Taidu. His palace stood a little to the west of Peking's present Forbidden City:

> As regards the size of this (new) city you must know that it has a compass of 24 miles, for each side of it hath a length of 6 miles, and it is four-square. And it is all walled round with walls of earth which have a thickness of full ten paces at bottom, and a height of more than 10 paces; but they are not so thick at top, for they diminish in thickness as they rise, so that at top they are only about 3 paces thick. And they are provided throughout with loop-holed battlements, which are all whitewashed.
>
> There are 12 gates, and over each gate there is a great and handsome palace, so that there are on each side of the square three gates and five palaces; for (I ought to mention) there is at each angle also a great and handsome palace. In those palaces are vast halls in which are kept the arms of the city garrison.
>
> The streets are so straight and wide that you can see right along them from end to end and from one gate to the other. And up and down the city there are beautiful palaces, and many great and fine hostelries, and fine houses in great numbers.[4]

Much of Polo's information is cribbed from an early Persian account, but is often accurate nevertheless; Khan-balik (or Cambalec; other variations exist) was the Mongol name, Taidu (or Dadu), meaning 'Great Capital', the Chinese name for the same place. Coleridge's imaginary picture of Peking, give or take a measureless cavern or two, was not far from accurate either:

In Xanadu did Kubla Khan
A stately pleasure-dome decree:
Where Alph, the sacred river, ran
Through caverns measureless to man
Down to a sunless sea.
So twice five miles of fertile ground
With walls and towers were girdled round:
And there were gardens bright with sinuous rills,
Where blossomed many an incense-bearing tree;
And here were forests ancient as the hills,
Enfolding sunny spots of greenery.[5]

In earlier times Peking had not been so grand. During the period of the Warring States a town existed there with the romantic name of Yanjing, the Capital of Swallows. To this day swallows fly at dusk from the eaves of the Forbidden City and the high roofs of the gates. Later it was a market town, then a military base. But from the tenth century it was adopted by successive waves of Mongolian invaders as their capital, the most powerful of whom arrived under Kublai at the beginning of the thirteenth century. They nurtured a true nomad's concern for their livestock, for which they needed a large enclosure; hence the great circumference of the outer walls enclosing the double city. A.B. Freeman-Mitford, an observant nineteenth-century attaché at the British Legation in Peking, with a developed skill as a letter-writer, explained the layout to his family at home thus:

Pe-king, which means the northern capital, as Nan-king means the southern, consists of two cities, the Chinese and the Tartar, and within this latter, again, is the Imperial city, which contains the palace and precincts of the court. Both cities are surrounded by walls of dark-grey brick; those of the Tartar city are fifty feet high, forty feet wide at the top, and about sixty feet below; the walls of the Chinese city are less important, being only thirty feet high. These walls have battlements and loopholes for guns. That of the Chinese city has fallen into decay, but that of the Tartar is more carefully repaired. At intervals are lofty watch-towers standing out against the sky. High towers stand also above the gates, which are closed at sunset, after which time ingress and egress are forbidden.[6]

The Mongols called their dynasty 'Yuan'. They provided Peking's water supply and established its grid street pattern. This layout survived the battles at the end of the Yuan in which many of the city's buildings were razed. When the Yongle emperor, second ruler of the succeeding Ming dynasty, decided in 1402 to make Peking his capital, the opportunity for extensive rebuilding therefore offered itself. This is when the true Peking of recent and splendid memory came into being. It is wonderfully described by Osbert Sitwell, easily the most sensitive and eloquent of all Peking's foreign prose portraitists:

From my room high up in the hotel . . . I obtained a first and most magnificent view of Peking. The Legation Quarter, a conglomeration of gardens, old temples and modern houses, lay behind me, out of the picture, as did 'The Chinese City', so called. But 'The Tartar City' extended shining below, almost untouched . . . the same now as it had always been; a sea of grey roofs surrounding the tall, vivid islands of the Forbidden and Imperial Cities, square and rectangular, one within the other; red-walled cities which occupied the centre of the picture and, because of the obvious grandeur and beauty of their temples, halls and pavilions, their moated gardens and canals, vast courts and parks, overshadowed their setting. Orange-tiled roof after orange-tiled roof, with bright green and vermilion eaves, further emblazoned by the clear, clean sunlight of this pure air, stretched away to two hills – the only ones for many miles around; until, indeed, you reach the perfect contours of the Western Hills. Both of these tall mounds are artificial and have buildings on them; the five summits of the nearer are studded with tiled pavilions, in which formerly the Empress and her ladies used to take the air, and see what was going on below them in the streets and alleys of the palace; while the further carries on its height a curious, white, bottle-shaped structure known as the White Dagoba, erected by the order of the Emperor Shan Chih in 1651, to mark the first visit of the Dalai Lama to Peking. Behind the White Dagoba, but still within the limits of the Imperial City, flashed in the sun a great sheet of water, the beautiful lines of its shores littered with derelict temples. This lake, famous for its lotuses, and the extensive wooded park which surrounds it, are known as Pei-Hai, or North Sea Lake. Now a public playground, it had once been the pleasance of Kubla Khan.[7]

It was the Yongle emperor who erected the walls of the inner city. The grid of its major streets formed squares each enclosing a tangle of little alleyways, the *hutongs*, once memorably described as 'fine and numerous as the hairs on a cow'. It was in one of these that Acton and his Philip Flower lived. The same chequerboard street pattern prevailed in the outer city.

> Yung Lo . . . the founder of the present Peking, is said to have consulted for his plan an eminent astrologer, Lu Po. The thaumaturge handed the Emperor a sealed envelope containing the plans of the new capital, based on the recognized principles of his magic. The city was to represent No-Cha, a mythical being with three heads and six arms, and a corresponding space or building was allotted to each part of his body. . . . Thus, to take a' few instances, No-Cha's head – or heads – is the Ch'ien Men, the principal gate of the Tartar City . . . an open gutter, now covered over, in the West City, represents his large intestine; a well in the Western Section of the Forbidden City, his navel; two gates, facing the Yellow Temple and Black Temple respectively, symbolize his feet, treading on 'Wind and Fire Wheels', while the red painted walls of the Imperial City constitute his red silk stomach protector.[8]

When the Tartars' Qing dynasty ousted the Ming in 1644, Peking's inner city became their territory, leaving the rest to the Chinese. Today the division of Peking into Tartar and Chinese cities has been obliterated by the demolition of city walls and infilling of moats. But a number of the gates survive because of the huge masses of masonry they contain, isolated now amid pressing suburbs and choking traffic. Peking boasted nine main outer gates, that number having superstitious significance. Each had a particular function: some were reserved for the imperial army's exits and entrances, one was for the passage of commercial goods, another was reserved solely for night-soil to be carried out, by appropriately named *fu* wagons, to neighbouring sewage farms. Every evening, after the sounding of a great bell, the gates were shut, and no-one could pass through unless the circumstances – or the person -- were exceptional. The diplomatic wife Lady O'Malley, writing as novelist 'Ann Bridge', describes how the immense gates once divided the city from its hinterland:

> The gates of walled cities have caught man's imagination from the time when King Solomon compared the nose of his beloved to the tower which looked towards Damascus, or King David bade the gates of Jerusalem lift up their heads that the King of Glory might come in. There is a splendid formality about the sharp line of masonry where the city ends at a stroke, and the open country spreads up to its very foot; the gates are the breaches in this line, sluices through which the life of the fields pours in to nourish the life of the town. A glamour of past events hangs about them – the lifted heads of the gates have looked on the entrances of kings and the exits of armies; they are grey with the dust of departures on great journeys; their outlines have been caressed from afar by the glad eyes of return. This interior thrill, this sense of the past, is intensified in a city such as Peking, where past and present meet; where the city's daily food still pours in, on donkeys' backs, on ancient carts and on shoulder-yokes, through the grey gateways beneath their mighty towers; where the motors of golfers and race-goers mingle their dust with that stirred up by the feet of long files of camels, coming in as they have come for centuries laden with coal from the

hills, or with who knows what strange burden of silks or carpets or furs, from Tibet and from beyond the Gobi Desert.[9]

After 1949 Peking became a barren and dusty urban sprawl. Mao Zedong ordered all grass to be grubbed up because it harboured mosquitoes, and birds became less numerous than formerly because they were assiduously trapped and eaten. But until then Peking was a greenly wooded place. Each courtyard house boasted its trees, the best-loved being the flowering varieties. Pierre Loti, writing in 1902, called the city a 'forest', and a member of the British Legation a few years earlier described Peking as 'a green wood surrounded by a high wall' when viewed from the battlements. For Pierre Teilhard de Chardin the city's trees gave it much of its loveliness: 'I have now been three days in Pekin. At this time of year the city is much less beautiful than in June. The trees, of which there are so many that the thousands of low-gabled houses look like rows of tents pitched in a forest, have shed their leaves. You no longer see the red and gold of the Imperial City reflected in the moats full of water lilies.'[10] Not everyone was unable to see the wood for the trees. Freeman-Mitford characteristically took a less poetic view than Teilhard de Chardin: 'In another fortnight the trees will all be bare, and Peking, throwing off the green clothes which it puts on in summer, in order to delude stray visitors into the idea that it is a pretty place, will stand naked, dirty and ashamed.'[11]

After Mao Zedong's death ended the Cultural Revolution in 1976, replanting of Peking's groves began, the new saplings struggling up among the unimpeachably ugly new tower blocks of the modern city. They have already made a large difference.

The populousness of Peking has been a constant. To some the number, variety and condition of humanity in the great capital was worse than a positive nuisance:

Peking is like a vast curiosity shop, with all the dust and dirt which are among the conditions of bric-a-brac. It would be pleasant-looking and admiring were it not for the difficulties of riding through the city owing to the enormous crowds which block the way – carts, porters, camels, chairs, pedlars, beggars, lamas, muleteers, horse-copers from Mongolia, archers on horseback, mandarins with their suites, small-footed women, great ladies in carts, closely veiled to keep off the gaze of the profane vulgar. In short, every variety of yellow and brown humanity, not to speak of dogs and pigs, get into one's path at every moment, and raise clouds of dust, which fill eyes, ears, hair, mouth, and nose, and temporarily destroy every sense save that of touch.[12]

Of all Peking's human sights perhaps the most affecting was the distressful but traditional host on Beggar's Bridge, which had to be crossed on every occasion of entering or leaving the Chinese city. Freeman-Mitford continues:

The 'Beggar's Bridge' is the most loathsome and stinking exhibition that it ever was my fate to come across. Here every day a hundred or two of the most degraded speci-mens of humanity congregate and beg. By far the greater majority of them are clothed only in dirt, and all sorts of repulsive cutaneous complaints; some have a linen rag, but it is worn over the shoulders, and in no way serves as a decent covering. Lice, mange, scrofula, leprosy and filth are allowed to remain undisturbed by water or drugs. They are a stock-in-trade, and as such rather encouraged than not. It is a sickening sight when these creatures come and perform the koutou to us, prostrating themselves in the dust or mud, which is scarcely as dirty as themselves. I spare you the description of the food I have seen them eating. If ever I get back to Europe, I feel that the Beggar's Bridge will be a nightmare to me for the rest of my life.[13]

These remarks make it seem that the leprosy and indigence on display were somehow deliberate, a plot to annoy pass-ing foreigners. To W.H. Auden and Christopher Isherwood travelling in China half a century later, city streets appeared little different: 'Every third person in the crowd appeared to be suffering from trachoma, or goitre, or hereditary syphilis. And the foodstuffs they were buying and selling looked hateful beyond belief – the filthiest parts of the oldest and most diseased animals; stodgy excrement-puddings; vile, stagnant soups and poisonous roots.'[14]

The advent of Communist China in 1949 succeeded, until recently, in removing such misery from the streets.

Although Peking's palaces and temples grew more numerous and splendid after Kublai's time, especially during the Ming, the city itself did not change fundamentally until the middle of the twentieth century. But when change came it was drastic. Neither a sense of history nor an instinct for conservation troubled China's post-1949 rulers. Peking's walls were torn down to make way for ring roads. Most of the traditional *hutongs*, many of them insanitarily crowded slums, had to give way before an advancing forest of cheaply constructed tower blocks. Such temples and other antique structures as survived demolition were turned into factories or offices, much of their ornament destroyed or defaced to rid the New China of 'feudalism's' traces. Apart from its greatest architectural treasures, chief among them the Forbidden City, the Temple of Heaven and the Summer Palace, Peking survives largely in fragments.

The city's lost appearance is well captured by C.A.S. Williams, the Peking Customs College official who, while resident in the city in the 1920s, filled his leisure hours with a scholarly study of Chinese symbolism. Peking, he wrote,

> has a beautiful appearance as viewed from the surrounding wall, from which can be seen an entrancing vista of temples and palaces, their curving roofs glittering with blue, green and yellow tiles, among the groves of trees with which the city abounds. The ancient capital presents a rather unique aspect from an aeroplane, from which we can observe that it is not only one city, but a veritable conglomeration or nest of cities, one packed within the other – like a Chinese puzzle.[15]

But the most spectacular part of Peking remains unchanged: the Forbidden City. As Acton's memoirs show, its rose-madder walls and golden roofs define not just the geographical but also the historical hub of the city. It is a magnet and an inescapable presence for visitor and resident alike. An Ann Bridge character describes its impact:

As her rickshaw crossed the Da Chang An Jie, the great street running along the north side of the Legation Quarter, she turned her head to look at the Forbidden City. That was a sight on which, after all these years, she could never look unmoved. One behind the other, the great red gateways stood up in the evening light like immense double-decker Noah's Arks, roofed in golden tiles, above the high crimson walls. Close at hand, on the right, showed the silvery green of the secular thujas round the Temple of the Ancestors – the 'sunny spots of greenery' of Xanadu, planted, legend says, by Kublai Khan. The egrets had come back after their winter absence, and their white shapes showed among the ancient trees, their harsh cries filled the air above the clang of trams and the blasts of motor-horns. Changeless matchless beauty, holding the eye and the mind, as only beauty does! She remembered her first sight of it on the evening of their arrival in Peking. Henry had taken her arm and led her, tired and stiff and discouraged with the unpacking, with the allocation of rooms, the dispersal of blankets and linen and silver to various household destinations, out into the icy dusk. They went through the West gate of the legation, across the glacis outside the Quarter, and found themselves presently in a red-walled avenue a hundred yards wide, stretching down on their left to the immense green-tiled gate-tower of Qian Men, stretching up on their right to the red and gold Noah's Arks, with gleams of white marble at their base. 'There!' said Henry. They looked. 'It's the eighth Wonder of the World,' he said. And she had gone back to the house with them, partly reconciled to a place of exile which held such breath-taking beauty.[16]

The prosaic name now given to the Forbidden City is *Gugong*, meaning Ancient Palace. Its original Chinese name was *Zijincheng*. *Jincheng* means Forbidden City; *Zi* denotes the pole star. The combination signifies that the Emperor, as Son of Heaven, lived in the earthly equivalent of the heavenly zenith. The Forbidden City was designed and built to be an embodiment of this fact. Peter Quennell, on his single visit to the place, was stunned by its beauty and proportions:

> Size is the canon of this architecture, height, space and solid massive dignity. If anything could dwarf these great pavilions, it is the enormous open courtyards they surround and which are strung together like a system of quadrangular lakes, white and empty among the glittering roof-ridges. They seemed particularly spacious that afternoon, by that pale brilliant dusty blinding glare. We had found our way into an extensive inner courtyard, through which a deep marble-lined canal, spanned by five narrow marble bridges, describes a bow-shaped arc from side to side. Facing us, as we crossed the central bridge, was the porch of a courtyard which lay beyond, approached by a low shelf of marble steps; behind us, three pavilions looked down from a gigantic rampart substructure of pink masonry – 'pink' I write for want of a better word. Pierre Loti, with melodramatic expressiveness, has described the colour as that of dried blood. . . .
>
> The yellow roofs, too, of the pavilions and cloisters are beginning to lose their harshness with the passage of time. They are the tone of yellow lichen on a tree-trunk; while the grass, which is growing here and there unchecked between ridges of glazed tiles, makes them shimmer at every movement of the wind.[17]

A mere six years before Quennell visited the Forbidden City in 1930, the last emperor, Pu Yi, had been expelled from its precincts, and with him the remaining court eunuchs. (They refused to leave until the little boxes containing their testicles were returned to them; every Chinese must join his ancestors whole.) This explains the grass sprouting among the roof-tiles and the air of decay. Since the foreign-currency potential of tourism dawned upon post-Cultural Revolution China, the walls of the Forbidden City have been restored to their dried-blood hue, and the roofs have been weeded.

Nothing so well illustrates the Forbidden City and the culture of which it was once the fountain and apex as a tale collected by the Manchu folklorist Jin Shoushen. It concerns the stone monkeys carved on one of the Forbidden City's bridges:

> East of the Hall of Martial Valour in the Forbidden City is a bridge with a beautifully carved stone balustrade, called Broken Rainbow Bridge. On each stone pillar of the balustrade squats a stone monkey. One has a ladle in its left paw, while with its right it is hitching up its skirt. None see it but marvel at the skill of this spirited carving.
>
> One old eunuch said, 'Each time the imperial equipage passed this way, a yellow cloth cover was slipped over this stone creature. Why? So as not to let its uncouth appearance alarm the Emperor.'
>
> Another said, 'No, that wasn't the reason. It was because one Emperor lost his temper over something and kicked one of his own sons to death in front of this stone. Later he felt so remorseful that each time he passed here he grieved; so to spare him his attendants draped a yellow cloth over the stone, thinking, Out of sight, out of mind.'
>
> Both eunuchs were right, but now let us hear a folktale which tells a different story. Once an old Emperor had a favourite concubine, who used to go to a palace near Broken Rainbow Bridge each day to bathe.[18]

(The palace was the House of Bathing Virtue; the Qianlong emperor's favourite, Xiangfei, the 'Fragrant Concubine', had a Turkish-style bath-house built for her here.)

> Each time she was accompanied by palace maids and eunuchs bearing fans and censers as, like stars escorting the moon, they saw her to the bath-house. Then they rested in the annexes while she bathed.
>
> The windows of the bath-house had glass panes, but while she bathed strict watch was mounted and all the doors and windows were tightly shut. But after some days the concubine noticed the faint shadow of a little black figure on the window; and every time she bathed

thereafter she noticed it. But when she looked out there was no-one there. She began to take fright, but dared not tell the Emperor, for fear he would order her not to bathe there any more.

She told her maids about the figure. They said, 'The palace is so big, and has such vast courtyards with old trees in them, that some evil spirit might easily slip in. But just call us when you see it, madam, and we'll rush out and catch it.'

As each day passed the shadow grew more and more distinct, and the concubine more and more alarmed. One day she could see it very clearly, stretching out its shaggy arms as if to break into the window. Too frightened to call for help, she snatched up a jade ladle lying nearby and hurled it through the window. Crash! The glass was smashed and the little black shadow vanished.

When the maids and eunuchs ran outside to catch the culprit, no-one was to be seen. But neither could they see the ladle. 'Find it!' the concubine ordered them anxiously. 'The Emperor gave it to me and will be angry if it is lost.' But search as they might they could not find it – until they came to Broken Rainbow Bridge, where to their astonishment they saw it in the paw of one of the monkeys. It was stuck so fast that they could not budge it. When they told the concubine of this she stamped her foot in exasperation. 'If it were broken we could hide it. But what will happen if the Emperor sees it when crossing the bridge? If he hears that you let a stone monkey slip through your guard to the bath-house window, he will have all your heads cut off!'

The terrified eunuchs thought up a plan. This was to make a yellow cover for the stone monkey, and to put it on whenever the Emperor passed so that he would never notice the jade ladle.[19]

After the 1911 revolution which brought the Qing dynasty to an end, the Forbidden City began to die as a palace. Reginald Johnston served as tutor there to Pu Yi, and witnessed the decline; but it was not immediate:

Though the emperor and the four *t'ai-fei* or dowager-consorts were the only imperial residents in the Forbidden City, it must not be supposed that it was an unpeopled city. Before the revolution there was a staff of about three thousand eunuchs, of various grades. In 1919, about a thousand still remained. The others had retired with their fortunes to their homes on the borders of Shantung and Chihli, to sanctuaries in the foreign Concessions of Tientsin, to the shops in which they had deposited their strangely-acquired capital, or to their monasteries and hermitages in the Western Hills, ten miles to the west of Peking. Of the thousand who remained, some were the personal attendants and chair-bearers of the emperor and the four dowagers, others were in charge of the various palace-buildings and responsible for the safe-keeping of their contents, others performed more or less menial duties. Those of the highest grade were the *yu-ch'ien t'ai-chien* – Eunuchs of the Presence – who had the honour of serving the Son of Heaven himself. The different grades were kept strictly apart from one another and on ceremonial occasions wore distinctive uniforms. . . . Beside the eunuchs there were numerous ladies-in-waiting (*nu kuan*) and maidservants (*kung nu*), but most of the former did not reside in the Forbidden City.[20]

With a sensitivity to things Chinese almost Chinese itself, of that exquisite literary and aesthetic cast which resembles the mind of a Chinese scholar, Osbert Sitwell recognized that the Forbidden City, like everything else of artistic value in China, has its best life in an integrated setting which includes nature, the season of the year, the weather, and a backcloth of timelessness:

> If you divide the Forbidden City into two, the southern half roughly comprises the main halls of state, while the second, the Nei Ch'ao or Inner Court, contains the pavilions and living quarters that I have mentioned as being so opposed in spirit to the great apartments. Both sections I have visited many times, under snow and wind and spring calm and great heat, and the particular quality

of beauty which each part manifests leads me to choose a different kind of weather by which to see it. First, for the frosty beauty of the great courts and the dark sumptuousness of the State Apartments, I should select a typical Peking winter day of bright, yellow-fleeced sun in a blue heaven, of an intensely animating cold; but, for the appreciation of the residential quarters, and the facets and adjuncts of the Chinese life they represent, gay as the drawing of a flower or a bird upon a Chinese paper, we must have a spring day, a morning from that brief season, enduring only a fortnight, that falls, very regularly, about a month later than the Feast of Excited Insects, and is all too short, since, in it, after a winter when every twig and piece of earth looked hard and dead as iron, the year suddenly leaps into life, and the lilac and shrubs and fruit-trees rush within the space of a few days into intoxicating flower and scent.[21]

Although the Forbidden City, repainted and weeded, is now reduced to the role of echoing tourist attraction, its splendour and its significance remain. Pierre Loti, contemplating the throne in the Hall of Supreme Harmony, recognized this:

Like the avenues which I have followed, like the series of bridges and the triple gates, this throne is on the central axis of Peking, and represents its soul. Were it not for all these walls, all these various enclosures, the Emperor, sitting there on this pedestal of lacquer and marble, could see to the farthest extremities of the city, to the farthest openings in the surrounding walls. The tributary sovereigns who visit, the ambassadors and the armies, from the moment of their entrance to Peking by the southern gate, would be, so to speak, under the blaze of his invisible eyes.[22]

An echo of this remains, despite what has happened since. Simone de Beauvoir visited to applaud the achievements of New China, and felt the thrill of the old.

The barriers have tumbled. The Forbidden City has become a public place; now everyone strolls freely through its courtyards, sips tea under its porches; Young Pioneers in red neckerchiefs visit the exhibits mounted in its hallways; certain buildings have been turned into palaces of culture and libraries; in another part of it the government has its seat. Beneath this new life invading it the original meaning of the palace remains unimpaired; I seldom succeed in forgetting it.[23]

But the Forbidden City is not the only place of aesthetic magic in Peking. Another, of comparable importance to the city and the history of China, is Tiantan, the Temple of Heaven.

One of the most important observances of the year required the emperor to quit the Forbidden City and journey by elephant-drawn chariot to this magnificent temple in the southern quarter of Peking, accompanied by two thousand ministers. Here, on the eve of the winter solstice, he made obeisance to his ancestors. After a night spent in fasting and meditation in the Hall of Abstinence in the temple grounds, he stood at the circular open-air altar of white marble and, helped by rising fumes of incense and the presence of his ancestral tablets, reported to Heaven on the preceding year's events. A month later the emperor returned to implore Heaven's help for the forthcoming year, especially for a good harvest.

First built in the early Ming, the temple has two beautiful tiered-roof circular halls in addition to its open-air marble altar. The halls are elaborately decorated, with dark-blue tiled roofs surmounted by golden balls. Somerset Maugham found the altar on its white-balustraded platform peculiarly evocative:

It stands open to the sky, three round terraces of white marble, placed one above the other, which are reached by four marble staircases, and these face the four points of the compass. It represents the celestial sphere with its cardinal points. A great park surrounds it and this again is surrounded by high walls. And hither, year after year, on the night of the winter solstice, for then heaven is reborn, generation after generation came the Son of Heaven solemnly to worship the original creator of his house. Escorted by princes and the great men of the realm, followed by his troops, the emperor purified by fasting proceeded to the altar. In the scanty light of the great torches the ceremonial robes were darkly splendid. And before the tablet on which were inscribed the words: Imperial Heaven – Supreme Emperor, he offered incense, jade, and silk, broth and rice spirit. He knelt and knocked his forehead against the marble pavement nine times.[24]

The timelessness of these proceedings made Maugham conscious that what he next witnessed was peculiarly fitting:

And here at the very spot where the vice-regent of heaven and earth knelt down, Willard B. Untermeyer wrote his name in a fine bold hand and the town and state he came from, Hastings, Nebraska. So he sought to attach his fleeting personality to the recollection of that grandeur of which some dim rumour had reached him. He thought that so men would remember him when he was no more. He aimed in this crude way at immortality. But vain are the hopes of men. For no sooner than he had sauntered down the steps than a Chinese caretaker who had been leaning against the balustrade, idly looking at the blue sky, came forward, spat neatly on the spot where Willard B. Untermeyer had written, and with his foot smeared his spittle over the name. In a moment no trace remained that Willard B. Untermeyer had ever visited that place.[25]

In the precincts of the Temple of Heaven there grows an asparagus-like herb called dragonbeard or motherwort. The latter name derives from the fact that the stalks and leaves of the ripe plant are said to furnish highly effective medicine for women's complaints. Legend gives the reason why motherwort flourishes here:

Before the temple was built a family of poor peasants scratched a living from the soil there. When the mother of the family fell ill, her daughter undertook a difficult journey into the distant Fragrant Hills to find a magic herb she had been told would bring about a cure. Her filial piety and courage persuaded the immortals to let her find it. Some of the seeds she brought home with her scattered on the ground, and the herb flourishes in the temple precincts to this day. They were nearly prevented from doing so; after the Altar of Heaven was erected a young emperor was incensed to see weeds growing around it, and ordered the gardeners to pull them up. But his mother, at that moment treating herself with medicine from the plants, told him that his beard would not grow unless this herb flourished in the temple grounds. Because the emperor is likened to a dragon, the alternative name of the plant is dragonbeard.[26]

The Altar of Heaven has existed since the earliest days of Peking as an imperial city. In the moonlight it appears to float above the ground, a saucer of shimmering ethereal milky whiteness. The Temple of Heaven, the larger of the two circular halls nearby, was destroyed by lightning in 1889 and rebuilt soon afterwards, and is therefore a modern building. It is lovely nevertheless. Even when enormous crowds of Pekinese and visitors shuffle through the grounds, to picnic or take photographs or to provoke the acoustics of the whispering wall, the temple complex remains strangely and magisterially calm. When Bertrand Russell and Dora Black were teaching in Peking in 1921, it was the place they went to recruit themselves on their days off:

In spite of the fact that China was in a ferment, it appeared to us, as compared to Europe, to be a country filled with philosophic calm. Once a week the mail would arrive from England, and the letters and newspapers that came from there seemed to breathe upon us a hot blast of insanity like the fiery heat that comes from a furnace door suddenly opened. As we had to work on Sundays, we made a practice of taking a holiday on Mondays, and we usually spent the whole day in the Temple of Heaven, the most beautiful building that it has ever been my good fortune to see. We would sit in the winter sunshine saying little, gradually absorbing peace, and would come away prepared to face the madness and passion of our own distracted continent with poise and calm.[27]

It is only recently that Peking's residents and visitors have been able to stroll through the Forbidden City, the Temple of Heaven, the ruins of the Old Summer Palace and the delights of the New Summer Palace – both these latter just outside the city – and the other attractions which history has now yielded up to tourism. But a real hint of old Peking remains in a quarter of the city devoted to booksellers and antique dealers, called Liulichang. It was a favourite place of resort for Acton:

> To visit the antique shops in the Liu Li Ch'ang was like calling at the houses of private collectors who showed one their treasures if the spirit moved them, and otherwise left one to browse. The sober modesty of the houses contrasted with the riches they contained. Their most valued objects were seldom displayed, for every time a rare object was displayed it seemed to lose a fraction of its value; and they only unveiled the nudity of an exceptional bronze, jade carving or porcelain vase to a serious collector or a scholar, hardly ever to a dealer or a tourist. I was to become more familiar with their ways, but in the meantime I was captivated by their combination of reticence and affable courtesy. They were in no hurry to sell until the right buyer came along. They were content just to drink tea with you and chat about things in general, but in the meantime they were appraising your taste, and if you admired something they thought admirable, they would warm to the theme. Immediately you would notice the gleam of enthusiasm in their eyes and a tremulousness in their expressive fingers, which they kept supple for the 'tactile values' by revolving polished walnuts or agate balls in their palms without letting them collide. Then they would lead you to a cabinet in the back room and show you something of superior quality.[28]

Today Peking is Beijing, a modern city in which these glories are hidden among high-rise blocks and broad traffic-jammed freeways. It is a tense city, because of politics and suspicion; but every morning, as on every morning since an immemorial past, old men air their singing birds in graceful cages in the parks, and in the hour after dawn thousands of people perform silent slow-motion 'shadow-boxing', a gentle keep-fit art, on roadside pavements and any other patch of available space. And even on the busiest days the Forbidden City and Tiantan retain their awesome beauty.

There can be no greater contrast than that which obtains between imperial Peking and brash, new, foreign Shanghai, a city created during the course of the last hundred years specifically to serve as a piece of the West on China's shoreline. The only way to see Shanghai for the first time as it really should be seen is by ship, as Thomas Woodroffe describes in *River of Golden Sand*:

> For an hour the tender steamed through the darkness towards a red glare in the sky. Occasionally a light twinkled from the shore, or a ghostly junk running down on the tide brushed past them, and the rhythmic chant of her crew straining at the huge oar over the stern came eerily out of the night.
>
> Once or twice they steamed through a smell – or more than a smell. It was a devastating stench, pungent and nauseating.
>
> Someone up in the bows giggled and then the voice of the Man Who'd Been Out East Before came braying out of the darkness: 'Phew! Now we're back all right. Bouquet d'Orient. Good old foo-foo barges.' It was the night soil from the Chinese city being carried down the river – not to be dumped at sea but to be sold as manure to farmers. It was a smell that was to become very familiar to Toby, and after a while, because of its familiarity, almost unnoticed. It pervaded China – the cities, the villages, the paddy fields, the countryside. It was always there. The tender ran out of it, as a ship runs out of a fog, and when they rounded the next bend the lights of the Bund burst upon them. Toby was reminded of Piccadilly Circus.

The sky was incandescent with ingenious electric advertisements. Not far away a brilliant sign flared over the roof tops and advertised the Astor House, the hotel to which he had been recommended by experts. Rockets ascended, burst and floated down, a motor-car with whizzing wheels scattered glittering particles of dust; but best of all to Toby's mind was the man smoking a cigarette. He placed it between his lips, took a puff, breathed the smoke out of his nostrils, and finally finished the cigarette, whose tip glowed red with each draw. Then suddenly the mammoth smoker disappeared, leaving a flaming slogan behind him, only to start all over again a few seconds later. The smoker was a China-man, and the slogan consisted of two huge Chinese characters.

Cars buzzed up and down like fireflies, and as they neared the landing stage, Toby saw the dim bulk of huge buildings and heard the clank of trams, groaning round a corner.

This could not be China.[29]

But China it is, although a quite different aspect of it. Isherwood saw that the handsome skyscrapers of the main waterfront avenue, the Bund, were a mask of a more than merely physical kind:

Seen from the river, towering above their couchant guardian warships, the semi-skyscrapers of the Bund present, impressively, the façade of a great city. But it is only a façade. The spirit which dumped them upon this unhealthy mud-bank, thousands of miles from their kind, has been too purely and brutally competitive. The biggest animals have pushed their way down to the brink of the water; behind them is a sordid and shabby mob of smaller buildings. Nowhere a fine avenue, a spacious park, an imposing central square. Nowhere anything civic at all. Nevertheless the tired or lustful business man will find here everything to gratify his desires. You can buy an electric razor, or a French dinner, or well-cut suit. You can dance at the Tower Restaurant on the roof of the Cathay Hotel, and gossip with Freddy Kaufmann, its charming manager, about the European aristocracy or pre-Hitler Berlin. You can attend race-meetings, baseball games, football matches. You can see the latest American films. If you want girls, or boys, you can have them, at all prices, in the bath-houses and the brothels. If you want opium you can smoke it in the best company, served on a tray, like after-noon tea. Good wine is difficult to obtain in this climate, but there is enough whisky and gin to float a fleet of battleships. The jeweller and the antique-dealer await your orders, and their charges will make you imagine yourself back on Fifth Avenue or in Bond Street. Finally, if you ever repent, there are churches and chapels of all denominations.[30]

In Mao Tun's celebrated novel of 1930s Shanghai, *Midnight*, the city's character is powerfully portrayed through the per-ceptions of an old man, the ageing father of the city's most notorious Chinese capitalist (a character somewhat reminis-cent of Shanghai's real-life prince of gangsters, Du Yueshang). Just arrived from the country, the old man is being reluctantly conveyed through the streets of the 'sinner's paradise' by car, clutching to his chest, as a talisman, a copy of his favourite book, *The Supreme Scriptures*, his mind intent upon one text in it: 'Of all the vices sexual indulgence is the cardinal; of all the virtues filial piety is the supreme.' With him are his younger son and daughter, and the fashionable young woman who had come to pick them up:

The car was racing along like mad. He peered through the wind-screen. Good heavens! The towering sky-scrapers, their countless lighted windows gleaming like the eyes of devils, seemed to be rushing down on him like an avalanche at one moment and vanishing the next. The smooth road stretched before him, and street-lamps flashed by on either side, springing up and vanishing in endless succession. A snake-like stream of black monsters, each with a pair of blinding lights for eyes, their horns blaring, bore down upon him, nearer and nearer! He closed his eyes with terror, trembling all over. He felt as if his head were spinning and his eyes swam before a kaleidoscope of red, yellow, green, black, shiny, square, cylindrical, leaping, dancing shapes, while his ears rang in a pandemonium of honking, hooting and jarring, till his heart was in his mouth.

When some time had passed without mishap, the old man slowly recovered his breath and became conscious of voices humming about his ears:

'Shanghai is not so peaceful nowadays either, Huei-fang. Not long ago there was a big Communist demonstration in Peking Road. Hundreds of them were arrested, and one of them was shot dead on the spot. Some of the Communists were armed, too! Sun-fu says the factory workers are restless and might make trouble or riot at any moment. And the walls of his factory and house have often had Communist slogans chalked all over them.'

'Haven't the police ever caught them?'

'They have caught some, but they cannot catch all of them. Oh, dear! I really don't know where all these desperate characters come from. . . . But my dear, you do make me laugh with your get-up. Your dress might have been in fashion ten years ago but now you're in Shanghai you must follow the fashion. You must get yourself a new outfit first thing tomorrow morning.'

Old Mr Wu opened his eyes again and saw that he was surrounded by a sea of little box-like motorcars like the one he was sitting in, all standing quiet and motionless, while not far ahead a stream of cars and vehicles of all kinds was rushing higgledy-piggledy in one direction and another stream the other way. Among the cars men and women of all sorts and conditions were dashing along as if the devil were on their tail. From somewhere above a shaft of crimson light fell upon him.

Here, at the crossing of Nanking Road and Honan Road, the cars going across were being held up by the traffic-lights.

'I haven't met Sun-fu's wife yet, Fu-fang,' whispered Huei-fang. 'I'm afraid she'll die laughing when she sees what a countrified girl I am.'

She cast a furtive glance at her father, then gazed out at all the fashionable women sitting in the cars around them. Fu-fang giggled, and took out her handkerchief to dab her lips. A whiff of perfume assailed the old man's nostrils, and it seemed to upset him.

'I really can't get over you, Huei-fang,' said Fu-fang. 'When I went home to the country last year, I didn't see any of the country girls wearing such old-fashioned clothes as yours.'

'That's true. Even country girls like to look pretty and smart nowadays. But father won't let me. . . .'

All this talk about fashion acted like a needle on the atrophied nerves of the old man. His heart fluttered, and his eyes fell instinctively upon Fu-fang and he saw now for the first time how she was decked out. Though it was still only May, the weather was unusually warm and she was already in the lightest of summer clothing. Her vital young body was sheathed in close-fitting light-blue chiffon, her full, firm breasts jutting out prominently, her snowy forearms bared. Old Mr Wu felt his heart constricting with disgust and quickly averted his eyes, which, however, fell straight away upon a half-naked young woman sitting up in a rickshaw, fashionably dressed in a transparent, sleeveless blouse, displaying her bare legs and thighs. The old man thought for one horrible moment that she had nothing else on. . . .

But the worst was yet to come, for he quickly withdrew his gaze, only to find his youngest son Ah-hsuan gaping with avid admiration at the same half-naked young woman. The old man felt his heart pounding wildly as if it would burst, and his throat burning as if choked with chillies.[31]

To Harold Acton, the tumult and dazzle of Shanghai in its heyday cried out to be recorded by a writer of epic talent in the realist style:

In Shanghai Bernardine Szold-Fritz, whom I had met in London and Paris, was determined that I should see everything, taste everything, smell everything in this steaming oven. I only wished that my constitution were that of Balzac and Zola, for it would require their

combined capacities for assimilation and documentation
to construct the great novel that Shanghai clamoured for.
The story of this city's rapid development from mud-flats
to skyscrapers and of the extraordinary personalities who
had devoted their energies to it and were still making
fortunes in this clammy heat would be very like a saga.
Its symbol should be the cicada, of whom a Chinese poet
wrote in the eleventh century:

> 'Are you not he, cicada,
> Of whom I have heard told you could transform
> Your body, magically moulding it
> To new estate? Are you not he who, born,
> Upon the dung-heap, coveted the sky,
> The clean and open air?'

A cicada-city, inhabited by some four millions of cicadas
struggling from their chrysalides on the dung-heap.
After the geometrical quietude of Peking and the tremendous spaces of rice-field and hill and river we had
traversed, it was like coming to a Liverpool in the
tropics. The 'Chinese City' to which Bernardine took
me realized all that had ever been written of human ant-
heaps, and the International Settlement was almost as
constricted. On the Bund at midday human beings
became insects again.[32]

The Chinese city is a small irregularly circular enclosure
in the south of the city centre, surrounded by the foreign-
built areas once called 'Concessions', which enjoyed extrater-
ritoriality until 1943, meaning that the British, French,
American and other foreign nationals resident there governed
themselves – or more correctly, gave themselves licence. Like
most visitors before the Second World War Shanghai's International Settlement was Bertrand Russell's first point of entry
to China, and although he found his Chinese hosts charming – 'I had not realized until then that a civilized Chinese
is the most civilized person in the world' – Shanghai's foreign community disgusted him; in a letter to Lady Ottoline
Morrell he described them as looking 'villainous and ill', and
castigated his own countrymen in particular:

The Englishman in the East, as far as I was able to judge
of him, is a man completely out of touch with his
environment. He plays polo and goes to the club. He
derives his ideas of native culture from the works of
eighteenth-century missionaries, and he regards intelligence in the East with the same contempt which he feels
for intelligence in his own country. Unfortunately for
our political sagacity, he overlooks the fact that in the
East intelligence is respected, so that enlightened Radi-
cals have an influence upon affairs which is denied to
their English counterparts.[33]

Because Acton knew China well his judgement of Shanghai is especially interesting. He saw it as a city of exiles, not
least among them the enormous immigrant community of
White Russians, true exiles with no other place to go, many
of whom made their living in one or another department of
Shanghai's vice industry:

Everywhere in Shanghai one jostled adventures and
rubbed shoulders with people who had no inkling how
extraordinary they were: the extraordinary had become
ordinary; the freakish commonplace. But I was seeking
adventures of the mind.
   The White Russians in the night clubs had lived
several lives, and they looked it. One must be singularly
blinded by racial prejudice to prefer these voracious
Medusas to the Chinese 'taxi-girls', so-called since one
bought tickets to dance with them. Paradise indeed to
wake up and find such grace beside one on a pillow, but
I was maddened by my inability to converse. Unfortunately for me the language of eyes and lips has never been
sufficient, and the paltry words we were able to exchange
struck a metallic chill, and brought me back to earth
with a clash of coins. Not only with a clash, but with
a bump of humiliation. Such ludicrous words as, 'Master,
please give one piecie dollar more to number one good
girl,' would pursue one, exploding the little wind that
was left in one's sails, leaving one to sink in squalid
quicksands. 'Dollars, more dollars,' was the burden of all
such lyrics. Had one merely represented a cheque-book?

In most cases I am afraid one had. One's other gifts did not matter. I had never encountered such hardness combined with such softness. It was galling that the true nature of those who fulfilled one's dreams of unearthly beauty was entirely earthbound, but with the standard of living so low it was easy to understand and to forgive. Beauty demands every sacrifice, even of one's pride.

The Russians who spoke one's language, ungainly as they were, could produce an illusion of the tenderness that most men craved – hence, paradoxically, their intercourse may have had a more spiritual value. The choice lay between tenderness and plainness on the one hand, indifference and beauty on the other. I chose indifference and beauty every time.[34]

This was the setting for Marlene Dietrich's portrayal of 'Shanghai Lily' in the film *Shanghai Express* – an unforgiving, raucous place, exemplifying what human life becomes when coin is the chief measure of things.

Then as now, Shanghai was China's leading industrial city. Its success as such was based on sweated labour. Every visitor with a modicum of social concern was appalled at the exploitation that Acton here describes:

Shanghai was the most cruel and merciless of cities; half the industrial workers of China subsisted within its area on miserable wages. Hours were long and competition was fierce. The Japanese mills ground the bodies and souls of the girls who toiled for them. Having been bought by contractors and sold to factories, these girls were practically slaves. In the average year some 29,000 corpses were gathered on the streets. These facts were inescapable; one could not feel happy for long in such a place.[35]

It is no surprise that China's Communist Party came to life here, born in 1921. On a July morning in that year a 28-year-old school-teacher from Hunan Province walked along the plane-tree-lined avenues of the French Concession to 106 rue Wantz, where, after pausing and looking round carefully, he slipped inside. Pan Ling records what followed:

There were perhaps a dozen men in the room. One was a fellow-Hunanese, but would not otherwise have been particularly noticeable. Two were not Chinese: a representative of the Trades Unions International named N. Nikolsky, and another Soviet agent called Hendricus Sneevliet, a Dutch Communist assuming the pseudonym G. Maring. The gathering was clandestine, and none of those present was to remember the details very well. But the 28-year-old delegate, and the resolves he took home with him to Hunan, were presently to change the world. The man was Mao Zedong, and the meeting was the opening congress of the Chinese Communist Party. Five of the men at the meeting were to lay down their lives for the Party; the fellow-Hunanese, Zhou Fohai, was to turn traitor.[36]

Tsai Chin, the woman who helped set the tone for London's 'Swinging Sixties' by her eponymous performance in *The World of Soozie Wong*, was brought up in Shanghai, and in her autobiography records the life of a well-off Chinese family in the years before the Communist takeover. Not even money could insulate a child from the less pleasant realities of the place:

> Once outside the haven of home, theatre and school, a child in Shanghai, no matter how protected, was . . . inevitably exposed to the life of the city, mostly hostile and inhumane. Much that I saw at this time baffled me. In the crowded thoroughfare of the Bund in the British zone, for instance, I tried hard to be immune to the aggressive way the Sikh policemen directed the traffic, leaping from their rostrums to beat defenceless Chinese rickshaw-pullers whenever it suited them. These hated subjects of the British Raj had been imported from India, like opium, but as slaves to control slaves. Parks in the foreign concessions were forbidden to Chinese, although they were paid for from Chinese taxes. Outside one was a sign which has become infamous: 'Dogs and Chinese Not Allowed'.
>
> As the city filled, the streets were lined with all manner of human misery and deformity. The fortunate were

allowed to spill over into the foreign concessions where a day's begging or thieving was more lucrative. They were controlled by the syndicates. Once, walking down the street with a woman servant, I noticed a man with a horrible face, with only a hole where his nose should have been. I asked my servant the reason for this deformity. She threw a quick glance at the man and quickly pulled me away. 'Never you mind. Disgusting!' she said scornfully. I was too young to have heard of syphilis. The beggar heard my servant's remark and shouted: 'Hey, your mother! Don't begrudge me the only bit of fun I've got left!'

Servants in Shanghai were plentiful, as labour was cheap. The poor after all had always relied on their only capital, their bodies, to make a living. Men sold their *ku li*, or 'bitter strength', from which the word 'coolie' derives. Women had various physical commodities to sell in different parts of their anatomy. Besides plain prostitution, a concubine's womb was used to perpetuate an otherwise extinct male line. And as wet-nurses, their babies' milk was sacrificed to nourish another mother's children.[37]

'Every war in the country', wrote Vicki Baum in *Shanghai '37*, 'must come to Shanghai.' In the Taiping Rebellion of 1850–64 the city was besieged for two years, precariously defended by a mixed body of Chinese and European troops officered by Europeans. One or two small defensive successes by this informal regiment prompted the emperor in Peking to accord it the title of 'The Ever-Victorious Army', whereupon it embarked on a series of defeats which threatened the very existence of the new entrepôt of Shanghai. Into this dangerous situation stepped the extraordinary figure of General Gordon, appointed to save the hour. He promised to defeat the Taipings within eighteen months; 'and', as Lytton Strachey memorably reports, 'he was as good as his word':

The Ever-Victorious Army, recruited from the riff-raff of Shanghai, was an ill-disciplined, ill-organised body of about three thousand men, constantly on the verge of mutiny, supporting itself on plunder, and, at the

slightest provocation, melting into thin air. Gordon, by
sheer force of character, established over this incoherent
mass of ruffians an extraordinary ascendancy. He drilled
them with rigid severity; he put them into a uniform,
armed them systematically, substituted pay for loot, and
was even able, at last, to introduce regulations of a
sanitary kind. There were some terrible scenes, in which
the General, alone, faced the whole furious army, and
quelled it; scenes of rage, desperation, towering courage,
and summary execution. Eventually he attained to an
almost magical prestige. Walking at the head of his
troops, with nothing but a light cane in his hand, he
seemed to pass through every danger with the scathless
equanimity of a demigod. The Taipings themselves were
awed into a strange reverence. More than once their
leaders, in a frenzy of fear and admiration, ordered their
sharp-shooters not to take aim at the advancing figure
of the faintly smiling Englishman.[38]

At the height of Shanghai's flourishing in the early 1930s
unpleasant rumours of war were again afoot. Sir Victor
Sassoon had not long since built that jewel of Art Deco
design, the Cathay Hotel on the Bund which, because of its
distinctive pyramidical roof, immediately became the city's
emblem. This is where the fashionable of the world thronged,
to Roof Garden dances and the smoky jazz bar. Everyone
knows that Noël Coward had flu at the Cathay Hotel in 1929,
and wrote *Private Lives* as he recuperated in one of its suites.
It is less well-known that in Shanghai he discovered the Royal
Navy and fell in love with it; they ferried him to Hong Kong
in the gaiety of an officer's mess, and he repaid them later
with *In Which We Serve*.

But the rumours of war were serious. There was civil
war in the land, and Japan was threatening China. In 1932
Shanghai witnessed a portentously ugly incident, in which
Japanese troops, by marching into the International Settlement, attempted to enforce their country's claim to be counted
among the community of nations there. And on 'Bloody
Saturday' in August 1937 there was a fatal sign of the
approaching end:

The year is 1937, the year when the Sino-Japanese War
started with a minor skirmish (if it can be so termed)
at the Marco Polo Bridge [in Peking]. Soon the conflict
spread to the environs of Shanghai and fighting broke
out between Chinese and Japanese troops in the Chinese-
administered areas of Shanghai, which surrounded the
International Settlement and the French Concession. . . .
As Dick Wilson writes, 'on Saturday afternoon – 14
August 1937 – foreign residents sipping cocktails in the
Palace Hotel bar saw two Chinese aeroplanes coming
towards them high over the river. . . . The two planes
circled under the clouds and then dropped four bombs,
two on a crowded crossroads, one on the roof of the
Palace Hotel and another on the neighbouring Cathay
Hotel. Over a thousand people were killed.' This sombre
event – a massacre of innocents – was a sign of things to
come, the end of sanctuary . . . both Nationalists and
Japanese showed scant regard for the neutrality of
European-controlled Shanghai. In 1943, at the Cairo
Conference, the Allies agreed that *all* Shanghai should
come under Chinese jurisdiction. It was the end of the
special status that foreigners had enjoyed for almost a
century.[39]

It was plain to everyone that the end was approaching;
yet Shanghai went on its frantic way, pretending otherwise, dancing to the edge of doom. Isherwood paints a
picture of the hysterical make-believe, and the proofs of its
absurdity:

It is the Ambassador's turn to give an official garden-
party. The preparations are elaborate. They require the
co-operation of the ladies of the British colony, the Sea-
forth Highlanders, the Embassy staff. Invitations are sent
out. The drinks and the cold buffet are organized. The
portico is decorated with flags. Bowing deeply, the doll-
butlers usher in their national enemies, the bandy-legged,
hissing Japanese generals. Everybody is present, including
the journalists. Next morning, the local newspapers will
carry photographs of the most distinguished guests. Out
on the lawn the Scottish pipers play their airs.

Everything goes off like clockwork. It is a beautifully
contrived charade, the perfect image of another kind of
life – projected, at considerable expense, from its source
on the opposite side of the earth. Such functions, no
doubt, are well worth the money they cost, for here and
there, amidst the regulation small-talk, a serious word
is exchanged, a delicate but pointed hint is dropped.
This afternoon certain minute but important readjust-
ments have been made in the exquisite balance of international relationships. At any rate, thank goodness, it
hasn't rained.

But gaily as the charade-players laugh, and loudly as
they chatter, they cannot altogether ignore those other,
most undiplomatic sounds which reach us, at intervals,
from beyond the garden trees. Somewhere out in the
suburbs, machine-guns are rattling. You can hear them
all day long. Everybody in the Settlement knows what
they mean – the Chinese guerrilla units are still active
here in the enemy's stronghold. But if you are so tactless
as to call the attention of the Japanese officers to these
noises they will reply that you are mistaken – it is only
their own troops at firing-practice.[40]

A graphic account of the Japanese takeover, when it came,
is given by J.G. Ballard in his autobiographical novel, *The
Empire of the Sun*. As it had done in Manchuria, Japan took
Shanghai by force and then installed a puppet Chinese leader-
ship. Its troops then looked menacingly on at the Looking-
Glass world that resulted:

Wars always invigorated Shanghai, quickened the pulse
of its congested streets. Even the corpses in the gutters
seemed livelier. Throngs of peasant women packed the
pavements of the Avenue Foch, outside the Cercle Spor-
tif Français the vendors locked wheels as they jostled
their carts against each other, lines of pedicabs and rickshaws ten abreast hemmed in the cars that edged forward behind a continuous blare of horns. Young Chinese
gangsters in shiny American suits stood on the street corners, shouting the jai alai odds at each other. In the
pedicabs outside the Regency Hotel the bar-girls sat in

fur coats with their bodyguards beside them, like gla-
morous wives waiting to be taken for a ride. The entire
city had come out into the streets, as if the population
were celebrating the takeover of the International Settlement, its seizure from the Americans and Europeans by
another Asian power.

Yet when Jim reached the junction of Avenue Petain
and the Avenue Haig a British police sergeant and two
Sikh NCOs of the Shanghai police force still directed
the traffic from their cantilever bridge above the crowd,
watched by a single Japanese soldier standing behind
them. Armed Japanese infantry sat like sightseers in the
camouflaged trucks that moved along the streets. A
party of officers stood outside the Radium Institute,
adjusting their gloves. Pasted over the Coca Cola and
Caltex billboards were fresh posters of Wang Ching-wei,
the turncoat leader of the puppet regime.[41]

But before the curtain fell life was lived at full pace. For
visitors and residents alike one of the chief ports of call in
Shanghai – a place to take on the fuel of desire, perhaps, in
preparation for the *maisons de plaisir* along the Bubbling Well
Road – was the Shanghai Club with its famous long bar. Noël
Coward's navy friends would have recognized the experience
of the characters in Thomas Woodrooffe's Yangtse gunboat
novel, who make a foray to the Club from their ship. It begins
when a shore sampan is summoned to scull officers across to
the Bund – a sometimes hazardous proceeding because the
Huangpo River was always crowded with boats:

> The old man at the stern threaded his way through the
> traffic with amazing skill. Apparently there was no rule
> of the road on the Whangpoo; smaller craft got out of
> the way of the larger, whatever the rights of the matter,
> and the tugs that came roaring up and down made no
> effort to miss anything that got in their way. . . . The
> sun was setting as they went ashore and for a moment
> the yellow river looked like the Thames, muddy after
> rain, and the forests of masts and variegated funnels
> might have been in the Pool of London; a smoky pall
> hung over the Chinese city, and the modern European

buildings on the Bund seen through a murky haze might have been on the Embankment and the green patch round the British Consulate, the Temple Gardens. It gave Toby a feeling of homesickness. Faintly across the water, now a brilliant orange where the sun caught it, he heard the song of some ship loading: 'Oh he, he ho', and once again he was back in China.

Outwardly, the club had a certain restrained dignity; inside it was a palace. A marble staircase led up to a vast colonnaded hall, also of marble. It was more like a Hollywood director's idea of the palace of an Emperor than the drinking rendezvous of half the business men of Shanghai. On one side of this hall was the bar, which, as every schoolboy knows, is the longest in the world, ranking with the Pyramids, the Grand Canyon, the Crystal Palace, Mount Everest, the Empire State Building and other giant phenomena. Toby had heard all about it, of course, from the Man Who'd Been Out East Before. He even knew that there existed an heretical sect that believed that there was a longer bar in San Francisco, a sect that did not show its head in Shanghai.

Blair led the way through a heavy mahogany swing door with a glass peep-hole in its upper half. Toby was prepared for a fairly large bar but not for this monstrosity stretching away to right and left, as long and narrow as a tube station. Along its whole length stretched a shining and resplendent mahogany counter that must have denuded whole forests in the making and massive enough to withstand the charge of a herd of elephants. It could safely support the non-drinking elbows of the elite of Shanghai. Behind this rampart were rows and rows of bottles on shelves, multiplied to infinity in shining mirrors behind them until the whole wall seemed composed of a mass of bottles ten deep. A cheering sight for a thirsty man. Between this glittering background and the bar itself, the upper portion of a row of Chinamen spaced at regular intervals, dressed in spotless white, stood as motionless as the bottles winking over their impassive heads. They looked rather like a row of unassuming flowers that are sometimes planted between the flaring riot of a herbaceous border and the grass verge. On the floor brass spittoons twinkled invitingly. Two-bladed fans spun lazily and noiselessly around overhead. It was an incredible room.[42]

The famous long bar is over thirty metres long; the Club is now the Dongfeng (East Wind) Hotel. Woodrooffe was not alone in being reminded of London by Shanghai's waterfront. Acton saw the resemblance too:

In fog or rain the muddy Whangpoo evokes the Thames. Perhaps the first British settlers had been struck by the resemblance when they chose this site for their godowns. Humanity begins on Soochow Creek, a forest of masts and hulls: here the hulks fold their wings at night, a huge family of sea-birds. Beyond are the seething alleys of Hongkew, and stretched along the nether shore, fading into distance, the great ichthyosauria of industrialism, the gaunt factories, warehouses and skeletons of cranes standing up from the docks.

At night the vast Bund is silent; your footsteps echo. But turning down any of the squinting side-streets you come towards a confused hum like a bee-hive magnified and dispersed. The hum increases as you walk on, louder and louder, and from the dead dark weight of the soulless deserted Bund you are transported in a few minutes into the glare and cacophony of Asia. From grotesquely sculptured doorways come blasts of hot shrill music, piercing falsetto and shattering gong, whiffs of aromatic odours impossible to define, olfactory variations of sandalwood, and leisurely torrents of people in long gowns, spilling everywhere, hardly bothering to dodge the passing rickshaws, neat and sociable, absorbed in their sociability, advancing casually against the avalanche of sound. . . .

The rickshaw coolies would yell at the top of their lungs to make way, but they yelled in vain, against a blank wall as it were. And inside the rickshaws were girls like bejewelled goddesses from a shrine, sitting stiffly erect in dazzling sheaths of silk, impassive under their brilliant make-up. All the colour and electricity in the street seemed concentrated in and upon them, as they passed, instantaneous visions of beauty never to cross my path again. The wall of the throng would crumble for an occasional motor-car, hooting desperately and barely slowing down. It was a flood predominantly indigo, but the roses and violets of women's head-dresses tinkled like bells on the surface. Very few wore Western clothes, and you forgot that you were in an International Settlement.

During these aimless walks one's curiosity was constantly excited – by the multicoloured merchandise in the shops and especially by the natural history museums of pharmacy windows, the strange claws, animistic herbs, mandrake roots, pickled salamanders, and powdered antlers. Subjects for poems came crowding upon one at every turn. The single-storied wooden houses with upturned roofs did not shut out the sun and air in the daytime, unlike the gloomy masonry near the Bund where the streets conspired to blackball daylight. I was generally the only European wanderer, 'alone like the rhinoceros', but I was never made uncomfortable by that fact. In a sense I was as isolated as in the depths of a jungle, but it was a friendly jungle.[43]

Shanghai still stands where it did, on the confluence of the Huangpo and the stinking Suzhou Creek, which mingle their polluted waters for the short distance to the Yangtse mouth and the Yellow Sea. But it has not been the place it was. In the Communist decades since 1949, taking its cue from the dreary repression everywhere in China, Shanghai was like a fire that had died out, a bed of grey ash. It was still of course overpopulated, noisy, industrial, crowded, sodden with heat in summer – but somehow not fully alive. As recently as 1982 Pan Ling, Shanghai's recording angel, claimed that

Much of the fascination of life in Shanghai in the decades before the 1949 Liberation lies in its strange remoteness from the world of China today. Strange that so contemporary an experience can vanish so completely – the street names changed, the capitalists fled, the glitter faded, the foreign residents chased out of town, the bubble burst. It was only yesterday, after all, that

Shanghai was the 'Paris of the East', the 'capital of the tycoon', the 'whore of Asia' and the 'paradise of adventurers', where missionaries declared that if God let Shanghai endure He owed an apology to Sodom and Gomorrah. Its very name was unsavoury, being an English nautical slang meaning 'to drug and ship as sailor when drunk'. No other city fell to Communism in so feverish a whirl of pleasure, dissoluteness, rapacity and squalor. Now, that image of last-fling decadence, of Shanghai dancing even while Communism knocked on its door, survives only as a cliché in the minds of the people, and those who witnessed it will almost certainly never see its like again.[44]

But Pan Ling is too pessimistic; things are changing again. Something of the vivid thrill of old Shanghai is returning – swiftly, one senses, like the high tides of the Yangtse which flood up the Huangpo and which in the old days brought back the coffins launched from the bund of the Chinese city. As China's economy booms, the ebullient and wicked ways of the past are coming back to Shanghai.

2

MUTUAL PERCEPTIONS

Barbarians, even when they have a ruler, are inferior
to Chinese, even when they do not have a ruler.

Confucius, *The Analects*, 3.5

British and American gun-boats were moored alongside the outer shore. Their crews were playing football – hairy, meat-pink men with powerful buttocks,
they must have seemed ferocious, uncouth giants to
the slender, wasp-waisted Cantonese spectators, with
their drooping, flowerlike stance and shy brilliant
smiles.

W.H. Auden and Christopher Isherwood,
Journey to a War, p. 31

The question of how Chinese and Westerners view each other
is a highly educative one. When any two peoples are unaccus-
tomed to one another's appearance and practices, they account
the other freaks, and believe them capable of anything.
Ignorance liberates the imagination in this respect. Without
question, much of what the Chinese have thought about foreigners, and foreigners about the Chinese, has been of this
order: ill-informed, fanciful and racist.

In the late nineteenth century an English missionary, A.H.
Smith, published *Chinese Characteristics*, a popular study of
'the Chinese character' containing many generalizations, some
insights, and not a few prejudices. It served as a bible for
foreigners visiting China, and was highly influential in shap-
ing the West's general view of the Chinese as inscrutable Fu
Manchus with pigtails and drooping moustaches who, when
not enfeebled by opium, were always up to no good.

This stereotype was repeated in films and novels galore.

And when the Chinese were neither narcotically depraved nor mysteriously wicked, they were merely comic, a view some visitors to China delighted in emphasizing. One, for example, assiduously collected Chinese efforts at English, like the sign in Chongqing advertising 'False Eyes And Dental Plumbing Inserted By The Latest Methodists' and the book called *Correctly English in Hundred Days* which states in its preface:

> This book is prepared for the Chinese young man who wishes to served for the big firms.
> It divided nearly hundred and ninety pages.
> It contains full of ordinary speak and write language.
> This book is clearly, easily, to the Chinese young man or scholar. If it is quite understood, that will be satisfaction.

The discoverer of the book comments:

> To me this book was extraordinary. . . . In its oblique chapters a whole fantastic world was unfolded. The section devoted to the farmyard referred to 'chickens and duckens' while the chapter on animals described the 'tigar' as having 'two bright eyes and very sharp legs'. Probably I can best suggest its unhinged universe by quoting in its entirety an essay on a familiar subject:

WATER

> Water is the most useful thing. If we want to cook something we must use the water. We wash face and body must use the water. Everything must have water to living in anytime in anywhere except the dead things. Young man should do something. Young man should obey his parent. Young man should not gumbling. Young man should be diligent. Young man should be fairthfil. Young man should on quarrel. Post no bill. Spitting prohibited. No smoking. No admittance. Stop talking. Public telephone. Please shut the door.[1]

In the eighteenth century, Europe was filled with admiration for China and things Chinese. Porcelain, gardens, styles of dress and even architecture felt the influence of what visitors there had seen. But in the nineteenth and first half of the twentieth century, opinion among most foreigners living in China was typical of colonists everywhere: it was racism of an often contemptuous kind, an attitude bred in missionary insensitivity and merchant ignorance, and carried home by them to the West. The anonymous curmudgeon of *China As It Really Is* who calls himself 'A Resident of Peking', writing just before the First World War, illustrates their outlook perfectly:

> The Chinese are probably the most ceremonious race in the world. The Frenchman or the Italian excites the good-humoured derision of the stay-at-home Briton: the Chinaman is more than ridiculous; he is frankly absurd. He attaches an extravagant importance to the due observance of an elaborate code of etiquette, for which the go-ahead people of the West have neither the time nor the inclination. His daily conduct is regulated by this code, and he has great and genuine contempt for all who, from ignorance or disinclination, do not conform to it. The contempt for the foreigner that is characteristic of the heathen Chinee is in no small way connected with our – to him – incredible ignorance and disregard of the conventions of social intercourse. The Chinaman, devoid of independence and self-reliance, intellectually warped and physically inferior, yellow and unwashed, is only just – after a long series of unprecedented humiliations – waking up to the fact that the foreigner is not of an inferior race that has everything to learn and nothing to impart. The Chinaman has everything to learn, and the task is more difficult because he has so much to forget before he can make progress. He is bound up in national and personal conceit. Conceit is the most prominent characteristic of the *literati* – the upper and official class of China: conceit totally unjustified and absolutely hidebound. . . .
>
> The Chinaman of all classes is essentially unwashed, and in this differs from the Japanese. Cleanliness is not a lost art in China; it is an art that has never been discovered. He washes his summer clothes occasionally, his person once in a blue moon. The wadded garments

that he affects in winter beggar description. His bed-clothes and his beds, his houses and his hotels, pass all understanding. . . .

The Chinese gentleman always affects long nails. It is an indication that he is a man of position. A manual labourer is obviously precluded from growing his nails three inches or so long. These long nails – their very length ensures a larger area for the accumulation of foreign matter – are peculiarly disgusting to the Westerner. . . .[2]

And so on. But the opposite – a love-affair between the foreigner and his China – could and did happen too. Thomas Woodrooffe provides an illustration of this. The officers of his fictional Yangtse gunboat are ashore, guests of an upriver British consul. Their conversation turns inevitably to 'the Chinese'. Between the ship's doctor and the host, Newton, sharply contrasting points of view are aired:

'What do you think of the Chinese?' said Blair.

Newton thought for a moment. 'I should take days to answer that question and then not do it to my satisfaction. Shortly, I consider that they are unquestionably the greatest race – or rather collection of human beings with a continuous history – that has ever been or ever will be. The greatest civilization, shall we say?'

'But they're finished,' said the doctor.

'What makes you say that?'

'Well, look at their Army and their Government. And . . . er . . . their lack of sanitation . . . and well, the Treaty Ports. Anybody can grab a bit of China who wants to, and the Japs will grab the lot in a few years. As a people they're effete. Their civilization is too old – played out.'

'Yes,' said the host, 'they have no Army and precious little Government and what there is is rotten with corruption and I agree their sanitation leaves a lot to be desired. But I think you are taking rather a gloomy view. They've been conquered before – many times. But, of course, you know that. But have you noticed that whoever may be in the position of conqueror,

Mongol, Tartar, the hordes from the West or North, the Chinese people have never been really conquered. The so-called conquerors have either been absorbed or merely grafted on to the Chinese people who, in spite of misgovernment and rapacity and bloodshed and all the rest of it, have gone steadily on. I never feel depressed about the future of China; I didn't, even when the Revolution [of 1911] turned out so badly. Their great sage, you know, lived during a time of chaos and repression, and Confucius lived five hundred years before Christ. Troubled times are nothing new in China – they pass by and leave the people unruffled.

'Walk down a street, watch the craftsmen at work or the coolies, go into the countryside and where have you ever seen a more industrious, peace-loving, happy lot of people? A million may die in a famine; two million may be homeless through floods, but in an incredibly short space of time the floods are under control and the country is again dotted with homesteads and paddy-fields, and the famine area is full of farm-houses and as densely populated as before. It's their vitality – their fertility – it's tremendous and thank heaven it is all directed to peaceful ends. The Chinese are not a warlike race; in their literature the warrior is always despised. They do not want conquests – they want peace. It is the man of letters, the poet who can imprison in a single phrase the glinting beauty of the dragon-fly's wing, the painter who can capture the movement of bamboos trembling in a breeze, the man with exquisite calligraphy – these are the men who are honoured in China above all others, and still are – though you might not think it. They have a respect for knowledge and therefore old age is revered, not because it is pathetic or helpless, but because it has learnt so much.'[3]

But such appreciative views were rare. Bertrand Russell's characterization of the foreigners he met in China as ignorant and imperceptive was much closer to the mark.

It was ignorance that did most harm. A good example is the way Western engineers, building railways and telegraph lines across China, neglected ancient sensitivities over *fengshui*, the geomantic spiritual properties of places:

> Earlier in the century European countries had viewed the advent of railways with mistrust and alarm; and China could hardly be expected to welcome what she still calls the 'fire-cart'. But the grounds on which she objected to it were much more diverse and fanciful. . . .
>
> That the railway was an innovation was bad; that it was a foreign thing was worse. Because of the haphazard ubiquity of Chinese burial-places, scarcely a mile of track could be laid without desecrating the graves of somebody's ancestors. Serious and frequent offence was caused to the *feng-shui*. The well-known foreign custom of burying Chinese babies in the foundations of important structures, like cathedrals, gave rise to macabre suspicions about the permanent way. . . .
>
> Telegraph lines were a further source of alarm and despondency. To the country people across whose patchwork fields the tall poles strode, their purpose was unfathomable and their appearance forbidding. When the wind blew, a low moaning, very piteous to hear, diffused itself from the wires. As these rusted, the rainwater dripping from them acquired a gruesome tinge of red and strengthened the belief that the spirits were being tortured by these alien contraptions.[4]

But the writer of these remarks, Peter Fleming, was alert to the other, less fanciful, reasons for Chinese disquiet too:

> These were some of the objections on what may be called the ideological plane. Others were more concrete and easier to sympathize with. . . .
>
> The official class, who knew better, disliked the telegraph because it was an agent of remote control and narrowed the area of legitimate delay which, seemly and expansive as a well-kept lawn, surrounded every *yamen* in the Empire. . . .
>
> The foreign businessmen who negotiated the [railway] concessions were often boors; the overseers who supervised the work were often bullies. Though the

railway might on a long view bring prosperity as well as progress, it immediately threatened the livelihood of thousands. Carters, chair-bearers, muleteers, camel-men, innkeepers and other humble folk faced, or thought they faced, ruin. Junks and the ponderous house-boats of officials could not pass under the bridges, so that riverine trade-routes which had flourished for centuries were interrupted. Minor functionaries who controlled and preyed on traffic using the roads and waterways found their importance and their illicit revenues sharply reduced. Although the rolling-stock itself, and especially the locomotives, excited wonder and delight in a people who have an inborn relish for ingenuity and loud noises, the railways aroused deep misgiving in the districts through which they passed or were projected; and in parts of the Empire where they were as yet only a bogy, rumour saw to it that the bogy was very alarming indeed.[5]

Foreign insensitivity thus bred suspicion and fear among the Chinese, and it extended beyond railways and telegraphs:

We went for a walk one morning on the other side of the river, and took the photographer with us and left him to his own devices. When we returned home he told us that the people had thrown stones and bricks at the camera. He said that his attempts had not been very successful. The Chinese people believe that foreigners make a juice out of children's eyes for photographic purposes; they say, 'A man, or a dog, or a horse cannot see without eyes; how then can that machine? If it has not got eyes of its own, it must have the eyes of somebody else.' Their logic is unanswerable, especially the brickbats and stones.[6]

These excitements, related by Captain William Gill, happened to a nineteenth-century photographer. A twentieth-century one found that suspicion had somewhat waned:

Auden did a lot of photography among the platform crowd. Shortly after his return from one of these camera-expeditions we looked out of the window to see a beggar rolling on the ground and roaring as though in fearful pain. The Englishman, he yelled, had stolen his spirit and put it into his little box. He wanted five dollars compensation. We were both rather alarmed by this new form of blackmail, but the onlookers seemed to be on our side. They merely laughed.[7]

But earlier the suspicions and anxieties were real enough, and deep-rooted. As Fleming noted, uneducated Chinese were especially fearful about foreigners' interest in Chinese children:

In China female children were often exposed at birth or – later in life, and if times were hard – offered for sale; no organization, and indeed no impulse, existed to care for waifs and strays. The missionaries, accordingly, opened orphanages. 'It is,' wrote Smith in 1901, 'impossible for the Chinese to understand the motive for beneficence of this sort: and the presence of so many helpless infants, especially when the mortality is large, is immediately connected with the invincible superstition that foreigners wish to mutilate the bodies for the purpose of alchemy, thus turning lead into silver.'
    Similar fables abounded, and plausibility was lent to them by garbled accounts of such rites as extreme unction and the baptism of the dying. The medical work done by many of the missionaries earned the gratitude of sufferers all over China, but the ill-disposed (including, for obvious reasons, the native doctors and pharmacists) saw to it that the most gruesome interpretation was put on any cure or operation that failed.[8]

Such fears counted among the sources of the celebrated Boxer rebellion of 1900, aimed at expelling foreigners from China. The Boxers directed their propaganda at peasants anxious about the drought then affecting large parts of the empire. One of their posters proclaimed:

The Catholic and Protestant religions being insolent to the gods, and extinguishing sanctity, rendering no obedience to Buddha, and enraging Heaven and Earth, the rain-clouds no longer visit us; but eight million Spirit Soldiers will descend from Heaven and sweep the Empire clean of all foreigners. Then will the gentle showers once more water our lands; and when the tread of soldiers and the clash of steel are heard heralding woes to all our people, then the Buddhist Patriotic League of Boxers will be able to protect the Empire and bring peace to all its people.

Hasten, then, to spread this doctrine far and wide, for if you gain one adherent to the faith your own person will be absolved from all future misfortunes. If you gain five adherents your whole family will be absolved from all evils, and if you gain ten adherents your whole village will be absolved from all calamities. Those who gain no adherents to the cause shall be decapitated, for until all foreigners have been exterminated the rain can never visit us.

Those who have been so unfortunate as to have drunk water from wells poisoned by foreigners should at once make use of the following Divine Prescription, the ingredients of which are to be decocted and swallowed, when the poisoned patient will recover:

> Dried black plums . . . half an ounce.
> Solanum dulcamara . . half an ounce
> Liquorice root . . . . . . half an ounce.[9]

The Boxers need not have used the excuse of drought; to most Chinese then, and to many now, foreigners were by themselves horrible enough to be obviously a source of evils. 'To a Chinaman's eyes,' wrote Gill,

a Western is as hideous and strange as a Chinaman at first is to ours; to his mind our clothes are not only uncouth and uncomfortable, but indecent; and to his ideas a light-haired being is diabolic – indeed the very animals seem to share this belief. A story is told of a red-haired, red-bearded Englishman who one day was walking in a country place; meeting a cart, the animals were so frightened by the extraordinary apparition, that they started, and upset the vehicle into a ditch. The Anglo-Saxon good-naturedly went to assist in setting matters straight, when the carter entreated him to get out of sight as soon as he could, as his awful appearance only terrified the animals the more.[10]

While Chinese oxen and donkeys dislike foreigners, Chinese dogs, it seems, dislike them even more:

This dog had been almost entirely amongst Chinese, and either the appearance or the smell of a European was distasteful to him. The Chinese, who to a European nose always emit a peculiar odour, declare that they can perfectly well distinguish the smell of a European. There can be no doubt that 'Tib' could detect, even at a distance, a European by his smell, for he invariably barked at the French missionaries directly they entered the courtyard of my house at Ch'eng-Tu, although they were always dressed in Chinese clothes.[11]

If foreigners looked odd to the Chinese and their animals, foreigners in return always felt it necessary to explain one or another aspect of Chinese appearance – in addition to the almond eyes, high cheekbones and smooth golden skin, that is. A favourite topic was the pigtail, plait or queue universally worn until the early decades of the twentieth century. Gill continues:

The plait was first imposed upon the Chinese as a badge of servitude by the Manchus when they took the country; but the origin of the appendage has been long forgotten – it is now valued almost as dearly as life, and to be without one is considered the sign of a rebel.
I was told that once a Chinese gentleman was riding in the settlement of Shanghai in a jinnyrickshaw, when he allowed his plait to fall over the side; it was a long one, and the end was soon caught in the axle, which gradually wound it up. The poor fellow shouted to the man drawing him to stop, but the coolie, imagining that he was being urged to greater efforts, only went the faster, until the unfortunate occupant, with his plait nearly wound up to the end, and himself nearly dragged out of his carriage, was in a pitiable plight. A British sailor at this moment happened to pass that way, and

observing the desperate predicament, with the readiness
of resource for which nautical people are famed, he drew
his knife and in an instant severed the plait from the
Chinaman's head. He thought he had done a kindly act,
but instead of thanks he received curses, and his life was
not considered safe until his ship was well beyond the
limits of the Shanghai river.[12]

Some nineteenth-century travellers in China reckoned that
hostility to them was felt chiefly by educated people – the
literati – whereas ordinary people, at least in rural areas, were
more likely to be friendly:

Besides the officials, the people of this province are
mostly either merchants or agriculturists, the literati –
that generally highly-favoured class in China – being
held in light esteem by the men of Ssu-Ch'uan; and to
this is probably owing the fact that foreigners are always
treated with great politeness, as wherever opposition to
foreigners is carried to any great extent, it will generally
be found to be owing to the influence of the literati class.
There were of course some literati here, and so good an
opportunity of showing their talents was not to be lost.
So they wrote a poem in very bad rhyme, which Baber
translated and headed, 'As others see us':

AS OTHERS SEE US.
The Sea-folk, once a tributary band,
In growing numbers tramp across the land
English and French, with titulary sounds
As of a nation, are the merest hounds!
Nothing they wot of gods, in earth or sky;
Nothing of famous dynasties gone by!
One of their virgins, clasped in my embrace
Told me last year the secrets of their race,
Taught me the foulness of the Western beast,
And, fouler still, the foulness of the Priest.
I know their features, Goblins of the West!
I know the elf-locks on their devil's crest!
Cunning artificers, no doubt, but far beneath our
    potency in peace, or war!

But now our opportunity is near;
Learning and valour are assembled here;
Let all to the cathedral doors repair,
Grapple the dogs, and never think to spare!
I rede ye right! Shall savages presume
To harry China and escape the doom?
No! Let us all with emulous might combine
To crush the priests, and save the Imperial line.
First slay the Bishop, tear away his hide,
Hack out his bones, and let his fat be fried;
And for the rest who have confessed the faith,
Drag them along, and roast them all to death!
For when these weeds are rooted from the plain,
No magic art can give them life again.[13]

Feeling that his readers need a gloss on this Chinese
Dunciad, Gill annotates it as follows:

The author begins by inquiring why foreigners should
come to China; and though he shows an unusual amount
of knowledge by stating that the French and English are
different people, yet he denies nationality to either one or
the other, who, he adds, are all mere dogs, and ignorant
of the true religion. In the sixth line he refers to the
features of foreigners, which all Chinamen consider worse
than hideous. Foreigners are usually also credited with red
hair, which, in their eyes, is an abomination; hence the
reference to elf-locks. The author exhibits unexpected
discrimination in crediting foreigners with being cunning
artificers; Chinese generally think, or pretend to think,
that we are ignorant of everything. In the eighth line,
reference is made to the approaching examinations, when
thousands of literati and students for degrees would be
assembled at Ch'ung-Ch'ing. The last line refers to the
popular belief that foreigners can after death return to life;
and, once more showing more knowledge than might
have been expected, combats this belief.[14]

Today Chinese people call foreigners 'lao wai', short for 'lao
waiguo ren', which literally means 'old foreigners' but has a

pejorative slant to it. Another, older, epithet is '*yang guizi*', meaning 'foreign devils'. Gill's remarks about how unpleasing the Chinese find Western coloration are true; blue eyes are regarded as especially weird. Hence the epithet 'devil' is apt. 'One of our subjects of complaint at the Chinese Foreign Office', writes a nineteenth-century diplomat,

> has been our being insulted in the streets of Peking by the riffraff of the place. Their means of annoyance is to howl out 'Kwei-tzu' (devils) after us when our backs are turned, and then, of course, to look as if they had not done it. Well, the other day M. de Mas, the Spanish Minister, being about to leave Peking, exchanged compliments p.p.c. with all the members of the Foreign Board. Amongst them all Heng-Chi distinguished himself by his *empressement*, sending M. de Mas a magnificent dinner *à la Chinoise*. M. de Mas went to thank him, and after the two old gentlemen had exchanged banalities to their hearts' content, the Spaniard knowing that Heng-Chi had a little son, the child of his old age, of whom he was inordinately proud, thought it would be a very pretty compliment if he asked to see the little boy, who was accordingly produced, sucking his thumb after the manner of his years. Him his father ordered to pay his respects to M. de Mas – that is to say, shake his united fists at him in token of salutation, instead of which the child, after long silence and much urging, taking his thumb deliberately out of his mouth, roared out 'Kwei-tzu' at the top of his voice and fled. Imagine the consternation of the two old twaddles! Heng-Chi was horrified, for after all his protestations of friendship to us, which by the bye took nobody in, it bothered him not a little that we should find out that his child was brought up in the privacy of his harem to look upon us as devils.[15]

What Heng-chi risked losing was 'face', a matter of tremendous importance to the Chinese then as now:

> Saving face might be described as a national industry.
> . . . The Chinese proclivity for ready-to-wear excuses

and the general talent for light fiction of an extemporaneous character have undoubtedly been fostered by the face-saving habit. The system probably grew out of a desire to conserve personal dignity on all occasions and to follow the usual Chinese practice of handling social situations with velvet gloves. . . . Fear of losing face follows a Chinese more persistently than his shadow. If he dies in a Western country, his remains must be shipped back to China, otherwise his ghost will lose face by having to mingle with haughty foreign ghosts. . . .[16]

But just as some foreigners loved and admired the Chinese, so matters were not all bad in the reverse direction, at least so far as the British were concerned:

The Chinese regard our nation as pre-eminently the honourable nation among whites in commercial matters, and adopting the nation as unit, extend to travelling Britons a credit not easily obtained by others. 'Englishman honour,' as an acceptable guaranteed bond, is one of the few things the Briton may be proud of in China. Even a little middy off an English man-of-war can obtain goods from shops on the promise to send a chit from the ship, or even pay when his ship returns, so many weeks later.[17]

And this positive view extended to respect for the efficacy of Western medicine:

My landlord was a Mahometan, and his respect for me was much increased by my reputation for never eating pork or ham. He told me that he had been to the Ko-Ko-Nor, and that the journey occupied three months in going, and the same time in returning; the road, he said, passed over dreadful mountains, the very recollection of which made him shiver. In winter-time the cold is intense, and the wild winds that sweep across the frozen plateaux cut great gashes in the face or any part of the body exposed. He asked me to give him some medicine against the wind; and as Chin-Tai declared that the possession of a bit of diachylon plaster would render him exceedingly happy, I felt I could not deprive him of the pleasure, although I rather spoilt the effect by telling him I was afraid he would not find it a certain remedy.

The . . . Chinese attributes to the foreigner all kinds of supernatural powers, which are even extended in their minds to European goods. Amongst many Chinese the application of grease from a foreign candle is considered a specific for small-pox; and European sugar is almost a pharmacopoeia in itself.[18]

Chinese attitudes to foreigners' appearance, although still widespread today, are not always unkind. Most travellers with some command of the Chinese language are guaranteed to hear themselves being discussed at length, and sometimes entertained thereby:

Riding through a town, where, as it was market-day, all the streets were crowded, I was much edified by the remarks passed by the crowd upon my person. I wore a helmet, and one man said, 'Does not he think himself a swell with a hat like a ram's horn?' 'Yes,' replied another; 'but look at his nose; he might be an official with that nose.'

The Chinese are great physiognomists, and always admire a good-sized nose; generally, their own noses are perfectly flat, without any bridge, and by saying I might be an official, the man meant that my nose was good. . . . Another man said that I had tremendously long legs. The Chinese always wear such loose baggy raiment, that in appearance the length of their legs is very much diminished.

The observations that are made are not as a rule very flattering, and forcibly illustrate the old proverb about listeners. I once heard of an English gentleman of whom an educated Chinaman remarked with the intention of being highly complimentary: *'Why, he is not so dirty as a Mongol.'* A Mongol never takes his clothes off all the winter, eats fat and grease by the pound, wipes his fingers on and drops messes all over his leather coat, and is about as greasy and dirty a personage as can well be imagined. On another occasion, an Englishman was told that he did not smell so bad as a Man-Tzu. However little it may flatter our Western vanity to admit it, there can be no doubt that every nation has its peculiar odour.[19]

Chief among the many things that amazed pre-1949 visitors about the Chinese was their attitude to human life, which seemed unfathomable and in some respects terrible. To a modern Westerner the idea of selling children is repugnant in the extreme; but poverty so often obliged Chinese to do it before the Communist era that it was commonplace. One deed of sale that Freeman-Mitford came across read as follows:

> Wan Cheng, of the village of Wan Ping, has a child the offspring of his body, being his second daughter and his seventh child, aged eight years. Because his house is poor, cold, and hungry, he has determined to sell his daughter to one named Ma. He sells her for twenty eight dollars, every dollar to be worth seven tiaos and a half.

What this implied was not always bleak. The report adds:

> Ma declares as soon as the girl is grown up he shall let her marry. He says, 'My no wanchee do that black heart pidgin.' I believe he will keep his word – it is a matter of business, and in business the southern Chinese trader is scrupulously honest. As for the child, she was simply in a fever of delight at leaving her parents. I dare say her poor little life had been none too rosy; for what says the proverb? 'Better one son, though deformed, than eighteen daughters as wise as the apostles of Buddha.'[20]

But not all purchasers were like trader Ma, and not all children were happy to be sold into what was, often enough frankly in name as always in fact, slavery:

> During last year it was . . . stated that no less than three thousand children from this neighbourhood, chiefly female children and a few boys, were sold to dealers.

. . . Girls are bought in Chaotong up to the age of twenty, and there is always a ready market for those above the age of puberty; prices then vary according to the measure of the girl's beauty, an important feature being the smallness of her feet. They are sold in the capital for wives and *yatows*; they are rarely sold into prostitution.[21]

But many children – again almost always girls, because of the enormous value of sons to the Chinese – were not sold but killed at birth. Somerset Maugham recounts:

Behind this row of arches the land rose sharply and since, in this part of the country, the Chinese bury their dead by preference on the side of a hill, it was thickly covered with graves. A trodden path led to a little tower ten feet high, perhaps, made of rough-hewn stone; it was cone-shaped and the roof was like a Pierrot's hat. It stood on a hillock, quaint and rather picturesque against the blue sky, amid the graves. At its foot were a number of rough baskets thrown about in disorder. I walked round and on one side saw an oblong hole, eighteen inches by eight, perhaps, from which hung a stout string. From the hole there came a very strange, a nauseating odour. Suddenly I understood what the little building was. It was a baby tower. The baskets were the baskets in which the babies had been brought, two or three of them quite new, they could not have been there more than a few hours. And the string? Why, if the person who had brought the baby, parent or grand-mother, midwife or obliging friend, were of a humane disposition and did not care to let the new-born child drop to the bottom (for underneath the tower was a deep pit), it could be let down gently by means of the string. The odour was the odour of putrefaction.[22]

In many places infants were simply exposed, and eaten by dogs and carrion birds; or were drowned in rivers, where the sight of their floating bodies occasioned no surprise:

Infanticide in a starving city like this is dreadfully common. 'For the parents, seeing their children must be doomed to poverty, think it better at once to let the soul escape in search of a more happy asylum than to linger in one condemned to want and wretchedness.' The infanticide is, however, exclusively confined to the destruction of female children, the sons being permitted to live in order to continue the ancestral sacrifices.

One mother I met, who was employed by this mission, told the missionary in ordinary conversation that she had suffocated in turn three of her female children within a few days of birth; and, when a fourth was born, so enraged was her husband to discover that it was a girl also that he seized it by the legs and struck it against the wall and killed it.

Dead children, and often living infants, are thrown out on the common among the gravemounds, and may be seen there any morning being gnawed by dogs. Mr Tremberth of the Bible Christian Mission, leaving by the south gate early one morning, disturbed a dog eating a still living child that had been thrown over the wall in the night. Its little arm was crunched and stripped of flesh, and it was whining inarticulately – it died almost immediately.[23]

The practice of selling children continues in today's China, but it has been made illegal. Infanticide also continues, and is indeed very widespread. An added reason for it these days is the one-child-per-family policy operated with strictness in the cities (it is more difficult to enforce in rural areas). Mothers who inadvertently fall pregnant may be at the end of such a long abortion queue that they come to term while waiting, so the resulting infants are disposed of in the time-honoured way.

Foreigners were equally disturbed by public executions and their attendant circumstances. Public executions were common in the West until not very long ago, so the mere fact of them was not the problem; it was the attitudes of the condemned which provoked comment, here from Freeman-Mitford:

One bright cold morning, about a fortnight ago, three of us witnessed a Chinese execution. The place of

execution is at the opening of the vegetable market in
the Chinese city. The market is held in a broadish street,
into which a number of large thoroughfares, at right
angles to it, lead. All these inlets were fenced off, and
the street itself filled with soldiery and officials. . . . The
whole of the shops in the street were closed, but the flat,
low roofs were crowded with spectators; among them
not a single woman or child was to be seen.

At one end of the space closed off was a matting
shed. Inside this were the condemned prisoners, who
were waiting for the Imperial decree for their death to
be brought on to the ground. We went in, and I shall
not easily forget the scene. There were fifteen criminals,
of whom one was a woman, one was a murderer. . . .
The murderer was to be decapitated, it being a severe
punishment to a Chinese not to take his body out of
the world as his parents gave it to him. . . . We gave
all the cigars we had with us to the poor condemned
criminals, who were very grateful for them, and I was
glad to leave so painful a scene. A little farther down
the street another large booth had been erected. Here
sat the high officials in a semicircle, with a red-button
mandarin from the Board of Punishments at their head.
On one side of this booth was a tiny sort of altar on
which were displayed the tools of the executioner – the
swords and bloody string, and the tourniquets and
strings for strangling. In front of the altar a small brick
stove had been built, over which was a cauldron of boiling water, like a huge barber's pot, to warm the swords.
The executioner's men were huddled round it toasting
their hands. The swords are short broad blades, almost
like choppers, with a long wooden handle on which is
carved a grotesque head. They have been above two hundred years in use, and are regarded as genii and invested
with preternatural powers. They are five in number, and
their names are Great Lord, second Lord, third Lord,
fourth Lord, and fifth Lord. When they are not in use
they are kept at the chief executioner's house, a tower
on the wall, where, as my teacher gravely informed me,
they are often heard at night to sing gruesome songs of

their past feats. When they are wanted their Lordships are 'requested' to come out.

The executioners have all sorts of stories and traditions about them. One is supposed to be younger than the others, and of a skittish, frolicsome nature, dallying and toying with the heads, not striking them off at one blow like the others, who are older and more sedate. There were many false alarms that the decree had come and announced the fatal moment. But at last the chief heads-man (Kwei-tzu-shou) came out, and throwing off his fur coat put on a bloodstained apron of yellow leather. He was a short, thick-set, but not ill-looking man, with that curious, anxious, *waiting* expression on his face that a man wears with serious work before him. It was horrid to see how completely he was the hero of the occasion, the soldiers round him treating him with the greatest deference, and evidently proud of a word from him. The five swords were carried in line near him. His assistant stripped his outer coat, and then all was ready. So soon as the decree arrived the prisoners were led out one by one to the booth where the mandarins were sitting, and there made to go through the form of acknowledging the justice of their punishment. They were then handed over to the executioner. The headsman and his men had to beat back the other soldiers with sticks in order to clear a space. Nothing could be more indecent and revolting than the behaviour of the latter. All order and discipline were at an end; they were like hounds yelling, snarling, and struggling to tear a fox into pieces rather than men ostensibly employed to keep the peace. The murderer was the first man brought forward. Happily he had raved himself into a state of insensibility, so his pains were over. The decapitation is done with marvellous speed. A string is passed round the prisoner's neck, close under the chin, and his head is thus held up by the assistant so as to offer resistance to the sword. When a mandarin is executed, the headsman meets him and says, 'Ching ta jen kwei tien,' 'I pray that your Excellency may fly to heaven' – much as our executioners used to ask the pardon of their victims. The man is made to kneel, in an instant the sword is raised, the executioner gives a shriek supposed to represent the words 'I have executed a man' (Sha liao jen), and at one blow the head is severed from the trunk and carried off to be inspected by the mandarins. As the blow falls the people all cry out, 'A good sword' (hao Tao), partly in praise of the headsman's skill, but more especially from a superstitious feeling of *um berufen*. The strangling is done with the same merciful quickness. It is far less lengthy than hanging. Two pieces of whip-cord are passed round the neck with a loop. The criminal is placed with his face to the ground, and the two executioners turn the tourniquet as quick as thought. Apparently there is no suffering. As I passed the big booth on my way out – for you may imagine that when I had seen how the matter was conducted I stayed for no more – I heard a loud voice shout out a name. Immediately out of the shed where the rest of the condemned were waiting, I saw a tall man walk out between two others as leisurely and composedly as if he had been going to his dinner. It was one of the young fellows with whom I had spoken so short a time before. The last act of horror is consummated in the Pit of the 10,000 (Wan Jen K'eng) by the wolves and foxes, a pit in the Chinese city where the bodies of executed criminals are thrown. Rich people's are bought back by their families that they may receive decent burial.

I was glad to see that the execution was conducted far more mercifully than one is led to suppose by certain writers. It is true that this is not the 'Ling Chih,' or disgraceful slow death, which is the punishment of parricide and high treason. But an Englishman who has witnessed that assures me that the criminal he saw so executed was put out of his misery at once, and that the mutilation took place *after* death and not before. I was specially struck by the excessive kindness of the soldiery to the criminals. The only sign of cruel disposition was the eagerness with which they pressed forward to see the death. That was revolting.

Of all the men who died that day not one appeared to be in the slightest degree affected by the solemnity of his position, or to show any apprehension for what was to follow. Where there was any emotion it was simply abject terror of the immediate pain of dying. Beyond that their thoughts did not seem to penetrate.[24]

Today executions are carried out by shooting. Condemned prisoners are driven through the streets of the town in open trucks, hands tied and signs affixed detailing their crimes and punishments. The standard method is a bullet in the head; families of the executed prisoner have to pay for the bullet, and if the prisoner's retinas and other organs are to be used for transplant purposes – often sold abroad through Hong Kong – they are removed before sentence is carried out.

These are matters of high drama, but it is as well that they be known. The Chinese are not alone in practising infanticide and capital punishment, a fact that does not excuse their doing so but, at least, places it in perspective. Moreover, there are plenty of educated Chinese who oppose these practices, just as there are plenty in the Western world who would like to see them reintroduced into their own societies.

One practice which is peculiarly Chinese, however, and does not invite any excuse in the perceptions of the West, is footbinding. It is no longer done, although one can still see many elderly women hobbling painfully about in minuscule slippers:

> The nature and origin of footbinding has been greatly misunderstood. Somehow it has stood as a symbol of the seclusion and suppression of women, and very suitably so. The great Confucian scholar Chu Hsi of the Sung Dynasty was also enthusiastic in introducing footbinding in southern Fukien as a means of spreading Chinese culture and teaching the separation of men and women. But if it has been regarded only as a symbol of the suppression of women, mothers would not have been so enthusiastic in binding the feet of their young daughters. Actually, footbinding was sexual in its nature throughout. Its origin was undoubtedly in the courts of the licentious kings, its popularity with men was based on the worship of women's feet and shoes as a love-fetish and on the feminine gait which naturally followed, and its

popularity with women was based on their desire to curry men's favour.[25]

Lin Yutang, a great interpreter of pre-Communist China to the West, hypothesizes that footbinding was made fashionable by a ruler of the Southern Tang dynasty who combined poetic talent with a developed sense of the exotic: 'One of his girls with bound feet was made to dance with light tiptoe steps on a golden lily six feet high, hung all over with jewels and pearls and golden threads. Thereafter, the fashion was set and imitated by the public, and the bound feet were euphuistically called "golden lilies" or "fragrant lilies", which enabled them to pass into poetry.'[26] The aim was for a girl's feet to be less than three or at most three and a half inches in length when fully grown. The process was agonizing; a girl's toes were forced to curl under a tightly up-arched instep, the whole foot strongly bound throughout her period of growth.

> The small feet of the Chinese women are not only pleasing in men's eyes but in a strange and subtle way they influence the whole carriage and walking gait of women, throwing the hips backward, somewhat like the modern high-heeled shoes, and effecting an extremely gingerly gait, the body 'shimmying' all over and ready to fall at the slightest touch. Looking at a woman with bound feet is like looking at a rope-dancer, tantalizing to the highest degree. The bound foot is indeed the highest sophistication of the Chinese sensual imagination.
>
> Then, entirely apart from the feminine gait, men had come to worship and play with and admire and sing about the small feet as a love-fetish. From now on, night shoes were to occupy an important place in all sensual poetry. The cult of the 'golden lily' belonged undoubtedly to the realm of sexual psychopathology. As much artistic finesse was exercised in the appreciation of different types of bound feet as was ever expended over the criticism of Tang poetry.[27]

In Qing times an enthusiast called Fang Xian devoted an entire book to the art of footbinding, classifying 'golden lilies' into five main divisions and eighteen separate types. The ideal bound foot, says Fang Xian, should be fat, soft and elegant, because

thin feet are cold, and muscular feet are hard. Such feet are incurably vulgar. Hence fat feet are full and smooth to the touch, soft feet are gentle and pleasing to the eye, and elegant feet are refined and beautiful. But fatness does not depend on the flesh, softness does not depend on the binding, and elegance does not depend on the shoes. Moreover, you may judge its fatness and softness by its form, but you may appreciate its elegance only by the eye of the mind.[28]

From time to time in imperial history efforts were made to stop footbinding. The Kangxi emperor of the Qing issued a decree banning it, but it had to be revoked after a few years owing to public pressure. Manchu mothers began to imitate their Chinese counterparts by binding their daughters' feet, but the Qianlong emperor stopped them by edict. Three eminent Chinese scholars railed against footbinding: Li Ruzhen, author of the feminist novel *Romance of Mirrored Flowers*, written in 1825, the eighteenth-century writer Yuan Mei, and his younger contemporary Yu Chengxie.

Christian missionaries campaigned against footbinding and in large measure it is owing to them that the practice began to die out in the early decades of the twentieth century. 'But,' says Lin Yutang gleefully, 'in this the missionaries have been fortunately helped by the force of circumstances, for Chinese women found in the modern high-heeled shoes a tolerable substitute. They enhance the women's figures, develop a mincing gait and create the illusion that the feet are smaller than they really are.'[29]

Both footbinding and high-heeled shoes have had little place in Communist China; recently, in the reopening of brothels and karaoke bars, the latter have been making a comeback.

Of all perceptions, China's perception of itself in the tumultuous twentieth century has been the most profound and easily the most biting. China's greatest modern writer, Lu

Xun, in his story of the pusillanimous, cowardly, bragging, ineffective, unfortunate Ah Q, savagely satirized what he saw to be the failings of the Chinese character, and the explanation for China's thraldom to tyrants, whether Manchu invaders or foreign capitalists:

> Ah Q . . . saw Whiskers Wang sitting stripped to the waist in the sunlight at the foot of a wall, catching lice; and at this sight his own body began to itch. Since Whiskers Wang was scabby and bewhiskered, everybody called him 'Ringworm Whiskers Wang'. Although Ah Q omitted the word 'Ringworm', he had the greatest contempt for the man. Ah Q felt that while scabs were nothing to take exception to, such hairy cheeks were really too outlandish, and could excite nothing but scorn. If it had been any other idler, Ah Q would never have dared sit down so casually; but what had he to fear by the side of Whiskers Wang? To tell the truth, the fact that he was willing to sit down was an honour for Wang.
>
> Ah Q took off his tattered lined jacket, and turned it inside out; but either because he had washed it recently or because he was too clumsy, a long search yielded only three or four lice. He saw that Whiskers Wang, on the other hand, was catching first one and then another in swift succession, cracking them in his teeth with a popping sound.
>
> Ah Q felt first disappointed, then resentful; the despicable Whiskers Wang could catch so many while he himself had caught so few – what a great loss of face! He longed to catch one or two big ones, but there were none, and it was only with considerable difficulty that he managed to catch a middle-sized one, which he thrust fiercely into his mouth and bit savagely; but it only gave a small spluttering sound, again inferior to the noise Whiskers Wang was making.
>
> All Ah Q's scars turned scarlet. Flinging his jacket on the ground, he spat and said 'Hairy worm!'
>
> 'Mangy dog, who are you calling names?' Whiskers Wang looked up contemptuously.
>
> Although the relative respect accorded him in recent

years had increased Ah Q's pride, when confronted by loafers who were accustomed to fighting he remained rather timid. On this occasion, however, he was feeling exceptionally pugnacious. How dare a hairy-cheeked creature like this insult him?

'Anyone whom the name fits,' said Ah Q, standing up, his hands on his hips.

'Are your bones itching?' demanded Whiskers Wang, standing up too and putting on his coat.

Thinking that Wang meant to run away, Ah Q stepped forward raising his fist to punch him. But before his fist came down, Whiskers Wang had already grabbed him and given him a shove which sent him staggering. Then Whiskers Wang seized Ah Q's pigtail and started dragging him towards the wall to knock his head in the time-honoured manner.

'A gentleman uses his tongue but not his hands!' protested Ah Q, his head on one side.

Apparently Whiskers Wang was no gentleman, for without paying the slightest attention to what Ah Q said he knocked his head against the wall five times in succession, and gave him a great shove which sent him staggering two yards away. Only then did Whiskers Wang walk away satisfied. . . .

Ah Q stood there irresolutely.

From the distance appeared another of Ah Q's enemies. This was Mr Chien's eldest son whom Ah Q also despised. After studying in a foreign school in the city, it seemed he had gone to Japan. When he came home half a year later his legs were straight (when the Chinese of those days saw foreigners walking with big strides – unlike the usual Chinese gait – they imagined that foreigners had no joints in their knees) and his pigtail had disappeared. His mother cried bitterly a dozen times, and his wife tried three times to jump into the well. Later his mother told everyone, 'His pigtail was cut off by some scoundrel when he was drunk. He would have been able to be an official, but now he will have to wait until he has grown it again before he thinks of that.' Ah Q did not believe this, however, and insisted

73

; him 'imitation Foreign Devil' and 'traitor in
pay'. As soon as Ah Q saw him he would start
under his breath.

t Ah Q despised and detested most in him was
e pigtail. When it came to having a false pigtail,
could scarcely be considered human; and the fact
that his wife had not attempted to jump into the well
a fourth time showed that she was not a good woman
either.

Now this 'Imitation Foreign Devil' was approaching.

'Baldhead – Ass' – in the past Ah Q had cursed under
his breath only, inaudibly; but today, because he was in
a bad temper and wanted to work off his feelings, the
words slipped out involuntarily.

Unfortunately this 'baldhead' was carrying a shiny
brown stick. . . . With great strides he bore down on
Ah Q who, guessing at once that a beating was impend-
ing, hastily braced himself to wait with a stiffened back.
Sure enough, there was a resounding thwack which
seemed to have alighted on his head.

'I meant him!' explained Ah Q, pointing to a nearby
child.

Thwack! Thwack! Thwack![30]

Lu Xun delivered a sound thrashing to his countrymen
thus; and perhaps it is true, as it would be true of any people
anywhere, that some deserved it. But to perceive the Chinese
aright it is not enough to compare eyes and noses and social
customs, or to observe them castigating themselves; it is to
see some way into their history and culture, and to get a sense
of its richness as a whole. We would ask for no less for
ourselves in return.

3

RIVERS AND ROUTES

Is it not a pleasure to have friends come from distant places?

Confucius, *The Analects*, 1.1

While your parents are alive, you should not travel far away and, when travelling, your whereabouts should always be known.

Confucius, *The Analects*, 4.19

The great Western travellers of the last two centuries in China and their numerous modern-day counterparts follow trails well-worn by countless journeyers of the past. The missionary Mildred Cable, about to enter the Gobi desert, might be describing a scene from any time over the past two millennia:

The third category of human beings to be met in Kiayükwan were the travellers who came, lodged for a night or two at the inns, and forthwith went their way. Every sunset and every sunrise they arrived, some taking night-stages and some travelling by day, but all were travel-worn and weary. They hailed from every part of China's dominion and were bound for her remotest frontiers. For one day or one night they used the place like masters, commanded the innkeeper's time and resources, fed their beasts in his stables and visited the shops, turning over the poor goods. . . .[1]

She observes how the residents viewed the itinerant strangers and their stories:

These formed the stream of living men and women who moved up and down the great road, acquainted with life and full of knowledge about distant places. They were familiar with the large cities and the great waterways of China, and had traversed her wide plains by the 'iron track' at a speed which seemed fabulous to the owners of these little shops. The static inhabitants saw them come, heard them talk, watched them go, but failed to understand the matters of which they spoke, for, to them, everything which they had never seen was unreal, vague, remote and seemed to bear no relation to everyday life.[2]

Sitwell understood well the corresponding remoteness felt by the traveller, coming as a stranger to a strange land:

Again, with China, my judgements and impressions may, for all I know, be more *chinoiserie* than Chinese, for I cannot – nor in any case would I – divest myself of Western ideas and of the culture which, such of it as I possess, comes from the shores of the Mediterranean, and not from those of the China Seas. And so I remain a traveller, overcome with wonder at strange sights and events, but often, I dare say, not fully grasping their cause or implication. My understanding is that of the eye; my only sure claim, to know and appreciate both beauty and character when I meet them.[3]

Marco Polo's expedition to China had a more specific motive: 'the hope of a profitable venture'. And when one reads a second-century BC account of the wealth of China's borders it does not seem surprising that throughout history merchants of many nationalities have braved the considerable hardships and risks of travel and trade in China:

The region west of the mountains has an abundance of timber, bamboo, grain, mulberry, hemp, yak hide and jade; the region east of the mountains is rich in fish, salt, lacquer, silk, musicians and beautiful women. South of the Yangtze are catalpa, cedars, ginger, cassia, gold, tin, lead, cinnabar, rhinoceros horn, tortoise shell, pearls, ivory and hides; and north of Longmen and Jieshi are horses, cattle, sheep, felt, furs, tendons and horns in plenty. As for copper and iron the mountain ranges which stretch for hundreds of miles are dotted with mines. All these commodities are valued by the people of China who use them for food and clothing, to supply the living and to bury the dead.[4]

Most foreign merchants travelled the Silk Route, running west from the long-time capital of China – Xian – to Central Asia. Mildred Cable was writing from Jiayuguan, the Ming dynasty terminus of the Great Wall whose great gate straddles the ancient way and separates the settled, familiar lands of China from the desert vastness of Central Asia. Despite the poverty of the land outside the gate it has been fought over since early times as China sought to retain control of the trade. But its constant military and diplomatic endeavours could not stop this vital road passing into other hands for long periods.

Among the items of trade which commanded high prices in China were the 'heavenly horses' of Ferghana and jade boulders from the rivers of Khotan. Reports of these were brought back in 125 BC by the envoy Zhang Jian after his thirteen years away, much of it as captive of the Xiongnu peoples. His mission, to persuade the more distant Yuezhi tribes into a treaty with the Chinese against these threatening nomads, was unsuccessful, but his detailed report of the lands he had travelled through, and their riches, tantalized the emperor. The earth ramparts constructed under Qin rule were accordingly extended into the desert as far as Dunhuang. Their terminus was Yumenguan – Jade Gate Pass – which stood some 200 miles west of the Ming gate. The walls were not the finished stone-faced structures of the Ming but nevertheless considerable traces survive and continue to impress travellers on this route. Aurel Stein, with his archaeologist's eye, gives a detailed description of their construction:

> we came upon a remarkably well preserved bit of wall, quite unbroken for 256 yards, and rising in places to fully seven feet. . . . Here the particular method of construction could be studied with ease. Layers of fascines, six inches thick, made up of mixed tamarisk twigs and reeds, alternated with strata three to four inches thick of coarse clay and gravel, as taken on the spot. Where I photographed the wall . . . I counted eight double

layers of fascines and stamped clay, respectively. . . . The salts contained everywhere in the soil and water and attested in the wall itself by a great deal of efflorescence, had given to the strange wall thus constructed a quasi-petrified consistency. In such a region it could hold its own against man and nature – all forces, in fact, but that of the slow-grinding and almost incessant wind erosion. The thickness of the wall measured close on seven feet across the top, and allowing for the loss which the upper-most fascine layer had suffered on its edges through erosion, about one foot more at the base.[5]

The Silk Road's most influential cargo was not brought by the merchants, but by itinerant Buddhist monks who, seeking safe passage, often joined the caravans. They moved along the Silk Road, founding monasteries and influencing both the local people and their rulers. The monasteries were endowed with frescos by local grandees and took local young men as students, teaching them both the Confucian classics and Buddhist scriptures. As they encroached eastwards the monks therefore created a legacy of literature and art.

The Silk Road divides to skirt the Tarim Basin at the heart of the Taklamakan Desert – 'you go in but never come out'. The oasis where the branches rejoin in the east, Dunhuang, became a thriving community, but when Marco Polo reached there it was past its Tang dynasty prime and under Muslim rule: 'The Idolaters have a peculiar language, and are no traders, but live by their agriculture. They have a great many abbeys and minsters full of idols of sundry fashions, to which they pay great honour and reverence, worshipping them and sacrificing to them with much ado.'[6]

He does not mention the real wonder of Dunhuang: the Mogao Caves. Stein arrived long after both the Buddhist and the Muslim communities had left the place to the sands:

It was getting dusk before I could tear myself away from this wonderful beehive of temples in its setting of barren rocks and sand. The route we followed when returning clambered up the riverine terrace by a steep detritus-covered slope, and then crossed the bare gravel plateau which edges the foot of the outer hills. The west wind which now swept it was piercing, and in the dust-laden atmosphere complete darkness soon overtook us. So there was nothing to interfere with the pictures full of vivid colour and grave pomp, all of ages of long gone by, which that day's over-abundant sightseeing had left impressed on my mind's eyes.[7]

But Stein was just as keen as Marco Polo on the bounties offered by the desert. Having heard of a recently discovered cache of manuscripts in one of the caves, he relied on his Chinese 'patron saint', the Tang dynasty pilgrim Xuanzang, to persuade the self-appointed keeper, the 'Tao-shih' (Daoist monk), to give him access: 'I confess, it never cost me any effort to grow eloquent on the subject of my "Chinese patron saint", whose guidance had proved so often fruitful for my own work. But now it was made doubly easy by the gleam of lively interest which I caught in the Tao-shih's eyes, otherwise so shy and fitful.'[8] The ruse was successful; to Stein's delight the cave was opened: 'The sight of the small room disclosed was one to make my eyes open wide. Heaped up in layers, but without any order, there appeared in the dim light of the priest's little lamp a solid mass of manuscript bundles rising to a height of nearly ten feet.'[9] There were thousands of sutras written on the finest yellow-dyed paper, contracts, letters and poems, and the earliest dated printed document in the world: a copy of the Diamond Sutra from 868. Dunhuang was not a desert outpost, but a rich and strategic part of the Chinese empire.

It may seem surprising that a Daoist priest was moved by the story of a Buddhist pilgrim. But accounts of travel in this desolate land quickly turn into legend, and it had long been believed among Daoists that Laozi, their founder, had left China in the seventh century BC, had passed along the Silk Route and had 'transformed' into Sakyamuni, the historical Buddha.

Xuanzang played a major role in the development of Buddhism in China, but he too has become the subject of legend. In 629 he set out for India without imperial permission to find Buddhist scriptures. On his return he was fêted by the emperor who sought intelligence of the Central Asian and Indian lands and peoples. Xuanzang obliged him, then settled down to translation of the texts he had brought back. It was not long before the account of his journey became linked with tales about one of China's favourite legendary figures, incorrigible Monkey, who, despite his mischievous ways, which had led him to steal the peaches of immortality from the Daoist Jade Emperor, was allowed to accompany the monk to the west. By the thirteenth century the story was common on the theatrical stage and two centuries later formed the central theme of the novel *The Journey to the West*. The account is fanciful – Acton, impressed by the poetic imagination of the author, said it embraced

> Grandeville's litany to which the Surrealist congregation have responded so feebly: 'Transformations, visions, incarnations, ascensions, locomotions, explorations, peregrinations, excursions, sojournings, cosmogonies, phantasmagorias, reveries, drolleries, facetiae, extravaganza, metamorphoses, zoomorphoses, lithamorphoses, metampsychoses, apotheoses, and other things.'[10]

But it represents the real dread of the desert beyond the gate. An earlier Buddhist monk, Fa Xian, kept a diary of his own journey to the west:

> Le Hao, the prefect of Dunhuang, had supplied them with the means of crossing the desert in which there were many demons and hot winds. Those who encounter these perish to a man. There is not a bird to be seen in the air above, nor an animal on the ground below. Although you look round most earnestly to find where to cross, you know not where to make your choice, the only mark and indication being the dry bones of the dead.[11]

Monkey joined the other animals who had travelled this road, the mules and dogs, and, most importantly, the camels, described by Ann Bridge with their precious moulting fur tied to their legs with bits of string as 'badly done-up brown paper parcels'. Camels are consummate desert travellers; a Chinese account describes one of their less-known skills: 'In the northwest of the land of Qiemo there are a hundred miles of flowing sands. During the summers hot winds sweep these lands and imperil the traveller. Only the old camels know when the wind is about to come. They then cry out and huddle together sticking their mouths and noses into the sand.'[12]

The archaeologists, adventurers, diplomats, merchants, monks and legendary Monkey were not the only travellers along the Silk Road. The others, however, were not there from choice. These were the soldiers, political exiles and criminals, as Mildred Cable and Francesca French relate:

> The most important door was on the further side of the fortress, and it might be called Traveller's Gate, though some spoke of it as the Gate of Sighs. It was a deep archway tunnelled in the thickness of the wall, where footsteps echoed and re-echoed. Every traveller toward the north-west passed through this gate. . . .
>
> The long archway was covered with writings, and anyone with sufficient knowledge to appreciate Chinese penmanship could see at once that these were the work of men of scholarship, who had fallen on an hour of deep distress. There were lines quoted from the Book of Odes, poems composed in the pure tradition of classic literature, and verses inspired by sorrow too heavy for the careful balance of literary values, yet unbearable unless expressed in words.
>
> Who then were the writers of this Anthology of Grief? Some were heavy-hearted exiles, others were disgraced officials, and some were criminals no longer tolerated within China's borders. Torn from all they loved on earth and banished with dishonoured name to the dreary regions outside, they stood awhile within the tomb-like vault, to add their moan to the pitiful dirge of the Gate of Sighs.[13]

Today this is still a region of prisoners and exiles, living in the harshness of China's gulag. The tens of thousands of modern-day prisoners form whole villages not marked on most maps but often frighteningly close to nuclear test sites, or adjacent to the mines for which they provide slave labour. When their sentences are finished most are refused permission to return to their homes and remain in these anonymous villages. Zhang Xianliang was imprisoned for eight years in a camp in Qinghai Province:

> The skeleton I could never forget had a long, black braid growing from its skull. It was approaching noon when a middle-aged labour reform convict cried out, 'Quick! Come see! There's a woman over here!' In the dry, barren desert even the spoken word 'woman' could lubricate a man. Convicts who had not seen a woman for years swarmed over to him from the various patches they had declared their own. If one was unable to see a woman, the sight of a woman's skeleton was almost as good, especially this one, which could hardly be more naked.
>
> I was the last one to make it over to the side of her pit and she had already been fully exposed by digging. She slept peacefully in her tiny bed, as though drunk or insane. She must have died quite early, perhaps in 1958 when this camp's convicts began to die in groups. The flesh of her body had gone cleanly, as if the bones had just emerged from a bath. The bones the yellow earth had so long concealed were now delectably pure and white. An ink-black braid wound down from her skull, three feet long with not a hair out of place. It ended just between her legs. On the end of the wavy braid was a smartly tied blue ribbon.[14]

As in the past, China today still struggles to retain control over this vast land, important now for its oil wells and anonymity: the separatist movement among the Turkic Muslims of Xinjiang is gaining in strength, despite massive Chinese colonization.

The Silk Road leads eventually to Xian. Capital of the Zhou in the first millennium BC, it continued as the most important city of China until nomads pushed the Chinese court south in the eleventh century and went on to gain control of the empire. Xian, known for much of its history as Chang'an, was always vulnerable to incursions from the west and northwest, and both the Zhou and the Han dynasties had to move their capital further east along the Yellow River valley during the later part of their rule. Even in the Tang, which saw the height of the city's glory, Tibetans made frequent raids across China's borders and once reached the capital, causing the emperor and his court to flee. They stayed only temporarily: they were a nomadic people with their own country, only interested in the spoils of China and not the complications of rule. But the military unreadiness of the capital to repel the attack was blamed on the emperor's beautiful concubine, Yang Guifei, and, while the court was fleeing the city, the emperor's generals forced him to have her killed.

It is not unusual for a woman to be blamed for China's political ills. The Tang Empress Wu and the more recent Empress Dowager Cixi are both portrayed in the histories as evil women who brought the empire to its knees. But the reaction to Yang Guifei was more ambivalent, and she has been a popular subject for literature and art. The Tang dynasty poet Bai Juyi's piece 'Song of Unending Sorrow' is the best-known on this theme:

> Having travelled over thirty miles beyond the western gate,
> The six armies would not go on
> Until in front of their horses those deadly moth-eyebrows were destroyed.
> Flowery hairpins fell to the ground but no one picked them up,
> Kingfisher feathers, golden birds and jade combs.
> The Emperor could not save her, he covered his face.
> Turning back to look, bloody tears seemed to fall.[15]

Courtesans and imperial princesses being sent off to marry a prince of a tributary state were among the few women seen on the roads, at least in late imperial China. Social and physical restrictions had been imposed on women from the early Song dynasty: young women and widows were not expected to go out, and footbinding became common among the upper classes. Shen Fu, a nineteenth-century writer, expressed his frustrations at the social conventions to his wife: 'Once I said to her, "It's a pity that you are a woman and have to remain closeted at home. If only you could become a man we could go to famous mountains and search out historical sites. . . .

Together we would be able to travel through all the lakes
south to west, and all the mountains from the north to the
east." [16]

Westerners came too late for Xian's heyday in the less conservative Tang. When Marco Polo visited China the capital
had been transferred to the Mongol heartlands in the north,
the site of Peking, and Auden and Isherwood writing in the
1940s saw only a shell:

> Sian has shrunk too small for its own immense peni-
> tentiary-walls. Most of the houses are mere shacks,
> dwarfed by the crazy old medieval gate-towers. Like
> shabby, dispirited spectators of a procession, they line the
> edges of the wide, rough cart-track streets. Everywhere
> there are plots of waste ground littered with ruins.
> When the sun shines the city is swept by great clouds
> of dust blowing down from the Gobi; when it rains the
> whole place is a miserable bog. Beyond the walls, all
> along the southern horizon you can see the broken line
> of the big, savage, bandit-infested mountains. [17]

The American art historian Langdon Warner also only finds
traces of the city's glorious past:

> But the best thing in the town for us, and one of the most
> impressive in all China, was Pei Lin – the Forest of
> Tablets. Back in dim times when Britons were painting
> themselves blue and Europe was barbarian, these great
> slabs of close-grained ringing stone had been inscribed
> with the ancient lore of China by imperial order. In later
> evil days they were proscribed and many were broken or
> lost. But now for centuries the scores that were saved,
> together with hundreds of later ones, have been gathered
> together under the shadow of long-roofed buildings
> where all day the wooden mallets hammer wet paper into
> the deep-cut stone characters as the makers of rubbings
> produce their stock in trade for Peking scholars and
> literary men. One series of inscriptions, cut in the ninth
> century after Christ, is copied by the thousand and used
> for a copy book by the children of the Chinese primary
> school because of its perfect calligraphy. [18]

But he delights in the city's antiquity:

Every walk out of doors in Sianfu leads you of necessity under the great drum tower, straddling the four roads which meet in the centre of the city. No sun enters here, but beggars crouch in antique slime, and enormous piles of red peppers are exposed for sale, like red coals in a dark smithy. Beside them lie egg-plants of royal purple two feet long, and light green sleek melons splashed with cool water in the shade. The very roofs and shop fronts here show something of older days, more mouldy and more gentle than Peking. There is a sagging slant of lichened tiles different from the roof lines of any other Chinese city. The ridges are great flat lace-work of flowers and of fruit in pressed tales which make one think of the silver-grey inks which the twelfth-century painters used for distant hills, and mountain nunneries by waterfalls. Perhaps Peking seemed thus before the Legations came and before it was desecrated by even partial sanitation.[19]

In its heyday Xian was a bustling and cosmopolitan city. Foreigners were welcomed, as long as they conformed to the laws of China. But then the empire started to weaken and was threatened by nomad invasions. A Japanese monk on pilgrimage to China in the ninth century records the bloody fruits of increasing xenophobia: 'The Uighur army has entered China, invading the frontiers, and at present is at Ch'in-fu. The nation has drawn troops from six regional commanderies and is sending them to the Uighur frontier. There are several hundred Uighurs in the capital, and they have all been executed in accordance with an Imperial command.'[20]

Auden and Isherwood, travelling in equally troubled times, recounted more recent atrocities:

If Cheng-chow smells of disease, Sian smells of murder. Too many people have died there throughout history, in agony and terror. In 1911 the Chinese population fell upon the Manchus and massacred twenty-five thousand of them in the course of a single night. In 1926 the city endured a terrible seven-months' siege. The Guest-House itself has been the scene of more than one execution.[21]

Xian is also the terminus of the many other roads that traverse the nomad territories stretching along the north and north-west frontiers of China. When China was not fighting the nomads she bribed them into peace by sending 'gifts'. Nomad leaders and Chinese generals have therefore long travelled these roads. From the north-east came Korean embassies, monks and women who found work as courtesans. In the seventeenth century the Manchus entered China as conquerors, while some of the cities carry the traces of the two waves of Russian occupation: the White Russian exiles from the revolution left dachas and ice-cream, while the Russian Communists abandoned the bare shells of heavy industrial plants, removing the machinery when they left. This road too has its legacy of sorrow. The north-east is the site of many labour camps and home to some of the Japanese and Korean women who were sent here to serve as prostitutes for the Japanese soldiers during the Sino-Japanese War.

In more recent times the lands on China's northern borders have fascinated Western adventurers and archaeologists, among them Teilhard de Chardin:

> The past fortnight the steppe has been piercingly beautiful. The sun – golden, and not so fierce – has cast a gentle glow over the great, grey undulations dotted with clumps of still-green artemisia and clusters of yellowing asclepia. Here and there in the salt hollows the fat-leaved salsola formed its crimson carpet on the snow-white salt, while against the horizon stood out the jagged blue outline of the Alta-Shan, already capped with white. No sound but the calls of little red-beaked crows, or the strange cry of camels at pasture, or the tinkle of some caravan. All my memories of autumn . . . came crowding in on me: autumns on the high plateaux of Auvergne, with the Forez or the Mont-Doré in the distance; autumns in Egypt when evening is almost cool as it falls over the violet desert; autumns at Hastings with the golden beeches and the sea wind over the rounded '*downs*' of the wide salting.[22]

He was presented with a very different picture as he tra-velled into the land north of Xian:

> After crossing the Great Wall . . . you leave the region of the Mongolian steppes and dunes and enter the astounding zone of the great loess or 'yellow earth' (though 'grey' would be better) of China. In the past . . . this area must have formed a wide undulating plateau. And then, suddenly, the base level of the water-courses must have fallen; from the small rivers down to the merest streams, everything that flows started to dig deeply into the soil. And since the soil in this region is formed of compacted earth (loess) the gullying has taken on formidable proportions. Today the ancient plateau is cut across by an astonishing network of cre-vasses of which the largest are 600 feet deep, while even the smallest, owing to their sheer walls, are impass-able obstacles. The few inhabitants live in caves scooped out of the walls of the crevasses and cultivate millet, sorghum, buckwheat and hemp – everything that ero-sion has spared. No paths except along the river-beds, or else tracks, just about wide enough for a mule that wind, corniche-wise, over the crevasses, snake their way up the slopes, or zig-zag along the crests between the mouth of the crevasses. The tracks often cave in and the river-beds are dangerous in the stormy season. I have seen with my own eyes a stream one could jump over, suddenly turn into a raging torrent 10 or 12 feet deep – and this in dry weather; there had simply been a bad storm upstream. What an odd country! At this moment it is charming, with the black hanging ears of the millet, and the sorghum from 6 to 9 feet high. But with its great folds of impassable land, that block the view and prevent you from going where you want to, you have the stifled feeling of being in a forest.[23]

Some of the travellers of the Cultural Revolution – both the idealistic and the unwilling – found themselves in this strange and poverty-striken land. Among them were Chen Kaige and Zheng Yimou who went on to make the film

Yellow Earth. It tells of another traveller to this land, a young People's Liberation Army (PLA) soldier, who has a tragic effect on a small community. He has been sent to collect intelligence about the people and their life through their folksongs, a Confucian tradition: *The Book of Odes* is traditionally described as folksongs collected on the order of the Zhou emperors in the first millennium BC.

This land of loess is skirted by the Yellow River, one of China's arteries. It does not leave this land behind: the loess is carried south and east to the great plain where it is deposited and, like a bad penny, continues its legacy of woe. The river, its level heightened by these deposits of loess, frequently bursts its banks and floods vast areas of the surrounding land. It is not surprising that the river running through the heart of China is seen as a source of both life and death.

But the Yellow River has another role: apart from the loess, it carries numerous travellers and goods across the country east from Xian. On its way it passes several other ancient capitals: Zhengzhou, the site of the Shang kings, Luoyang, and Kaifeng. It joins the sea in Shandong province, the birthplace of Confucius and home to Mount Tai, the easternmost of the five sacred mountains of China. When Confucius climbed Mount Tai he was surprised at how small the towns on the plains below appeared. Today thousands puff their way up the 7,000 steps to see the sun rise, passing many temples and examples of rock-carved calligraphy left by travellers of the past:

> In 1814 I visited the famous Mount Tai. On reaching the top we sat down to wait in the 'Basking Sun and Rising Cloud Pavilion'. It was summer but when we woke before dawn we were surrounded by darkness. A strong wind was blowing and we put on our fur coats. At first, a light appeared in the north-east; then it looked like white hair transforming itself into a golden snake. The distant clouds seemed to surge and boil, and soon the red sun appeared on the horizon.[24]

In this heartland of China there was a constant stream of travellers: officials moving to new posts, visiting home or friends, or making excursions to famous places; monks and lay-believers on pilgrimages to the holy sites; merchants; peasants on corvee duty; and deserting soldiers, along with the indefatigable foreign missionaries; and, in more recent times, the ubiquitous tourist, the Chinese far outnumbering the foreigner.

The Yellow River, which formed the main thoroughfare of central China and linked with the road west, also led to another ancient and much-travelled route, the road south. This mainly riverine route, starting from the Grand Canal linking the Yellow and Yangtse Rivers, was followed by exiled officials, merchants, missionaries and foreign embassies on their way to and from the southern ports, and by the emperor on his periodic tours of inspection.

This was the route taken by the Macartney Embassy on its way out of China in 1793. Macartney, like many other travellers, seeks the familiar in this foreign land: 'The river here appeared to be as broad as the Thames at Gravesend. Great numbers of houses on either side, built of mud and thatched, a good deal resembling the cottages near Christchurch in Hampshire.'[25]

The Embassy surgeon, Barrow, was not impressed by Chinese boatmen: 'the Chinese have no great dexterity in the management of their vessels'. The judgement is surprising given the antiquity of both this route and the method of transport. But other travellers told a different story, especially those who had survived the Yangtse gorges, whose fast waters had been long put to good use by the Chinese:

The two banks along the 200 mile stretch of the Three Gorges link directly with the mountains without the slightest opening in between. Tiered crags and layered cliffs hide the sky and block out the light of the sun, so that unless it is noon or midnight the sun and moon cannot be seen. With the arrival of summer the level of the water rises up the hills and travel is prevented in both directions. Sometimes, when the emperor commands the speedy dispatch of a proclamation, the court sends it by boat from the city of Baidi. By sunset the boat has already reached Jiangling, having covered 400 miles.

Even if one were to mount a swift horse and ride with the wind you would not go faster. In spring and winter white torrents rush into the green tarns, and the swirling clear ripples cast their reflections. Strangely formed cypresses grow on the sheer stacks of rock while springs and waterfalls fly and scour among them.[26]

G.E. Morrison, an Australian doctor travelling across China and later renowned as *The Times* correspondent in Peking, was too preoccupied to notice the scenery:

I sat in the boat stripped and shivering, for shipwreck seemed certain, and I did not wish to be drowned like a rat. For cool daring I never saw the equal of my boys, and their nicety of judgement was remarkable. Creeping along close to the bank, every moment in danger of having its bottom knocked out, the boat would be worked to the exact point from which the crossing of the river was feasible, balanced for a moment in the stream, then with sail set and a clipping breeze, and my men working like demons with the oars, taking short strokes, and stamping time with their feet, the boat shot into the current. We made for a rock in the centre of the river; we missed it, and my heart was in my mouth as I saw the rapid below us into which we were being drawn, when the boat mysteriously swung half round and glided under the lee of the rock. One of the boys leapt out with the bow-rope, and the others with scull and boat-hook worked the boat round to the upper edge of the rock, and then, steadying her for the dash across, pushed off again into the swirling current and made like fiends for the bank. Standing on the stern, managing the sheet and tiller, and with his bamboo pole ready, the laoban yelled and stamped in his excitement; there was the roar of the cataract below us, towards which we were fast edging stern on, destruction again threatened us and all seemed over, when in that moment we entered the back-wash and were again in good shelter. And so it went on, my men with splendid skill doing always the right thing, in the right way, at the right time, with unerring certainty.[27]

Chinese boatmen were not only skilled at negotiating the deep waters of the Yangtse. The route south made use of many smaller tributary rivers and streams. Barrow was forced to praise the boatmen's ingenuity, although his tone is rather grudging:

> The whole of the three last days' navigation might, with propriety, in England be called only a trout stream; upon which no nation on earth, except the Chinese, would have conceived the idea of floating any kind of craft; they have however adapted, in an admirable manner, the form and construction of their vessels to the nature and depth of the navigation; towards the upper part of the present river, they draw only, when moderately laden, about six inches of water. They were from fifty to seventy feet in length, narrow and flat-bottomed, a little curved, so that they took the ground only in the middle point.[28]

He was on surer ground again when talking about sanitary arrangements: 'there is not a water-closet, nor a decent place of retirement in all China'; and on roads, or the lack of them, in which respect China 'fell far short of most civilized nations'. The water-closet, a comparatively recent invention in the West, was not to be found in China but inns were expected to provide separate sanitary arrangements. Fan Chengda, a twelfth-century traveller on the road south, was not impressed by the arrangement in what is now Hunan Province: 'None of the resthouses and restaurants provide outhouses and privies, causing travellers great anguish.'[29]

Toilet paper was in use by the Tang, information gleaned from its purported medicinal uses in an eighth-century book. 'Privy slips' were alleged to be efficacious in relieving cholera or a difficult childbirth if burnt under the sufferer's bed. But up to the present the water-closet remains scarce in a country where everything has its use:

> Patriarch Mu came up with an idea. 'On my trips to town,' he said to himself, 'I see cesspits all along the road, although we have none in our village. We are obviously wasting this precious resource. What I have in mind will prove a more lucrative business than any

other I know of.' He summoned workers and had three cesspits dug below the large room at the front of his house. He divided the room into cubicles and had the walls whitewashed. Then he bustled off to town to ask a relative of his for a quantity of painting and calligraphy to hang on the walls. 'Everything is ready to go. All I need is the name tablet,' he said, surveying his handiwork. So he invited the local elementary school teacher to think up a name. The teacher thought for a while. 'I test my pupils all the time,' he said, 'but the lines all come from classical poets. Now you are asking me to come up with something entirely on my own. That's murderously difficult.' The patriarch then brought out wine and delicacies as if making a formal request and the teacher could scarcely refuse. With wine cup in hand he ran through the names of all the halls in and around town but he could not come up with a single title. Then a thought struck him. 'Hold off the wine for a minute,' he announced with great satisfaction, 'I want to compose the title before indulging myself.' Mu promptly set to work grinding up the pungent ink. The teacher nibbled at the end of his brush, dipped it in the ink until it was fully loaded and then, with immense care and concentration, wrote three characters. 'Read it to me, won't you,' said Mu, 'so that I can memorize it?' 'Here is your title, Nobilitas Hall,' declared the teacher. Mu asked him to explain what it meant but the teacher had copied it from the memorial arch in front of Board Chairman Xu's house in town and had no idea of its meaning and so had to improvise. 'It is a very apt title,' he said, 'highly auspicious for business success. There is a classical allusion behind it which I will explain another time.' He departed without even drinking his wine. Old Mu was thoroughly embarrassed. He prepared two boxes of gifts and went to the school to thank him, 'This is much too considerate of you,' said the teacher, 'why go to all this expense a second time on my account?' 'There is another matter on which I would like to enlist your help,' said Mu, drawing a hundred or more sheets of red paper from his sleeve. 'You want me to write a couplet for your gate?' 'No,' replied Mu, 'I have recently set up these three lavatories and I am afraid that people may not know about them. I want to post notices to attract custom. I would like you to write the following: "The sweetly scented New Pits of the Mu family respectfully solicit the patronage of gentlemen from near and far. Toilet paper provided by the establishment." ' The teacher realized that the new text was already prepared, and that he had merely to copy it out and there was no problem. In a few hours he had finished the task.[30]

But even though travellers might find the sanitary arrangements uncomfortable, at least there are no records of anyone being bewitched by the goddess of the privy, as was the unfortunate eponymous hero of an early nineteenth-century story, 'The Biography of Red Li' by Liu Zongyuan:

He went to the privy and having been gone a long time his friend followed him and saw Red embracing the lavatory bowl. He was cackling and, having looked from side to side, was just about to stick his head into it. The friend rushed in and dragged him out upside down. Red was furious: 'I had already entered the hall and faced my wife. Her appearance cannot be matched. The hall is beautiful, with grand and ornate decorations, and there is the scent of peppers and orchids in profusion. Looking back on your world it is like a privy to me, while the residence of my wife is indistinguishable from that of the Heavenly Emperor in his Celestial City. Why do you keep pestering me so?'[31]

The aphrodisiac scent of the pepper and orchids continued to attract Red Li to his 'wife', and at the end of the story he is found dead with his feet sticking out of the lavatory bowl.

Inns, if basic and none too salubrious, have always lined the roads at regular intervals. Those in the north offered a communal bed, the kang, as William Gill explains:

The great feature in every room in every inn in Northern China is the 'kang'. There is a hollow raised dais, about eighteen inches high, covering half the floor, over which there is usually laid a bit of straw matting, the home of innumerable fleas. In the winter a fire is lighted under this, and through the bricks or mud of which it is built a pleasing warmth is imparted to the traveller, who, rolled up in his blanket, lies on it to sleep. During the day-time a little table about nine inches high stands on the kang; a person sitting on the latter can just make use of this by twisting himself round into an impossible attitude, which after any length of time eventuates in aches all over the back. There may be in addition a brokendown and exceedingly filthy table and armchair very clumsy, heavy, stiff, straight-backed, and uncomfortable, with legs which, thrust out in a sprawling fashion, seem to have the most unhappy knack of being always in the way; and the table with a ledge underneath just where an ordinary person wants to put his knees, and a bar below to interfere with the free movements of his feet.[32]

With the burgeoning trade from Canton and the rapid colonization of the Tang, the route south was improved, particularly the Yü Pass which led travellers across the mountains onto the Guangdong plain. Before engineering works commissioned in 716 it was a dreaded place:

> Abandoned previously, this road east of the pass,
> Extremely forbidding, causing men hardship.
> Struggling upward, the road was direct,
> Skirting several miles of dense forest.
> Bridges hovered, clinging to the edge
> Halfway up tall precipitous cliffs. . . .[33]

And perhaps travellers along it experienced some of the same terror expressed by Isherwood, undergoing the now all too familiar experience of being at the mercy of a Chinese chauffeur:

> Beyond Lanchi the road leaves the river-valley and turns off into the hills. Soon we were hurtling round the curves of a mountain pass. The scenery was superb, but we were too frightened even to look out of the

window. Instead, Auden tried to distract our thoughts from the alarming Present by starting a conversation about eighteenth-century poetry. It was no good: we could remember nothing but verses on sudden death. Meanwhile, the road twisted and struggled, and the car clung to it like a mongoose attacking a cobra. Pedestrians screamed, cyclists overbalanced into paddy-fields, wrecked hens lay twitching spasmodically in the dust-storm behind us. At every corner we shut our eyes, but the chauffeur only laughed darkly as befitted one of the Lords of Death, and swung us round the curve with squealing brakes. Neither Major Yang nor Mr Liu showed the least symptoms of nervousness. 'The road is very difficult,' Mr Liu observed peacefully, as we shot across a crazy makeshift bridge over a gorge, rattling its loose planks like the bars of a xylophone. 'It wouldn't be difficult', I retorted, 'if we weren't driving at seventy miles an hour.'[34]

For Fan Chengda on the more western route south, through Changsha and what was much later Mao Zedong's birthplace, a much lower pass led them into Guilin, a land that has always astonished (and not only for the excellence of its roads):

26th day: we passed over the border into Guilin. There is a large decorated sign spanning the road which reads: 'Guangan West District'. Everyone in our party looked up and cried in amazement at having got this far. From the time we had reached Xiang until now there had been continuous hills of red clay and although the landscape was delightful the paths beyond Mount Xiang were nasty and narrow. But now that we had crossed the border the countryside became broad and level and for several miles on both sides of the road there were rocky peaks, stocky and upright like yamen clerks in formation.

As we headed south, all in our party were excited and amazed. We all pointed to various sights, praised the scenery and exclaimed with delight, lamenting at the same time that we had been so tardy in visiting this place. Tall maples and ancient willows line the great throughfare which resembles a city road. . . . The landscape of

Guilin had been praised since Tang times for its singularity and beauty.[35]

Canton, the southern terminus of the road south, was another of China's great cities and also cosmopolitan, with merchants from many distant lands. But in later times it was chiefly known for its foreign factories and, like Xian, visitors here lamented its faded past, not least Harold Acton:

> The farther south I travelled, the more I regretted the north. Canton in mid-June was more Chinoiserie than the Chinese: George Chinnery and the early Victorian engravers have familiarized us with the landscape, lush and rococo and rickety. There was not much left of old Canton; most of the narrow lanes had been demolished; the picturesque Chan Ka Chi Temple, with its terracotta figures running along the roof, had been converted into a school, and the Flower Pagoda looked on the verge of collapse. The Pearl River was a floating city of junks and sampans where myriads spent amphibious lives. Here and there pretty little rain pavilions had been built along the shore to shelter travellers from a sudden storm, but the pagodas were sadly decayed, with trees pushing their roots out of the masonry. The bridges looked more decorative than practical. Pink water-buffaloes glared and snorted from their mud-baths: on the back of one buffalo I saw a tiny naked boy piping on a flute, as in a scroll I had bought in Peking. These buffaloes, terraced rice-fields and plantations of edible bamboo distinguished this landscape from what I had seen in the north. The graves were shaped like horseshoes, built in dips of the hill-sides where the good influences of Nature no doubt collected to soothe the dead, and horseshoes of trees protected them from the winds. The clumps of bamboos were singularly graceful, and their rustling was the finest music I heard in the neighbourhood of Canton.[36]

Roads and rivers are the traditional routes in China, but ships also crossed the seas in search of trade from her south and east coasts, or carrying envoys in search of the lands of the immortals. At Quanzhou in Fujian Province there is a monument to the eunuch admiral Zheng He who in 1405 led an argosy to Africa, and also to the non-Chinese writers who speak of the town Zayton, among them the Moroccan Ibn Battuta and Marco Polo, who described it as 'one of the two ports in the world with the biggest flow of merchandise'.

In the later nineteenth and early decades of this century great railway lines were constructed to make travel faster although not always more comfortable, as Noël Coward discovered: 'I will spare the reader a detailed description of a 24-hour journey to Peking in an unheated train in which we sat, wrapped in fur coats, in a wooden compartment trying unsuccessfully to conquer intestinal chills by eating nothing at all and drinking a bottle of brandy each, while the frozen Chinese countryside struggled bleakly by the window.'[37]

But in the spirit of a true traveller, Paul Theroux enjoyed the experience nevertheless:

> It was always like a fire-drill, getting on or off a Chinese train, with people panting and pushing; but the journey itself was a great sluttish pleasure for everyone – a big middle-aged pyjama party, full of reminiscences. It seemed to me that the Chinese had no choice but to live the dullest lives and perform the most boring jobs imaginable . . . and because of that, these people were never happier than when on a railway journey. They liked crowded compartments and all the chatter; they liked smoking and slurping tea and playing cards and shuffling around in their slippers – and so did I. We dozed and woke and yawned and watched the world go by.[38]

Today trains carry the 'floating population' of China – tens of millions of people looking for work – and are scarcely more convenient. The Party official, businessman and foreign tourist have taken to the air. But even Chinese airplanes have been known to squeeze extra passengers aboard by the addition of folding seats in the aisles. Theroux's observations remain accurate, although only the committed traveller will find pleasure travelling in present-day China: 'Transportation in China is always crowded; it is nearly always uncomfortable; it is often a struggle. The pleasures are rare, but they are intense and memorable. Travel in China, I suspected, would give me a lasting desire for solitude.'[39]

4

THE POET IN THE LANDSCAPE

The wise find pleasure in water, the benevolent find
pleasure in mountains. The wise are active, the benevolent are tranquil. The wise are joyful, the benevolent are long-lived.

Confucius, *The Analects*, 6.23

Teilhard de Chardin made demands upon China unusual
among foreign writers. But his search for spiritual solace in
the landscape was frustrated when he first encountered the
north China plain in 1913:

My impressions of this country are still almost non-
existent. They come down to this: China, to the north
of the Yangtze Kiang, is a region where there are fertile
sources of interest for anyone who wants to work and
search. But it is the last country in the world in which
to find rest and comfort. Just as Malaya enchanted me
with its flamboyant flowers and dense forests, so the
valleys of the Blue River and the Yellow River strike
me as austere and desolate regions in which the mind,
as well as the body, is exposed defenceless to all the great
winds of the earth. These immense expanses, grey and
flat, out of all proportion to our plains of western
Europe, and these completely bare and rocky mountains,
provide no moral hand-hold. One feels lost in such
undemarcated country.[1]

Familiarity, at least for Ann Bridge, changed her initial
impression. The heroine of her novel *Peking Picnic* explains
how the landscape of China had come to seem to her far more
benign:

Her eyes rested with pleasure on the scene before her. Beyond the river a wide stretch of alluvial flat ran up into the hills, brown and level, curiously sprinkled with young isolated poplars whose round fluffy tops resembled puffs of green shrapnel loose in the air, so inconspicuous were their straight, slender boles. On her right the hot yellow outline of the bluff, curving round, cut off this view with theatrical abruptness; downstream, on her left, wide sand-flats, glittering like water in the heat, gave place gradually to the dusty distances of the Peking plain – she could just see, far away, the outline of the Red Temple on its ridge above the river. Behind the green puffs of shrapnel rose the hills, lavender, pink, creamy, grey, with sinister black smears where the coal seams ran out on to the face, sharply coloured even in the distance under the pouring glittering brilliance of the intense light, detailed beyond European belief in the dessicating clearness of the bone-dry air of Central Asia. The delicate strange beauty of the whole landscape struck powerfully on her senses, rousing her to an active delight. What was the quality in this Chinese scene which so moved her, she wondered? She remembered with curious distinctness the distress she had felt during the first few months of her sojourn in Peking at the sheer unfamiliarity of the face of Nature. Her mind, accustomed to draw nourishment from the well-known scenes of England, the great elms standing round the quiet fields, the broad sweep of distant downs, the white roads winding over de Wint-like skylines, dotted with rick and barn, to the huddle of red village roofs, had ranged eagerly, vainly, over the Chinese countryside, finding no resting place. She remembered how alien at first had seemed these dusty flat fields, unmarked by hedge or tree, and the prevailing brown tone of the landscape; how unnatural the sharpness of outlines in crystal-dry air, the vivid colour of far-off mountain shapes – till her very spirit had sickened for green, for the touch of dew, for the soft aqueous blue of distances in a moist climate. The stylised, formal beauty of it she had seen at once – what was lacking was beauty in familiarity, the richness of association entwined with sights and scents, going back through the quiet swing of the seasons to the enormous days and tiny pleasures of childhood; going back deeper and further still, blood of her English blood and bone of her English bone, to the very roots of life. Cut off from all that, planted down in a life as strange as the world she looked upon, she had wilted within like an uprooted plant. She could still remember her own astonishment at the depth of her distress, at finding how much the spirit depends for its strength on the changing but familiar beauty without, the face of the earth, the changeful face of the sky. But gradually the alien beauty of China had awakened its own response in her, and now this scene too, under the blazing untempered life, had power to nourish her spirit. The eastern changes of the seasons, the sudden swing and rush from brown earth to a high waving sea of green, the autumn gold of willows, the pictures of Chinese country life . . . brought their own sense of stability and strength. What is it, she pondered, shifting her seat on the yellow rock, and sending the lizards shooting away with her movement – what *is* the sustenance that we draw from scenery? Why does the spirit live so much through the eye?[2]

Harold Acton was soothed on his first encounter: 'Not only Peking, but the open country outside the city walls was so beautiful and calming to the eye and nerves that I longed to discover the secret of this calm and beauty, unapproached by anything I had seen before.'[3] These feelings would have been familiar to the literati of China, as Ann Bridge noted: 'The Chinese do deeply love and honour the things of nature – air, water, flowers and trees; more deeply than almost any other people; not with a vague poetic yearning, as northern races do, but with a practical recognition, a visible universal allegiance. These things are, as it were, part of the Established Church, not lovely pagans or sly dissenters.'[4]

Appreciation for landscape, expressed in poetry and painting, was noticeable from the fourth and fifth centuries in China, a time when many literati, in order to avoid the intrigues and dangers of unstable courts after the fall of the Han dynasty, retired to their country villas.

But the south was still a foreign land for many, far different from the landscape of the northern plains and loess vistas. Teilhard de Chardin's anguish, therefore, echoes that of numerous Chinese writers who were exiled hundreds of miles away from the heart of China, to the south and west. In the Tang dynasty out-of-favour officials were punished with exile to posts in the most distant reaches of the empire: southern Guangdong, Yunnan and the Vietnam border, areas with tiny Chinese populations. Hainan island, off the south coast and named Yaizhou in the Tang, was as far as one could go; it was reserved for perpetrators of the worst acts of disloyalty. Such a one was Wei Zhiyi, upstart prime minister during the abortive reform movement of 805, and ridiculed by an opponent of the movement, Han Yü:

> Even in the days of his early obscurity he was obsessed by the idea that his career would end in banishment and he had a horror of mentioning any place south of the mountains. Later on it was noticed that whenever he and his fellow secretaries were looking at maps of China, as soon as they came to a map of the south, Wei shut his eyes and would not look. When he became Prime Minister and took over his new official quarters, he noticed at once that there was a map on the wall. For a week he could not bring himself to examine it. When at last he screwed up his courage and looked, he found it was a map of Yaizhou. And sure enough, it was to Yaizhou that he was banished in the end, and at Yaizhou that he died when not much over 40.[5]

Exile, however, was not usually a permanent state and at this time it had a functional as well as a penal role: it provided an ample source of talented officials to fill posts that otherwise would have attracted the least talented. Only in extreme cases would anyone spend more than two or three years so far removed from the political centre, and therefore few had time to gain familiarity with the exotic, semi-tropical surroundings. The despair and loneliness of these banished literati is expressed through their poems, often written to move those still in power to support their reinstatement. No-one expresses this better than Liu Zongyuan, exiled at the same time as Prime Minister Wei, but coming off more lightly – he received a sinecure near present-day Changsha in Hunan Province. He called this poem 'Prison Mountains':

Eternal mountains enclosing Chu and Yue
Like surging billows–
Joined in confusion, swirling upward and falling
  together, creating a natural barrier,
    or
Like layered battlements–
Soaring contentiously, thrusting one above the other,
  obliquely.
At the mountains' feet there is a cleft,
I am relieved to see them subside and suppressed,
But before the land levels out completely
  they rise once again.
Clouds and rain gather and saturate the rich earth,
Miasmas pour out their foetid odours.
There is not even diffuse sunlight; it is shut out and
The massed shade is cold like a prison.
I grieve for the added labour of these people,
Who have to plough and harvest on the mountains'
  sheer slopes.
The woods massed at the foot of the mountains serve
  as the gaol's thorn hedge,
While the roaring of tigers and leopards replaces the
  howling of prison dogs.[6]

Han Yü, exiled some years later, depicts the south as a place of extremes, in climate, fauna and disease; there is little comfort here:

Typhoons for winds, crocodiles for fish,
  afflictions and misfortunes not to be plumbed.
South of the country, as you approach the border
  there are swollen seas joining to the sky.
Poison toads and malarial miasmas,
  which day and evening flare and form.[7]

Their fears – not only of illness but, more importantly, of dying far from home – were not unfounded. Many contracted malaria; Liu Zongyuan himself died of beri-beri, despite prescriptions in contemporary *materia medica* for vitamin-rich concoctions. This was after fifteen years in exile, an extraordinarily long period, but it gave him time to appreciate the beauty of his surroundings and, like Ann Bridge's heroine, to come to love the landscape despite his constant longing for a return to the north. And, just as 'nature' had become popular a few centuries earlier, the landscape of the south started to be praised from Tang times onwards. Influential in this appraisal was a series of eight landscape essays by Liu Zongyuan which described his excursions into the local countryside:

> Flat-Iron Lake lies west of the western hills. At its entrance Ran Stream flows swiftly south, strikes the mountain rocks and is diverted eastwards. As it pours down the steep slope its force becomes increasingly violent. It has eaten into the bank and widened the sides and deepened the middle until it has reached the rock. Floating foam forms into wheels and then the water flows slowly into a clear level stretch of over an acre where there are trees and a spring which feeds it.
>
> Because of my frequent visits the man who lived there knocked on my door one day and told me that he could not meet his accumulation of tax and private debts. He had cleared a hillside and moved house and wished to sell this land to get him out of his difficulties.
>
> I gladly agreed to the proposal. I added to the height of his terrace, lengthened his railed walks, and led the spring up to a height so that it fell into the lake with the sound of meeting waters. This place is especially appropriate for viewing the moon at mid-autumn in that one here may see the loftiness of the heavens and the infinity of the air. What can make me delighted to dwell among the barbarian and forget my native land if not this lake?[8]

He also wrote many other pieces on the landscape theme. In the preface to a series of poems on the scenery of a local stream he gently teases himself for the folly of the actions which led to exile: the irony in this piece is typical of much Chinese literature, as is the political message. But it also reveals the Chinese preoccupation with the combination of mountains and water – the characters which together form the word 'landscape' in Chinese:

> The stream flows east from the south bank of the River Guan into the River Xiao. I was banished here for my foolishness, and here I found this stream and fell in love with it. A mile or so along there is an exquisitely beautiful stretch where I have made myself a home. Ancient texts make reference to a place called Fool's Valley. Because the name of the stream is not settled and even the local people would quarrel about it, I felt bound to choose my own name and so I called it Fool's Stream.
>
> I purchased a small hill next to the stream and this became Fool's Hill. Sixty paces to the northeast I found a spring which I also bought and it became Fool's Spring. The spring has six outlets on the level ground at the foot of the hill where it rises. The water from these flows together into Fool's Creek and meanders southwards. By damming a narrow section of the Creek with earth and piled stones I formed Fool's Pond. To the east stands Fool's Hall and to the south Fool's Pagoda, while in the pond there is Fool's Island. The fine trees and unusual rocks combine to make this an extraordinary and beautiful landscape yet I have disgraced it by calling it foolish. As Confucius said, 'Wise men appreciate water.' Why then should this stream be singled out for humiliation? . . . Like me it is of no use in the world, so it is appropriate to slander it by calling it foolish.[9]

Water is an enduring theme for the exile, especially the rivers of Hunan, site of the ancient state of Chu. This region played host to many banished exiles, but the most famous is undoubtedly Qu Yuan, a third-century BC statesman at the court of the Chu king and China's first named poet. His death – he threw himself into the Miluo River just north of Changsha – is now associated with the Dragon Boat Festival when people drop parcels of sticky rice into local rivers to feed the fish and so prevent them from eating his body. But his name does not only occur in folklore: he became an exemplar of the loyal but wronged official, a transformation greatly aided by the corpus of poetry he left behind in which he adopts the role of martyr:

> I mourn that my lot was cast in an unfit time;
> I grieve for the many woes of the land of Chu.
> My nature was one of spotless purity,
> But I fell on a time of disorder and met with disgrace.
> Hating the upright dealing of an honest man,
> The muddy impure world could not understand me.
> My prince and I – we were so much at odds,
> I removed myself from him to wander by Yuan and
>   Xiang.
> There I threw myself into the Miluo's waters,
> For I knew there was no hope that the world might
>   change.
> Anguish of parting and broken hopes assailed me,
> And I turned in the water, but already the current had
>   carried me far.
> I had entered the gloomy gates of the House of Darkness
> Hidden in caverns under the rocky cliff face.
> Henceforth water serpents must be my companions,
> And dragon spirits lie with me where I would rest.
> How sheer and awful were the towering rocks overhead!
> My fainting soul shrank back, oppressed;
> And as I lay, mouth full of water, deep below the
>   surface,
> The light of the sun seemed dim and very far above me.
> Mourning for its body, dissolved now by decay,
> My' unhoused spirit drifted, disconsolate.
> Remembering how Orchid and Pepper had lost their
>   fragrance,
> My soul was confused, it could see no real way ahead.
> If only I could be sure that my acts had been faultless
> I could still be happy, even in my dissolution.

Yet I grieved that the land of Chu was sinking to
    destruction;
I was sad that the Fair One had advanced so far in error.
Truly the fashion of this present age is folly;
Foggy of purpose, they lack sense of direction.
I remembered how selfish men had taken charge of
    policy,
And I had been forced into exile, far south of the River.
I remembered how Nü Xu had expostulated with me,
All the tears she had shed for me in sorrowful entreaty.
But I had resolved to die, to abandon the living:
There could be no returning now, even if I tried.
Standing in the pellucid water of the rushing shallows,
I gazed on the rugged peaks of high mountains;
Then, with sad memories of the red cliffs of Gaoqui,
Plunged once more in the water, never more to
    return.[10]

The Miluo is on the main riverine route south and since
then generations of literati have dedicated poems to Qu Yuan
on their way into exile, appropriating his name to assert their
own loyalty and righteousness. Liu Zongyuan was among
them:

On my way South I do not grieve like the Chu official
For I expect to re-enter the Capital's gate.
The spring winds return to the Miluo
But I do not take the choppy waters to mean that times
    of peace are impossible.[11]

Liu did indeed set foot again within the gates of the capital,
then Xian, but he was told immediately that he had been
re-exiled – at a longer distance but in a higher post: peace
was not to be. And his poem, written in 815 on this second
journey south to near present-day Guilin, has a very different
mood and is more openly critical of the government:

A thousand years after you, I am exiled for the second
    time and passing the Xiang River,
I seek you out at the Miluo, clutching fragrant
Heng and Ruo grasses.

And in this hurried moment I wish to devote some
  words
To you and thereby receive some understanding.
You did not follow along with the world
But only pursued the true Way.
World affairs were in disorder and society diseased,
Noble men were ignored and petty men served at court,
And while the hens cackled meaninglessly, the cock's
  beak remains closed.[12]

Perhaps Mao Zedong, born in this region, recalled Qu Yuan
when he threatened to drown himself in the village pond after
a family altercation. The students in Changsha certainly
remembered him and exploited the theme of political dis-
sent when in 1989 they mourned those killed in Peking on
4 June:

Was it the indignant still-beckoning spirit of Qu Yuan
from more than two thousand years ago which took
you away? You have gone, suddenly gone. You have left
behind only a river of fresh blood, only a deep love and
a deep hate. You have gone. Spirits of Beijing, where
do you rest? Where do you rest? The mountains and
the rivers weep, the sad wind whirls. Before the evil
gun muzzles, before the ugly face of fascism, before our
people in their suffering, and before the calm, smiling
face on your death masks, I can do no more than make
this offering to your spirits. . . . You are gone! Today,
two thousand years ago, Qu Yuan, his heart afire with
loyal ardour, leapt into the pitiless Miluo River. 'I sub-
mit to your crystal-clear depths, Oh Death, come now.'
Today, two thousand years later you, our loyal brothers
and sisters, fell under the guns of the so-called 'people's
own soldiers'; you fell under the tanks of the 'most
cherished ones'.[13]

Landscape is at the heart of the dilemma presented by Qu
Yuan's case, but already expressed two centuries earlier by
Confucius: whether to continue to serve in a corrupt court
or to retire from public life to the country. Qu Yuan received

both praise and criticism for his actions:

> People will not always follow your example:
> You turned your back on the kingdom,
> Disdained to follow custom,
> And were contemptuous of death itself.[14]

Both courses were, however, acceptable, as Mencius made plain:

> The actions of the sage are not always the same. Some live in retirement, others enter court . . . but it all comes to keeping their integrity intact.[15]

Chinese literature therefore abounds with officials extolling the pleasures of their country retreats and the 'simple life'. The whole of nature is encapsulated within the two extremes of the effusive motion of water and the quiet, eternal quality of the mountain. And, following both Confucian and Daoist traditions, these were regarded as a source of mystical, emotional and aesthetic pleasure. The literatus, forced for whatever reason to abandon the more worldly delights of city life, was not being entirely disingenuous when he wrote that he preferred country life:

> From my youth I have loved the mountains,
> Never was I suited to the world of men,
> Mistakenly I got entangled in these affairs
> And was caught in the snares for thirteen years.
> The caged bird longs for its old tree,
> The farmed fish for its original pool.
> I till the soil in the uncultivated southern borders, clinging to solitude in my return to the land,
> My plot is only an acre, and my cottage only has eight or nine rooms.
> Elms and willows shade the back while peaches and plums spread over the front,
> The sprawling village in the distance, and the wafting chimney smoke in the air,
> A dog barks in the hidden lanes, and the cocks crow on the mulberry tree.

My house is free from the dust of the world, and there
  is peace and quiet in the empty rooms.
Long I have been in the prison of men, but I have
  regained a return to nature.[16]

But, of course, the country cottage was never as humble
as the poets made out, nor did they literally till the fields: this
was a pretence of rusticity not unknown to poets in the West.

The 'return to nature' was usually only a temporary expedient to avoid the intrigues and dangers of court: few kept
it up for a lifetime. But there were compensations. The ensu-
ing gain to literature – working literati had little leisure time
in which to write for pleasure – was remarked by Sima Qian,
author of a celebrated history written in the first century
BC:

> Too numerous to record are the men of ancient time who
> were rich and noble and whose names have yet vanished
> away. It is only those who were masterful and sure, the
> truly extraordinary men, who are still remembered.
> When the Earl of the West was imprisoned at Yuli he
> expanded *The Book of Changes*; Confucius was in distress
> and he made *The Spring and Autumn Annals*; Qu Yuan
> was banished and he composed his poem 'Encountering
> Sorrow'; after Zuo Qiu lost his sight he composed *The
> Narratives of the States*; when Sun Zi had had his feet
> amputated he set forth *The Art of War*; Lu Buwei was
> banished to Shu but his *Lulan* has been handed down
> through the ages; while Han Fei Zi was held prisoner
> in Qin he wrote 'The Difficulties of Disputation' and
> 'The Sorrow of Standing Alone'; most of the three hun-
> dred verses in the *Book of Odes* were written when the
> sages poured forth their anger and frustration.[17]

Like Qu Yuan before him and Liu Zongyuan almost a
thousand years later, Sima Qian had fallen out of favour. His
punishment, which was intended to force him into suicide by
its severity, was castration. Sima Qian chose to live but for
a purpose. He continues:

> All these men had a rankling in their hearts for they were
> not able to accomplish what they wished. Therefore they

wrote of past affairs in order to pass on their thoughts to future generations. . . . I wished to examine into all that concerns heaven and man, to penetrate the changes of the past and present . . . but before I had finished my rough manuscript I met with this calamity. It is because I regretted that the work was not complete that I submitted to this extreme penalty without rancour. When I have truly finished my work, I shall deposit it in some safe place. If it is handed down to men who appreciate it, and it penetrates to the great cities and the villages, then even though I should have suffered a thousand mutilations, what regret would I have?[18]

Sima Qian presented another ideal for the literatus to emulate: the official famous in his lifetime for his service who ensured his fame after his death through his writings. Few had the time or talent to achieve both. All those who attempted to gain preferment through the official examinations had to be able to compose poems and prose but many stopped writing after attaining office, apart from the occasional poem or memorial tablet for a friend, or a commission to help eke out their meagre salary. It was only in late imperial China that large numbers of scholars entered the civil service by this route: in the Tang there were only a score of successful examinees each year and even then they did not automatically gain a place in a bureaucracy which numbered eighteen thousand. Those who had literary talent and entered the civil service on a fast track could expect to have little time for literature. Sima Qian's observation remained true: political exile provided both the opportunity and the motivation to develop a literary voice. It also provided the subject-matter: there are a vast number of poems on landscape and the beauties of nature.

Those few who freely chose long-term retirement for mystical reasons belong to an ancient and revered tradition of eremetism, of which Zhuangzi, the fourth-century BC Daoist, was an amusing and forceful proponent:

Zhuangzi was fishing in the River Pu when two ministers from the court of the King of Chu approached him. 'His Majesty', they reported, 'offers his whole state as bait to ensnare you.' Zhuangzi, concentrating on his fishing-line, did not even turn round, but replied, 'I hear that there is a sacred tortoise in Chu which has been dead for three thousand years. His Majesty keeps it wrapped in a box at the head of the hall in his ancestors' shrine. Do you think this tortoise would rather be dead and honoured as preserved bones, or alive and dragging its tail in the mud?' The Ministers replied, 'It would rather be alive and dragging its tail in the mud.' 'Leave me to drag my tail in the mud.'[19]

In these early Daoist writings public life is scorned and the individual is encouraged to seek a mystical knowledge of the Way – the *Dao*. The later concentration on the Daoist Yellow Emperor, a sage ruler whose government institutions were themselves a manifestation of the *Dao*, did nothing to dispel Zhuangzi's initial vision, although by this time the Daoist hermit was expected to nurture his vital force, to refrain from eating the five grains, and to search for special fungus and other substances to prolong his life. In perhaps the most important work on philosophical Daoism, *The Master Who Embraces Simplicity*, its third-century author emphasizes the importance of the landscape, instructing, for example, that 'you must be amid mountains of repute, in a place without men when you blend cinnabar elixirs'. Many of the most famous Tang dynasty poems encapsulate the eremetic ideal. For example, 'On Looking in Vain for the Hermit' by Jia Tao reflects the elusiveness of the true hermit:

> I questioned the boy under the pine trees,
> 'My Master went to gather herbs,
> He is still somewhere on the mountainside
> So deep in the clouds I know not where.'[20]

Paradoxically, retiring to the mountains, especially those around the capital, was also a way of gaining an official position as hermits were regarded as men of high virtue and integrity who would be an asset in government.

Literati in office were not, however, completely starved of 'mountains and water': their delight in nature was satisfied by excursions to places renowned for their scenic beauty and, on a smaller scale, by gardens, potted plants and miniature landscapes. The making of such a landscape is described by Shen Fu in the early nineteenth century:

Once when I was sweeping the family graves in the mountains, I came across some pretty patterned stones which I took home and discussed with Yün. 'If putty is used to set Xuanzhou pebbles into a white stone dish,' I said, 'it looks attractive because the putty, the pot and the stones are all the same colour. These yellow stones are delightful, but if I use putty the white and yellow will contrast and show up the chisel marks on the stones. What can we do?'

'Select the poorer stones', said Yün, 'and pound them into dust. Mix the dust with the putty and use it to fill in the chisel marks while it is still wet. When it dries perhaps the colours will be the same.'

We did as she suggested and built up a miniature mountain in a rectangular pot from the Yixing kilns. It inclined to the left with a bulge on the right. Along the mountain we scored horizontal lines so that it resembled the rocks in paintings by Yunlin. The cliffs were irregular, like those along a river bank. We filled in an empty corner of the pot with river mud and planted white duckweed and on top of the stones we planted morning glory. It took us several days to complete.

By the mid-autumn the morning glory had grown all over the mountain, covering it like wisteria hanging from a rock face, and it bloomed a deep red. The white duckweed also flowered and letting our spirits roam among the red and white was like a visit to the Isle of the Immortals. We put the pot under the eaves and discussed it in great detail; here we should build a pavilion on the water, there a thatched arbour; here we should inscribe a stone with the characters: 'Where blossoms fall and water flows.' We could live here, fish over there and gaze into the distance from this viewpoint. We were as excited as if we were actually going to move to those imaginary hills and vales. But one night some miserable cats fighting over something to eat fell from the eaves, smashing the pot in an instant.[21]

In this passage Shen Fu gives the ideal of the garden: not a formal affair, but made to reflect nature at its best and enhanced by man's artifice with pavilions, the judicious placement of miniature mountains and water, and with spots highlighted by a calligraphic phrase which would recall echoes upon echoes of lines from famous poems of the past. Such was the garden built for the return of the daughter of the household in China's most famous novel, *The Dream of Red Mansions* (also known as *The Story of the Stone*), by Cao Xueqin. She was an imperial concubine and protocol demanded a separate residence befitting her elevated status to house her when she visited her family. On completion of the garden her father, Chia Cheng, inspected it with his literary friends so that they could suggest appropriate quotations, and he ordered his son, Pao-yu, to join them, having received a favourable report of his couplet-composing skill from the tutor:

> Chia Cheng rose to his feet and set off at the head of the party, while Chia Chen went on in advance to let everyone in the garden know they were coming.
> . . . At the entrance to the garden, they found Chia Chen with a group of stewards lined up in wait.
> 'Close the gate,' said Chia Cheng. 'Let us see what it looks like from outside before we go in.'
> Chia Chen had the gate closed and Chia Cheng inspected the gatehouse, a building in five sections with an arched roof of semi-circular tiles. The lintels and lattices, finely carved with ingenious designs, were neither painted nor gilded; the walls were of polished bricks of a uniform colour, and the white marble steps were carved with passion-flowers. The garden's spotless whitewashed wall stretching to left and right had, at its base, a mosaic of striped 'tiger-skin' stones. The absence of vulgar ostentation pleased him.
> He had the gate opened then and they went in, only to find their view screened by a green hill. At this sight his secretaries cried out in approval.

1. The old city walls of Peking
'There is a splendid formality about the sharp line of masonry where the city ends at a stroke, and the open country spreads up to its very foot . . . with the long files of camels, coming in as they have come for centuries laden with coal from the hills, or with who knows what strange burden of silks or carpets or furs, from Tibet and from beyond the Gobi Desert.'

Ann Bridge, *Peking Picnic*

2. Daoist monks on Mount Hua
'The demon from the North fears that from the South, the East his
brother from the West, while all dread one another . . . temples,
therefore, built on the summits of high hills are free from their visitations,
for to a demon there would always be the chance of meeting a rival.
Those who have been pestered overmuch by demons, often spend an
unhurried week-end on some lofty pinnacle in peaceful contemplation.'
Thomas Woodrooffe, *River of Golden Sand*

3. 'From the road outside came the continual pig-squeal of wheelbarrows going past.'

           W. H. Auden and Christopher Isherwood, *Journey to a War*

'A demon hates a noise . . . and for this reason . . . the wheelbarrow coolie is able to go his way unmolested as long as his wheel is making a hideous din.'

           Thomas Woodrooffe, *River of Golden Sand*

4. A Peking bookshop
    'Thus moved, he will spread his paper and poise his brush
        To express what he can in writing . . .
          Writing is in itself a joy . . .
    In a sheet of paper is contained the infinite.'
                    Lu Ji, 'Essay on Literature'

5. A scholar airing his books
'The moment I awake, I long for my library and bound towards it, swift as a thirsty cat.'

Yuan Mei, 'Thoughts on Master Huang's Book Borrowing'

6. 'Here sat the high officials in a semicircle, with a red-button mandarin from the Board of Punishments at their head. On one side of this booth was a tiny sort of altar on which were displayed the tools of the executioner – the swords and bloody string, and the tourniquets and strings for strangling.'

A. B. Freeman-Mitford, *The Attaché at Peking*

7. The Dowager Empress Cixi

'I have often thought that I am the most clever woman that ever lived, and others cannot compare with me. Although I have heard much about Queen Victoria . . . still I don't think her life was half so interesting and eventful as mine . . .'

Cixi

8. Deng Xiaoping

'The handful of octogenarians and the privileged bureaucratic clique whom they represent will neither change their ways nor hand over power. Thus they are doomed to destruction. Yes, the people will pay a bloody price, but in the end they will shake off this monstrous thing that is draining them of their life's blood.'

Liu Binyan, *A Higher Kind of Loyalty*

9. The Monkey King, a popular opera character

' "How long has this pernicious monkey been in existence?" asked the Jade Emperor.

"He . . . was emitted three hundred years ago by a stone . . . Since then he has managed somehow to perfect himself and achieve immortality. He now subdues dragons, tames tigers and has tampered with the registers of death." '

Wu Cheng'en, *Monkey*, trans. Arthur Waley

'If not for this hill,' observed Chia Cheng, 'one would see the whole garden as soon as one entered, and how tame that would be.'

'Exactly,' agreed the rest. 'Only a bold landscape gardener could have conceived this.'

On the miniature mountain they saw rugged white rocks resembling monsters and beasts, some recumbent, some rampant, dappled with moss or hung about with creepers, a narrow zigzag path just discernible between them.

'We'll follow this path,' decided Chia Cheng. 'Coming back we can find our way out at the other side. That should take us over the whole grounds.'

He made Chia Chen lead the way and, leaning on Pao-yu's shoulder, followed him up through the boulders. Suddenly raising his head, he saw a white rock polished as smooth as a mirror, obviously intended for the first inscription.

'See, gentlemen!' he called over his shoulder, smiling. 'What would be a suitable name for this spot?'

'Heaped Verdure,' said one.

'Embroidery Ridge', said another.

'The Censer.'

'A Miniature Chungnan'.

Dozens of different suggestions were made, all of them stereotyped clichés; for Chia Cheng's secretaries were well aware that he meant to test his son's ability. Pao-yu understood this too.

Now his father called on him to propose a name.

Pao-yu replied, 'I've heard that the ancients said, "An old quotation beats an original saying; to recut an old text is better than to engrave a new one." As this is not the main prominence or one of the chief sights, it only needs an inscription because it is the first step leading to the rest. So why not use that line from an old poem:

A winding path leads to a secluded retreat.

A name like that would be more dignified.'

'Excellent!' cried the secretaries.

'Our young master is far more brilliant and talented than dull pedants like ourselves.'

'You mustn't flatter the boy,' protested Chia Cheng with a smile. 'He's simply making a ridiculous parade of his very limited knowledge. We can think of a better name later.'

They walked on through a tunnel into a ravine green with magnificent trees and ablaze with rare flowers. A clear stream welling up where the trees were thickest would its way through clefts in the rocks.[22]

Further on the garden emulated the ideal rural life, prompting praise from Chia Cheng:

As they walked on talking, their eyes fell on some green hills barring their way. Skirting these they caught sight of brown adobe walls with paddy-stalk copings and hundreds of apricot-trees, their blossoms bright as spurting flames or sunlit clouds. Inside this enclosure stood several thatched cottages. Outside grew saplings of mulberry, elm, hibiscus and silkworm-thorn trees, whose branches had been intertwined to form a double green hedge. Beyond this hedge, at the foot of the slope, was a rustic well complete with windlass and well-sweep. Below, neat plots of fine vegetables and rape-flowers stretched as far as eye could see.

'I see the point of this place,' declared Chia Cheng. 'Although artificially made, the sight of it tempts one to retire to the country. Let us go in and rest a while.'[23]

But Pao-yu was not so impressed:

Chia Cheng led the party into one of the cottages. It was quite free of ostentation, having papered windows and a wooden couch. Secretly pleased, he glanced at his son and asked, 'Well, what do you think of *this* place?'

The secretaries nudged the boy to induce him to express approval. But ignoring them he answered, 'It can't compare with "Where the Phoenix Alights."'

'Ignorant dolt!' Chia Cheng sighed. 'All you care for are red pavilions and painted beams. With your perverse taste for luxury, how can you appreciate the natural beauty of such a quiet retreat? This comes of neglecting your studies.'

'Yes sir,' replied Pao-yu promptly. 'But the ancients were always using the term "natural". I wonder what they really meant by it?'

Afraid his pig-headedness would lead to trouble, the others hastily put in, 'You understand everything else so well, why ask about the term "natural"? It means coming from nature, not due to human effort.'

'There you are! A farm here is obviously artificial and out of place with no villages in the distance, no fields near by, no mountain ranges behind, no source for the stream at hand, above, no pagoda from any half hidden temple, below, no bridge leading to a market. Perched here in isolation, it is nothing like as fine a sight as those other places which were less far-fetched. The bamboos and streams there didn't look so artificial. What the ancients called "a natural picture" means precisely that when you insist on an unsuitable site and hills where no hills should be, however skilfully you go about it the result is bound to jar. . . .'[24]

This could be a discussion taking place between eighteenth-century adherents of the 'natural' style of landscape gardening practised by Capability Brown and the newer 'picturesque' style. And indeed gardens were one aspect of China that, from the first, excited interest among Western writers, even though most of them gained their information second-hand. The first Englishman to remark on the irregularity of Chinese gardens was Sir William Temple writing in 1685 when English country houses had stylized, formal and symmetrical gardens: 'The Chinese scorn this way of planting, and say a boy that can tell a hundred, may plant walks of trees in straight lines. . . . But their great reach of imagination is employed in contriving figures, where that beauty should be great, and strike the eye, but without any order of disposition of parts, that shall be commonly or easily observed.'[25]

And his lead was followed by Addison and Pope, who both replanted their gardens accordingly, setting a new vogue which received a further stimulus in 1747 with Père Attiret's description of the Yuanmingyuan, the imperial summer palace north of Peking (it was razed by British and French troops in 1860). The method was put into effect by Sir William Chambers, architect to King George III and designer of the Chinese Garden at Kew, who had travelled to China in his youth. It was hardly surprising that Lord Macartney should feel completely at home in the grounds of the palace, comparing them to Luton Hoo, which had been landscaped by Capability Brown:

> We rode about three miles through a very beautiful park kept in the highest order, and much resembling the approach to Luton in Bedfordshire. . . . It would be an endless task were I to attempt a detail of all the wonders of this charming place. There is no beauty of distribution, no feature of amenity, no reach of fancy which embellishes our pleasure grounds in England that is not to be found here. Had China been accessible to Mr Brown or Mr Hamilton, I should have sworn they should have drawn their happiest ideas from the rich sources, which I have tasted this day; for in the course of a few hours I have enjoyed such vicissitudes of rural delight, as I did not conceive could be felt out of England, being at different moments enchanted by scenes perfectly similar to those I have known there, to the magnificence of Stowe, the soft beauties of Wooburn and the fairy-land of Paine's Hill.[26]

Barrow, who accompanied the embassy, felt bound to challenge the descriptions of Chambers regarding the Chinese picturesque: 'if an opinion may be formed from those parts of [the Yuanmingyuan] which I have seen, and I understood there is great similarity throughout the whole, they fall far short of the fanciful and extravagant descriptions that Sir William Chambers has given of Chinese gardening. Much, however, has been done, and nothing that I saw could be considered as an offence to nature.'[27]

The pavilions and Chinese bridges would not of course have spoilt Lord Macartney's sense of familiarity; after all, the

English gardens of this period were as well stocked with 'chinoiserie' as the houses:

> Where is the pastoral refinement of an Englishman's garden, here is an eruption of gloomy forest and towering crag, of ruins where there was never a house, of water dashing against rocks where there was neither spring nor a stone I could throw the length of a cricket pitch. My hyacinth dell is become a haunt for hobgoblins, my Chinese bridge, which I am assured is superior to the one at Kew, and for all I know at Peking, is usurped by a fallen obelisk overgrown with briars.[28]

The burgeoning appreciation of nature in eighteenth-century England was influenced not only by Chinese garden design, but by the art of watercolour landscapes which had been developed over a thousand years previously in China. Also at this time the first translation (into Latin) of the Daoist classic, the *Daodejing*, appeared with its vision of Arcadia in a corrupt world:

> Bring it about that the people will return to the use of the knotted rope, will find relish in their food, beauty in their clothes, will be content in their abode and happy in the way they live. Though adjoining states are within sight of one another, and the sound of dogs barking and cocks crowing in one state can be heard in another, yet the people of one state will grow old and die without having had any dealings with those of another.[29]

The ideal garden so precisely described in *The Dream of Red Mansions* is now thought to have been inspired by the private gardens of Prince Fu in Peking, although there is still considerable scholarly debate over this. The advantages of the private garden were explained in a Chinese treatise on gardening: 'If one can thus find stillness in the midst of city turmoil, why should one then forego such an easily accessible spot and seek a more distant one? As soon as one has some leisure time then one can go and wander there, hand in hand with a friend.'[30]

And some of the most exquisite private gardens in China are found in the city of Suzhou. The oldest, 'Lion Grove', originated as temple grounds laid out by a Buddhist monk in the fourteenth century. Others, with names such as 'The Garden of the Master of the Fishing Nets' and 'The Humble Administrator's Garden', exemplify Shen Fu's instructions on the design of small gardens:

> In laying out gardens, pavilions, meandering paths, layered stone mountains, and flowers try to give the sense of the small in the large and the large in the small, the real in the illusion and the illusion in the real. . . .
> This is the way to show the large in the small: the wall of a small garden should curve outwards and inwards and be covered with green vines. There should be large stones decorated with inscriptions set into them. Then one will be able to open a window and feel as if one were gazing out across a precipice.[31]

Their delights have been hidden from public view until this century, when admired by Colin Thubron:

> I spent two days wandering the gardens of Suzhou. My tourist brochure said that they 'crystallised the collective wisdom of the working people of our country', but in fact they were esoteric and profoundly exclusive. The retired officials and merchants, painters and poets who created and inhabited them were steeped in a refined conservatism. Their gardens lay secluded down lanes behind high walls through inconspicuous gates. They were places for *wu wei*, for stillness after the stress and pomp of a government career, for retreat into a precinct which did not dominate nature, but expressed and sanctified it.
> . . . I slipped into the 800-year-old Garden of the Master of the Fishing Nets, and here, in the compass of an acre, momentarily lost footing in Time. In the outer court stand quiescent rocks. They are a stilling, an announcement. A gallery opens on a little glade of trees. The way bifurcates. And thereafter the eye is bemused by possibility and contrast everywhere. Within a few paces the view is concentrated in gateways, splintered by lattices, unfolded from a terrace. Beyond black eaves

a camphor tree shines in isolated brilliance. A moon-gate circumscribes a boulder. In the villa's chambers the windows hang close against whitewashed walls outside: the framed rocks and leaves shine in the rooms' darkness. . . .

If a man would be happy for a week, ran a saying, he could take a wife; if he planned happiness for a month, he must kill a pig; but if he desired happiness for ever, he should plant a garden.[32]

The urban scenery of Hangzhou, the other 'heavenly city' in the oft-quoted saying, 'Above is Heaven, Below are Hangzhou and Suzhou', has always been accessible. Marco Polo, who calls it Kinsai, notes the allusion to heaven and extols its beauty, although, like many foreign writers on China, he was more concerned with the people and their pleasures than with the landscape:

On the Lake of which we have spoken there are numbers of boats and barges of all sizes for parties of pleasure. These will hold 10, 15, 20, or more persons, and are from 15 to 20 paces in length, with flat bottoms and ample breadth of beam, so that they always keep their level. Any one who desires to go a-pleasuring with the women, or with a party of his own sex, hires one of these barges, which are always to be found completely furnished with tables and chairs and all the other apparatus for a feast. The roof forms a level deck, on which the crew stand, and pole the boat along whithersoever may be desired, for the lake is not more than 2 paces in depth. The inside of this roof and the rest of the interior is covered with ornamental painting in gay colours, with windows all round that can be shut or opened, so that the party at table can enjoy all the beauty and variety of the prospects on both sides as they pass along. And truly a trip on this lake is a much more charming recreation than can be enjoyed on land. For on the one side lies the city in its entire length, so that the spectators in the barges, from the distance at which they stand, take in the whole prospect in its full beauty and grandeur, with its numberless palaces, temples, monasteries, and gardens, full of lofty trees, sloping to the shore. And the lake is never without a number of other such boats, laden with pleasure-parties; for it is the great delight of the citizens here, after they have disposed of the day's business, to pass the afternoon in enjoyment with the ladies of their families, or perhaps with others less reputable, either in these barges or in driving about the city in carriages.[33]

The singing girls also occupied much of Barrow's account, although he does admit that 'the natural and artificial beauties of the lake far exceeded anything we had hitherto had an opportunity of seeing'. Archie Bell, writing early this century, when he eventually reached the lake after a disappointing ride through the town of Hangzhou, was also won over to the charms of the landscape, although he was somewhat censorious about the pleasures, inquiring of his guide as to the marital status of the men on the barges:

My impression was that of passing from purgatory into paradise. The coolies spattered along through the filthy and vile streets of Hangchow. At the hotel I told them to take me to West Lake. My earlier experiences of the day had not been the sort that make me think that I was visiting the 'City of Heaven'. I began to think that the Chinese poets and even old Marco Polo himself, must have had lively imaginations. Either that or things had changed in a thousand years. Of course things do change in a thousand years, even in old China; and as the foul odours of the streets met my nostrils, as I looked into the faces of the weird crowds and saw almost savage life, I was about ready to give up my quest for beauty and go back to the houseboat and breathe the comparatively pure air of a Chinese canal.

I merely took one more chance and told Hong that if West Lake did not come nearer to living up to the classical reputation of Hangchow, we would go elsewhere and take the word of historians about the grandeur of the place which was no longer grand, or did not seem to be. But once we emerged from the tangle of streets the coolies put down my chair on flagstones that went down to the waters of a five-mile lake.

Immediately I realized tht my wily Chink boy had reserved this view for the great climax of our houseboat meanderings. Here, at last, was one of the great objects of all travel in China. From the depths of a squalid, filthy, miserable China I had emerged into the real Hangchow, City of Heaven. Before me lay the original of the great landscape gardens of the world.

Here I saw that Hangchow is still a city of great wealth and oriental indolence. Reconstructed palatial dwellings and pavilions of ancient courts still face the lake, and are tenanted by a dreamy class of Chinese who live in the China of one or two thousand years ago and do not care for the onward march of events. They much prefer that luxurious life of the past. . . .[34]

Bertrand Russell does not record whether he was so distracted but he was similarly struck by the impression Hangzhou gives of an old civilization: 'Our Chinese friends took us for two days to Hangchow to see the Western Lake. The first day we went round it by boat, and the second day in chairs. It was marvellously beautiful, with the beauty of ancient civilisation, surpassing even that of Italy.'[35]

His curious remark in a letter to Lady Ottoline Morrell describing Hangzhou, that 'apparently poets in ancient China were as rich as financiers in modern Europe', is completely unfounded. Poets were amateurs, mainly writing for pleasure, for friends, for influence, or to record a particular moment or feeling. The Hangzhou scenery inspired many of these; for example, Bai Juyi writing four centuries before Marco Polo:

Now spring is here the lake seems a painted picture,
Unruly peaks all around the edge, the water spread out
   flat.
Pines in ranks on the face of the hills, a thousand layers
   of green:
The moon centred on the heart of the waves, just one
   pearl.

Thread-ends of an emerald-green rug, the extruding
    paddy-shoots:
Sash of a blue damask skirt, the expanse of new reeds.
If I cannot bring myself yet to put Hangzhou behind me,
Half of what holds me here is on this lake.[36]

The other half may well have been the singing girls – Bai
Juyi's most famous poem was inspired by the song of a
courtesan. And Hangzhou's beauty also brought women to
Su Shi's mind three centuries later:

The shimmer of light on the water is the play of sunny
    skies,
The blur of colour across the hills is richer still in rain.
If you wish to compare the West Lake to the Lady of
    the West,
Lightly powdered or thickly smeared the fancy is just
    as apt.[37]

Hangzhou, with its mountains and lake, was a place where
worldly pleasure and the delights of the natural landscape met
to satisfy all the needs of the poet. Nowadays it is visited by
tens of thousands of tourists, but it retains its soothing
capacity to recall the China of old, and to make each of its
visitors a poet in a landscape, as Colin Thubron found:

As I strolled around the lake, it was the muted palette
of the Song painters which came to mind, with its
misty areas of empty silk. Already the quiet had purged
Shanghai from me. I felt indolent and empty-headed
– a figure in a watercolourist's landscape, wandering
between willows along a causeway.[38]

5

LITERATURE AND LITERATI

It is not easy to find a man who has studied for three years without thinking about earning a salary.

Confucius, *The Analects*, 8.12

From emperors to commoners, courtiers to hermits, there is no-one who does not tirelessly pursue merit and fame. Why is this? Because they have all set their hearts on immortality. And what is immortality? No more than to have one's name written in a book.

Liu Zhiji, *Generalities of History*

Chinese culture is in the highest degree a literary culture. This was true long before the system of civil service examinations was established in the Tang dynasty. Every scholar aspired to be a poet, for poetry was regarded as the prime vehicle for expression of feeling and truth; and the poetic tradition of China is very ancient. *The Book of Odes*, a collection of ballads, was venerable by the time of Confucius in the sixth century BC. The First Emperor, Qin Shi Huang Di (reigned 221–210 BC) – unifier of China and builder of the Great Wall, whose spectacular tomb near Xian is guarded by the famous terracotta army – proved the importance of books in his day by burning them on a massive scale. Sima Qian tells the tale. 'These scholars', says the First Emperor's prime minister, complaining to him of the literati,

learn only from the old, not the new, and use their learning to oppose our rule and confuse the people. . . . In former times when the world, torn by chaos and disorder, could not be united, different states arose and argued from the past to condemn the present, using empty rhetoric to cover up and confuse the real issues, and employing their learning to oppose what was established by authority. Now Your Majesty has conquered the whole world, distinguished between black and white, and set unified standards. Yet these opinionated scholars get together to slander the laws and judge each new decree according to their own school of thought, opposing it secretly in their hearts while discussing it openly in the streets. . . . If this is not prohibited, the sovereign's prestige will suffer and factions will be formed among his subjects. Far better put a stop to it!

I humbly propose that all historical records but those of our own time be burned. If anyone who is not a court scholar dares to keep the ancient songs, historical records or writings of the hundred schools, these should be confiscated and burned by the provincial governor and army commander. Those who in conversation dare to quote the old songs and records should be publicly executed; those who use old precedents to oppose the new order should have their families wiped out; and officers who know of such cases but fail to report them should be punished in the same way.

If thirty days after the issuing of this order the owners of these books have still not had them destroyed, they should have their faces tattooed and be condemned to hard labour at the Great Wall. The only books which need not be destroyed are those dealing with medicine, divination and agriculture. Those who want to study law can learn it from the officers.[1]

The emperor sanctioned this proposal. Imperial sanction meant action: the First Emperor not only burned books, he also killed those who wrote them. 'Over four hundred and sixty scholars', Sima Qian reports, 'were buried alive in Xianyang as a warning to the whole empire. Even more were banished to the frontier regions.'

H.A. Giles, one of the founders of Sinology, claims that we may regard Confucius as the founder of Chinese literature on the grounds that in the respites of a busy and itinerant life 'he found time to rescue for posterity certain valuable literary fragments of great antiquity, and to produce at least one original work of his own'.[2] The works of which Confucius is said to be editor are *The Book of History*, *The Book of Odes*, the *Yi Jing* (or *The Book of Changes*), *The Record of Rites*, and *The Spring and Autumn Annals*. Collectively they are known as the Five Classics.

When Neo-Confucianism became dominant in the eleventh century they were supplemented and eventually superseded by the Four Books, namely the *Analects*, or sayings of Confucius; the writings of Mencius; and two excerpts from *The Record of Rites*, the 'Great Learning' and 'The Doctrine of the Mean'.

The classics constituted the curriculum of study for the civil service examinations. They embody Confucian morality, and represent one major strand – if not indeed the chief strand – of influence on Chinese culture throughout much of the last thousand years.

An eloquent statement of Chinese love of letters, showing the profound respect accorded to the literary life, occurs in what is sometimes claimed to be the first work of criticism in China, *The Literary Mind and the Carving of Dragons* by Liu Xie (c. 465–522). After defining the 'literary mind' as the mind which strives after literary forms, Liu Xie says:

> Now with respect to the universe, it is everlasting and boundless, and in it we find people of all types. He who wants to stand out above the others must depend on his intelligence. Time is fleeting and life itself is transitory. If a man really wants to achieve fame, his only chance is to devote himself to writing. In his appearance, man resembles heaven and earth, and he is naturally endowed with five talents: his ears and eyes are comparable to the sun and moon; his voice and breath are like the wind and thunder; yet, as he transcends all things, he is really spiritual. His physical form may be as fragile as the grasses and trees, but fame is more substantial than metal and stone. Therefore, a man of virtue, in his relationship with the people of the world,

aims at immortalizing both his character and his
words. So it is not that I simply happen to be fond of
this argument; it is that I cannot do otherwise than
write.[3]

In the more exacting medium of poetry Lu Ji's *Essay on
Literature* hymns dedication to the writing life likewise:

Erect in the Central Realm the poet views the expanse
  of the whole universe,
And in tomes of ancient wisdom his spirit rejoices and
  finds nurture. . . .
The shining magnanimous deeds of the world's most vir-
  tuous are the substance of his song,
As also the pure fragrance which the most accomplished
  goodness of the past yields.
The flowering forest of letters and treasuries of poetic
  gems are his spirit's favourite haunts,
Where he delights in nothing less than perfection of
  Beauty's form and matter.
Thus moved, he will spread his paper and poise his brush
To express what he can in writing. . . .
Writing is in itself a joy,
Yet saints and sages have long since held it in awe.
For it is being, created by tasking the Great Void,
It is sound rung out of profound silence.
In a sheet of paper is contained the infinite,
And, evolved from an inch-sized heart, an endless
  panorama.
The words, as they expand, become all-evocative. . . .
Bright winds spread luminous wings, quick breezes soar
  from the earth,
And, nimbus-like amidst all these, rises the glory of the
  literary world.[4]

If the highest aspiration was to achieve immortality by writing, the next highest was to enjoy a life of collecting books
and reading them. In a touching reminiscence, the twelfth-
century poetess Li Qingzhao recalls her early years of marriage,
when she and her student husband began to apportion some
of their small income to the purchase of books:

On the first and fifteenth day of every month, my husband would get a short vacation from the Academy; he would 'pawn some clothes' for five hundred cash and go to the market at Hsiang-kuo Temple, where he would buy fruit and rubbings of inscriptions. When he brought these home, we would sit facing one another, rolling them out before us, examining and munching. And we thought ourselves persons of the age of Ko-t'ien.

When, two years later, he went to take up a post, we lived on rice and vegetables, dressed in common cloth; but he would search out the most remote spots and out-of-the-way places to fulfil his interest in the world's most ancient writings and unusual characters. When his father, the Grand Councillor, was in office, various friends and relations held positions in the Imperial Libraries; there one might find many ancient poems omitted from *The Book of Odes*, unofficial histories, and writings never before seen, works hidden in walls and recovered from tombs. He would work hard at copying such things, drawing ever more pleasure from the activity, until he was unable to stop himself. Later, if he happened to see a work of painting or calligraphy by some person of ancient or modern times, or unusual vessels of the Three Dynasties of high antiquity, he would still pawn our clothes to buy them. I recall that in the Ch'ing-ning Reign a man came with a painting of peonies by Hsu Hsi and asked twenty thousand cash for it. In those days twenty thousand cash was a hard sum to raise, even for children of the nobility. We kept it with us for a few days, and having thought of no plan by which we could purchase it, we returned it. For several days afterwards husband and wife faced one another in deep depression.

Later we lived privately at home for ten years, gathering what we could here and there to have enough for food and clothing. Afterwards, my husband governed two commanderies in succession, and he used up all his salary on scholarly materials. Whenever he got a book, we would collate it with other editions and make corrections together, repair it, and label it with the correct

title. When he got hold of a piece of calligraphy, a painting, a goblet, or a tripod, we would go over it at our
leisure, pointing out faults and flaws, setting for our
nightly limit the time it took one candle to burn down.
Thus our collection came to surpass all others in fineness
of paper and the perfection of the characters.

I happen to have an excellent memory, and every evening after we finished eating, we would sit in the hall
called 'Return Home' and make tea. Pointing to the
heaps of books and histories, we would guess on which
line of which page in which chapter of which book a certain passage could be found. Success in guessing determined who got to drink his or her tea first. Whenever
I got it right, I would raise the teacup, laughing so hard
that the tea would spill in my lap, and I would get up,
not having been able to drink anything at all. I would
have been glad to grow old in such a world.[5]

It was indeed part of the Chinese idea of a good time to
sit with friends making up poems, or capping one another's
quotations from the classics, while drinking long and deep.
In *The Dream of Red Mansions* the younger family members
arrange a 'verse-making' party. Some of them, provoking the
others' jocular complaints, begin with a feast of venison
cooked over an open brazier in Snowy Rushes Retreat, a corner of the mansion's elaborate gardens:

Hsiang-yun, still munching, replied, 'It's only after
eating this that I feel like drinking, and I need wine to
give me inspiration. Without this venison I couldn't
possibly write a poem today.'

'Where did all these beggars come from?' cried Tai-yu.
'Well, well! Red Snow Cottage is out of luck today,
all messed up by Hsiang-yun. My heart bleeds for it.'

'A lot you know,' retorted Hsiang-yun. 'A real scholar
can afford to be eccentric. You pretend to be so refined
and pure, it's disgusting! Stuffing ourselves now with
this venison will inspire us presently to produce some
fine lines.'

'If you don't make good that boast,' threatened Pao-
chai, 'you'll have to pay the penalty by bringing up that

meat and swallowing some of those reeds under the snow!'

When they had finished eating, they washed their hands and rinsed their mouths. Ping-erh, looking for her bracelets, found one missing. She searched everywhere but there was no trace of it, to everyone's surprise.

'I know where it's gone,' said Hsi-feng with a smile. 'There's no need to look for it now. Just get on with your poems. I guarantee you'll get it back within three days.' Then she asked, 'What are you writing today? The old lady says it will soon be New Year, and we should make some lantern riddles to amuse ourselves in the first month.'

'That's right,' they agreed. 'We'd forgotten. We must hurry up and make up a few good ones to guess in the first month.'

They went into the room with the heated floor, where refreshments and drinks were ready. Pasted on the wall was the subject on which they were to write, and the rhyme and metre. Pao-chai and Hsiang-yun, going over to have a look, saw that they were to compose a collective poem on the scenery in five-character lines using rhymes from the *hsiao* group of rhymes. The order in which to write was not stipulated.[6]

Although Lytton Strachey did not read Chinese, his response to H.A. Giles's evocative translations is both sympathetic and perceptive, so that he succeeds in conveying the character of Chinese poems better than many whose acquaintance with them is first-hand:

We hear them, and we are ravished; we hear them not, and we are ravished still. But, as in the m   t fluctuating sounds of birds or breezes, we can perceive a unity in their enchantment, and, listening to them, we should guess these songs to be the work of a single mind, pursuing through a hundred subtle modulations the perfection which this earth has never known. We should err; for through the long centuries of Chinese civilisation, poet after poet has been content to follow closely in the footsteps of his predecessors, to fit the old music to the old imaginations, to gather none but beloved and familiar flowers. In their sight a thousand years seem indeed to have been a moment; the song of the eighteenth century takes up the burden of the eighth; so that, in this particular literature, antiquity itself has become endowed with everlasting youth. The lyrics in our anthology, so familiar, so faultless, so compact of art, remind one of some collection of Greek statues, where the masters of many generations have multiplied in their eternal marbles the unaltering loveliness of the athlete. . . .

The Chinese lyric . . . aims at producing an impression which, so far from being final, must be merely the prelude to a long series of visions and feelings. It hints at wonders; and the revelation which at last it gives us is never a complete one – it is clothed in the indefinability of our subtlest thoughts.

> 'A fair girl draws the blind aside
> And sadly sits with drooping head;
> I see the burning tear-drops glide,
> But know not why those tears are shed.'

'The words stop,' say the Chinese, 'but the sense goes on.' The blind is drawn aside for a moment, and we catch a glimpse of a vision which starts us off on a mysterious voyage down the widening river of imagination. Many of these poems partake of the nature of *chose vue*, but they are not photographic records of isolated facts, they are delicate pastel drawings of some intimately seized experience. Whatever sights they show us – a girl gathering flowers while a dragon-fly perches on her comb – a lonely poet singing to his lute in the moonlight – pink cheeks among pink peach blossoms; whatever sounds they make us hear – the nightjar crying through the darkness – the flute and the swish of the swing among summer trees – all these things are presented to us charged with beautiful suggestions and that kind of ulterior significance which, in our moments of imaginative fervour, the most ordinary occurrences possess. Sometimes the impression is . . . particular, as in this charming verse:

'Shadows of pairing swallows cross his book,
Of poplar catkins, dropping overhead . . .
The weary student from his window-nook
Looks up to see that spring is long since dead.'

And sometimes it is more general:

'The evening sun slants o'er the village street;
My griefs, alas! in solitude are borne;
Along the road no wayfarers I meet, –
Naught but the autumn breeze across the corn.'

Here is the essence of loneliness distilled into four simple
lines; they were written, in our eighth century, by Keng
Wei.

Between these evanescent poems and the lyrics of
Europe there is the same kind of relation as that between
a scent and a taste. Our slightest songs are solid flesh-
and-blood things compared with the hinting verses of
the Chinese poets, which yet possess, like odours, for
all their intangibility, the strange compelling powers of
suggested reminiscence and romance. Whatever their
subject, they remain ethereal. There is much drunkenness in them, much praise of the wine-cup and the
'liquid amber' of the 'Lan-ling wine'; but what a contrast
between their tipsiest lyrics and the debauched exalta-
tion of Anacreon, or the boisterous jovialities of our
Western drinking-songs! The Chinese poet is drunk
with the drunkenness of a bee that has sipped too much
nectar, and goes skimming vaguely among the flowers.
His mind floats off at once through a world of delicate
and airy dreams:

'Oh, the joy of youth spent in a gold-fretted
    hall. . . .'

So wrote the drunken Li Po one summer evening in
the imperial garden eleven hundred years ago, on a pink
silk screen held up for him by two ladies of the court.
This great poet died as he had lived – in a trance of
exquisite inebriation. Alone in a pleasure-boat after a
night of revelry, he passed the time, as he glided down

the river, in writing a poem on himself, his shadow, and the moon:

'The moon sheds her rays on my goblet and
    me,
And my shadow betrays we're a party of
    three. . . .
See the moon – how she glances response to my
    song;
See my shadow – it dances so lightly along!
While sober I feel, you are both my good friends;
When drunken I reel, our companionship ends.
But we'll soon have a greeting without a
    goodbye,
At our next merry meeting away in the sky.'

He had written so far, when he caught sight of the reflection of the moon in the water, and leant over the side of the boat to embrace it. He was drowned; but the poem came safely to shore in the empty boat; it was his epitaph.[7]

Poetry is one of China's glories; but there is also drama, and a rich prose tradition in essays, philosophy, histories, stories and novels. Many Chinese think that *The Dream of Red Mansions*, a romance of love and youth, is their greatest novel; but there is a list of classics besides, chief among them *The Water Margin*, an adventure story; *Journey to the West*, full of comedy and supernatural wonders; *The Romance of Three Kingdoms*, an historical saga; *The Scholars*, a social satire; and the pornographic classics *The Golden Vase Plum* and *The Precious Mirror of Graded Flowers*, the latter dealing with homosexual relations. 'In looseness of plot,' says Lin Yutang,

the Chinese novel is like the novels of D.H. Lawrence, and in length like the Russian novels of Tolstoy and Dostoievsky. The similarity between Chinese and Russian novels is quite apparent. Both have an extremely realistic technique, both revel in details. . . . On the whole, the tempo of the Chinese novels reflects very well the tempo of Chinese life. It is enormous, variegated and never in a hurry. . . . A Chinese novel should be read slowly and with good temper. When there are flowers on the way, who is going to forbid the traveller from stopping to cull them?[8]

A Western reader who expects to find a plot in the fiction he reads should restrict attention to twentieth-century Chinese writers like Mao Tun, Shen Congwen and Lu Xun. In China's classic novels the structure is episodic and meandering, like the Yellow River; and they are every bit as likely to silt up at times, or to overflow their banks.

Literary life would not be possible without education, and education in China until very recently meant preparation for the civil service examinations. Their meaning and character is marvellously exhibited in Wu Qingzi's *The Scholars*, the eighteenth-century work listed above among China's classics. In it we meet Chou Chin, who passionately longs to further his career by taking the provincial examinations. Fortune has been against him, and although by now middle-aged, he is still a poor scholar of the lowest class. His brother-in-law, knowing his ambition, contrives a visit for him to the examination hall in the provincial capital, so that he can at least see what it looks like. When Chou Chin sees the cells in which the examinees write their essays he is so overcome that he faints, and upon recovering weeps bitterly. His brother-in-law's fellow merchants are astonished:

'What's your trouble, Mr Chou?' asked one of them. 'What made you cry so bitterly in there?'

'I don't think you realize, gentlemen,' said Chin, 'that my brother-in-law is not really a merchant. He has studied hard for a score of years, but never even passed the prefectural examination. That's why the sight of the provincial examination school today upset him.'

Touched on the raw like this, Chou Chin let himself go and sobbed even more noisily.

'It seems to me you're the one to blame, Old Chin,' said another merchant. 'If Mr Chou is a scholar, why did you bring him on such business?'

'Because he was so hard up,' said Chin. 'He had lost his job as a teacher; there was no other way out for him.'

'Judging by your brother-in-law's appearance,' said another, 'he must be a very learned man. It's because nobody recognizes his worth that he feels so wronged.'

'He's learned all right,' said Chin, 'but he's been unlucky.'

'Anybody who buys the rank of scholar of the Imperial College can go in for the examination,' said the man who had just spoken. 'Since Mr Chou is so learned, why not buy him a rank so that he can take the examination? If he passes, that will make up for his unhappiness today.'

'I agree with you,' rejoined Chin, 'But where's the money to come from?'

By now Chou Chin had stopped crying.

'That's not difficult,' said the same merchant. 'We're all friends here. Let's raise some money between us and lend it to Mr Chou, so that he can go in for the examination. If he passes and becomes an official, a few taels of silver will mean nothing to him – he can easily repay us. Even if he doesn't pay us back, we merchants always fritter away a few taels one way or another, and this is a good cause. What do you all say?'

The others responded heartily:

'A friend in need is a friend indeed!'

'A man who knows what is the right thing to do, but doesn't do it, is a coward!'

'Of course we'll help. We only wonder if Mr Chou will condescend to accept.'

'If you do this,' cried Chou Chin, 'I shall look upon you as my foster-parents. Even if I become a mule or a horse in my next life, I shall repay your kindness.' Then he knelt down and kowtowed to them all, and they bowed to him in return. Chin thanked them too. They drank a few more bowls of tea, and Chou Chin no longer cried, but talked and laughed with the others until it was time to return to the guild. . . .

As luck would have it, it was just the time for the preliminary test for the provincial examination. Chou

Chin took the test and came first of all the candidates from the Imperial College. On the eighth day of the eighth month he went to the examination school for the provincial examination, and the sight of the place where he had cried made him unexpectedly happy. As the proverb says, 'Joy puts heart into a man.' Thus he wrote seven excellent examination papers, then went back to the guild, for Chin and the others had not yet completed their purchases. When the results were published, Chou Chin had passed with distinction, and all the merchants were delighted.[9]

When Chou Chin returned home after this triumph he was ceremoniously visited by the magistrate and the local Commissioner of Examinations, and all the neighbouring officials sent their cards. Near and distant relations called, and local people who were not relations began to claim relationship, and perfect strangers introduced themselves as old acquaintances. Chou Chin was kept busy dealing with this access of good neighbourliness for an entire month. But then it was time to take the highest examinations, success in which would mean an official appointment: 'Soon it was time to go to the examination in the capital. Chou Chin's travelling expenses and clothes were provided by Chin. He passed the metropolitan examination too; and after the palace examination he was given an official post. In three years he rose to the rank of censor and was appointed Commissioner of Education for Kwantung province.'[10]

Like the shepherd in *A Winter's Tale*, Chou Chin was determined to put his good fortune to honourable use:

Now, though Chou Chin engaged several secretaries, he thought, 'I had bad luck myself so long; now that I'm in office I mean to read all the papers carefully. I mustn't leave them to my secretaries, thereby neglecting to give real talent a chance.' Having come to this decision he went to Canton to take up his post. The day after his arrival he burnt incense, put up placards, and held two examinations. . . .

Commissioner Chou sat in the hall and watched the candidates crowding in. There were young and old, handsome and homely, smart and shabby men among them. The last candidate to enter was thin and sallow, had a grizzled beard and was wearing an old felt hat. Kwantung has a warm climate; still, this was the twelfth month, and yet this candidate had on a linen gown only, so he was shivering with cold as he took his paper and went to his cell. Chou Chin made a mental note of this before sealing up their doors. During the first interval, from his seat at the head of the hall he watched this candidate come up to hand in his paper. The man's clothes were so threadbare that a few more holes had appeared since he went into the cell. Commissioner Chou looked at his own garments – the magnificent crimson robe and gold belt – then he referred to the register of names, and asked, 'You are Fan Chin, aren't you?'

Kneeling, Fan Chin answered, 'Yes, your excellency.'

'How old are you this year?'

'I gave my age as thirty. Actually I am fifty-four.'

'How many times have you taken the examination?'

'I first went in for it when I was twenty, and have taken it over twenty times since then.'

'How is it you have never passed?'

'My essays are too poor,' replied Fan Chin, 'so none of the honourable examiners will pass me.'

'That may not be the only reason,' said Commissioner Chou. 'Leave your paper here, and I will read it through carefully.'

Fan Chin kowtowed and left.

It was still early, and no other candidates were coming to hand in their papers, so Commissioner Chou picked up Fan Chin's essay and read it through. But he was disappointed. 'Whatever is this fellow driving at in this essay?' he wondered. 'I see now why he never passed.' He put it aside. However, when no other candidates appeared, he thought, 'I might at least have another look at Fan Chin's paper. If he shows the least talent, I'll pass him to reward him for his perseverance.' He read it through again, and this time he felt there was something in it. He was just going to read it through once more, when another candidate came up to hand in his paper.

This man knelt down, and said, 'Sir, I beg for an oral test.'

'I have your paper here,' said Commissioner Chou kindly. 'What need is there for an oral test?'

'I can compose poems in all the ancient styles. I beg you to set a subject to test me.'

The Commissioner frowned and said, 'Since the emperor attaches importance to essays, why should you bring up the poems of the Han and Tang dynasties? A candidate like you should devote all his energy to writing compositions, instead of wasting time on hetero-dox studies. I have come here at the imperial command to examine essays, not to discuss miscellaneous literary forms with you. This devotion to superficial things means that your real work must be neglected. No doubt your essay is nothing but flashy talk, not worth the reading. Attendants! Drive him out!' At the word of command, attendants ran in from both sides to seize the candidate and push him outside the gate.

But although Commissioner Chou had had this man driven out, he still read his paper. This candidate was called Wei Hao-ku, and he wrote in a tolerably clear and straightforward style. 'I will pass him lowest on the list,' Chou Chin decided. And, taking up his brush, he made a mark at the end of the paper as a reminder. Then he read Fan Chin's paper again. This time he gave a gasp of amazement. 'I failed to understand this paper the first two times I read it!' he exclaimed. 'But, after reading it a third time, I realize it is the most wonderful essay in the world – every word a pearl. This shows how often bad examiners must have neglected real genius.' Hastily taking up his brush, he carefully drew three circles on Fan Chin's paper, marking it as first. He then picked up Wei Hao-ku's paper again, and marked it as twentieth.[11]

But of course not all – perhaps, in the larger view, not many – stories of scholarly ambition ended so happily. One small girl was deprived of her father's companionship because of her grandfather's desire that he should succeed as a scholar.

The tale also reveals the hierarchical character of traditional Chinese family life, and its rigid discipline:

> As I grew older I began to discover the reason for one of my keenest regrets, that I had seen little or nothing of my father during these years. It was because for several years he was confined to his study by grandfather's orders and, as he was isolated in the courtyard where the unmarried men lived, neither my mother nor I could go there to see him. To explain this I must go into the past history of our clan again. Our clan held the highest official and scholastic status in our city. This went back several centuries to one of us who had taken first place in the national imperial examinations for the highest degree, known as Han Lin. He became a high official, which traditionally constitutes the chief claim to distinction in China in that it sets the seal of accomplishment and government recognition upon scholarship. It is also, with few exceptions, based on wealth, at least sufficient to provide leisure for the long years of study necessary. This, then, permanently established our prestige, but proved to be our highwater mark for both scholarship and official position. As grandfather's wealth increased he had become ambitious to revive this tradition. . . . So he took action. First Uncle was an able businessman but no scholar. Third Uncle was brilliant but lazy. My father was the only hope. Grandfather therefore ordered him confined to his study until he completed the requisite preparation for the government examinations, allowing him only one holiday in the year. This is the standard method of making a scholar. After grandfather's death, grandmother rigidly continued the same policy.
>
> I remember once when father wanted to come to see my mother to show her a new poem he had written for her. He cautiously inquired of a slave girl, found that grandmother was asleep, and came quietly to mother's room. Mother exclaimed over his paleness and weakened condition. This was the closest I ever saw her come to showing her feeling for him.

'Ai-ya, you are sick,' she whispered. 'Why can't you be where I can take care of you?'

Then she kept Wood Orchid and me busy preparing tea and a nourishing soup. I was happy to help serve my father, but inadvertently knocked over a bowl, which fell to the floor with a crash, and we heard grandmother clear her throat. We all stayed motionless and stared at each other anxiously for a long moment. Nothing happened, and we gradually relaxed. But grandmother's suspicions were aroused and after a little she sent for father. We could hear her scolding him. Mother and I wept together. The examinations came soon afterwards and father failed to qualify. He had begun too late to compete with men whose entire life had been given to study. Grandfather's attempt to mix business and scholarship had failed. We had definitely become a family of merchants. After this, father had more freedom, for it seemed useless to continue further. So he returned to his duties in the family business. This was not much better so far as mother and I were concerned, for he was away from home most of the time.[12]

His failure did not make scholarly ambition repellent to him, however; it simply made him transfer it, as his father had done, to his son; and with equally unhappy results, for his own experience evidently taught him nothing about how to encourage a love of learning:

When father returned from a business trip and had paid his respects to all and settled down comfortably in mother's room, his first question was always as to how we children were getting on with our studies. Nor was he content with a perfunctory or general answer but always had Third Brother bring his books, in which he would pick a passage at random, have brother repeat it from memory, and question him as to its meaning.

One night, father returned from a long trip after we were all asleep. The questioning had to go on just the same. Third Brother was routed out, but was so sleepy that he could not remember the passage, and father kicked him and beat him over the head with the book, until he wept bitterly, while mother and Wood Orchid looked on in pity and dismay but were powerless to interfere.

He wanted to get me up also, but mother dissuaded him. I was not in school, but was learning to repeat the rhymes all mothers teach their children about filial piety and family harmony, and father checked up on my lessons also. It was easy for me to remember these simple verses and I rattled them off with a glib assurance that always pleased him, and it was this that led him to direct that I should go to school when I was old enough.

Grandmother heard Third Brother crying that night, and scolded father the next day for being too hard on us. After that when Third Brother heard that father was returning he used to study all night in preparation.

'*Lao hu hsin* – the heart of a tiger,' he exclaimed bitterly to me at the end of one of these sessions. We were both afraid of my father when he was in this mood, but my brother had to stand at attention and take it, whereas I would retreat to the protection of my mother and stand near her. Furthermore, father was far more strict with him as a son than with me as a daughter. Mother used to try to get him to rest first, for he frequently returned utterly weary and half sick. But he would have none of it. Perhaps he felt himself a failure for not realizing grandfather's ambition and was implacably determined that we should succeed, at whatever cost to him or us, where he had missed out.[13]

Reform during the last century has brought a Western-style school and university system into being, but the authorities still dictate, on the strength of graduates' results, which post they will go to – such, at least, was the case until very recently.

Controversy surrounds recent and contemporary literature in China. Before the Communist success of 1949 writers of excellence like Lu Xun, Lao She and Shen Congwen kept Chinese letters in the first rank of world literature. But after that date Communist Party views of revolutionary correct-

ness in writing produced a lowering of standards. Among
the foreign novelists for whom ordinary Chinese readers have
a pronounced taste is Charles Dickens; it is his sentimentality
they chiefly relish, and their own revolutionary literature
exemplifies the same characteristic to the same often excessive degree. Poetry also, as ever, flourishes, although here too
in a manner influenced by the times, as Stephen Spender,
while travelling in China with David Hockney, found:

> Recently, 'Poetry Magazine' had broadened its interests
> but circulation had fallen. The motto of the magazine
> was 'Let the hundred flowers blossom', chosen because
> today so many magazines are permitted to be published.
> It struck me that, considering the fate that befell so many
> of Mao's hundred flowers, this seemed an ironic motto
> to choose. But I note a tendency to acquit Chairman Mao
> of responsibility for the consequences of his edicts.
>   Like Tang Mu-li, the artist, Mr Tsou dwelt on
> the difference between professional and amateur: the
> professional being by definition one whom the state
> permits to work full time at his art. He said that most
> poets over sixty received salaries. Recently the quality of
> poetry has been raised, he said, a bit as though he were
> speaking of livestock. The reason for the improvement
> was that poets are now permitted to cover a far wider
> range of subjects than some years previously. There was
> an opening up now of themes of nature, countryside,
> rivers, landscapes, also love and friendship. During the
> period of the Gang of Four these had been taboo, par-
> ticularly love. The idea then was that all poets should
> expatiate on the virtues of that heroine, Chairman Mao's
> wife. Criticism of the errors of the establishment was not
> allowed. For example, the government declared a village
> called Tachai (Dazhai) in Shensi (Shaanxi) province to be
> a wonderful example of the success of the rural produc-
> tion brigades. It became a place of pilgrimage for tours
> (until it became something of a laughing stock). Writers
> were expected to write saying how successful it was,
> though it was a failure. 'People had to say false words.
> . . . After smashing up the Gang of Four, we had the

opportunity to study the criterion of truth. . . . Now poets can write according to their wish.'

I tried to discover what was meant by the criterion of truth. The young poet, Ch'iu Hsiao-lung, explained that they could put a broad interpretation on their commitment to write poetry about people who were engaged in constructive tasks. 'For instance,' he said, 'if we today write poems about love and beauty and natural scenery, we think these can be good poems. Moreover, such poems can really educate people and enhance their ideological role.'

During the Gang of Four period, poems were labelled bad if they did not conform to directives by officials who were not poets. But today the criticism of poetry was the preserve of the poets themselves. Poets were encouraged to go in for self-criticism in the course of discussion.

I asked what were their aims in writing poetry. The first to answer was Miss Li Hsiao-yu. She was rather bashful. She explained that she had gone to the Victory Oil Field in eastern China. There she worked together with the oil workers, and wrote poems about their lives. She had published a volume called *Ode to the Feather of White Geese*. 'A charming title,' I said. 'She also writes love poems,' interposed Mr Tsou, to put her in the best possible light, I suppose.

She went on: 'I hadn't been writing long before I approached "Poetry Magazine". At that time I was in the army, and there I had the opportunity to live and work with the soldiers. I tried to write poems about army life. After making contact with "Poetry Magazine" I had the opportunity to go to different places, one of which was the oilfield. Then I thought I should write something about their life, their struggle.' She did not insist that the only kind of poetry that should be written was the socialist realist kind.

She said that young poets had different approaches to writing poetry. Some wished to express their own personal feelings and ideas, their way of thinking. She, however, constructed her poems on the foundations laid

by writers during the 1950s and 1960s, who were trying
to write about real conditions.

'Then what is your attitude towards the expression of
your feelings in your poetry?'

She answered, 'I feel satisfied with my poetry when
it expresses happiness and pleasure in the workers' lives.
I really do feel that my thinking is in accord with their
thinking, and so I am very happy with that.'

Her eyes shone. She said all this modestly, demurely
even, not as though she considered herself an example
for others to follow.

David asked, 'Do the oil workers read your poems and
find that they express their attitudes?' 'The workers read
my poems,' she answered, 'not only the workers in the
oilfield where I worked, but also other workers from
other oilfields. They write me letters expressing satisfaction with my poems. Moreover, members of the Ministry of the Petroleum Industry said my poems were good.'

I asked our local guide to translate one of her poems
for me. Miss Li did so, rather approximately, as was
inevitable. Later Mr Lin produced a more studied version
(which I have slightly amended). The poem is called
'Moon in the Meridian Transit' and runs – in what I suppose gives only a rough idea of it – as follows:

> Wind from the rigs brings over the smell of the
>   oil.
> The horizon is twinkling in the deep night,
> The hum of the machinery praises these most
>   memorable days.
> O, this moonbeam. . . .
> Tonight what shall I talk with you about,
> And how . . .[14]

Mao Zedoing himself was a poet, it must be remembered,
and although he hated intellectuals, whom he labelled 'the
stinking ninth category' (the ninth being the lowest among
'bad types' of people in Communist demonology), the love
of literature and respect for the life of letters survives in China.
Among the older generation there are still men one cannot
otherwise describe than by the phrase 'scholar gentlemen'.

Any comment on Chinese literature cannot pass without at least a glance at the language embodying it. Cognoscenti will tell you that Chinese is a language of marvellous suppleness and subtlety, a language of concise, allusive power of the kind applauded by Strachey. It is a simple language to learn for the purposes of basic communication; but a discriminating grasp of it for literary and philosophical reading is a work of dedication. This is especially true of classical Chinese, which can be bafflingly brief and bewilderingly elliptical.

At one time it was quite seriously proposed that Chinese is the world's original language. After the ark had beached atop Mount Ararat, so this view ran, a nephew of Noah set off for the East to people it, too far from Babel to be affected by God's confusion of the tongues there. In 1668 John Webb dedicated to Charles II his *Essay Towards the Primitive Language* in which this thesis is argued:

> The most remote parts then of the Eastern World, being planted before the dispersion at Babel, and until the Confusion of Tongues, the whole Earth being of one language and one lipp, it must indisputably succeed, that Noah and whoever remained with him, which came not with the rest to the valley of Shinaar, and consequently by their absence thence, had no hand in that vain attempt, could not be concerned in the Confusion there, nor come within the curse of the Confounded Languages, but retained the PRIMITIVE tongue, as having received it from Noah, and likewise carry the same with them to their several Plantations, in what part of the East soever they settled themselves . . . it may therefore be with much probability asserted, that the Language of CHINA, is the PRIMITIVE Tongue, which was common to the whole world before the flood; and that it could never be branched into several Languages, or Dialects of the same one language, by the Commerce and Intercourse which they had with Nations of a different Speech, when they never had Commerce or Intercourse with any; nor were ever known to these parts of the world (scarcely to their adjoining Neighbours) till, about an hundred and fifty years since, by the Portugals and Spaniards they were discovered.[15]

Had the bad-tempered anonymous author of *China As It Really Is* ever heard the suggestion that Chinese is Eden's language, he would have waxed apoplectic:

> The Chinese language is the most horrible that any sane man can be called upon to acquire. 'Sane' is said advisedly, for the general opinion among foreigners resident in China is that no Westerner who has anything like a deep knowledge of Chinese, is entirely sane. To call a man a sinologue is a very severe reflection on his intelligence and abilities. The time taken to acquire such knowledge, and the all-absorbing interest that is waiting for the unwary, give some justification for this opinion. . . .
>
> A Chinese book is written in vertical colunms, which follow each other from right to left. The strain on the eye and brain of the foreign reader entailed by this radical subversion of the method of reading to which he and his ancestors have been accustomed, accounts more for the weakness of sight that afflicts the student of this language than does the minuteness and illegibility of the characters themselves. The Chinese language must go.[16]

The Chinese invented printing nearly a millennium before it reached Europe, but even before then no educated man was without his lovingly collected library, central to it the Five Classics, most of which he could quote verbatim. It did not matter which dialect a Chinese spoke, whether Mandarin or Cantonese – mutually unintelligible as spoken tongues – or one of the many others; the written language was the same for all, and so the literature was available to all. 'The moment I awake,' said Yuan Mei, 'I long for my library and bound towards it, swift as a thirsty cat.'[17] Nothing better expresses the Chinese relish for literature.

6

PLEASURES

> To be fond of something is better than merely to
> know it; to find joy in it is better than merely to
> be fond of it.
>
> Confucius, *The Analects*, 6.20

Pleasure is the aesthetic emotion, and every least aspect of life
offers its opportunities of pleasure to the Chinese sensibility.
Raindrops pattering on leaves, the fragrance of tea, a view
across a lake, a maiden's 'moth-like' eyebrows, the texture of
ornamental rocks in a delicately laid-out garden: they all yield
their increments of delight. Appreciation of literature and the
plastic arts is central to the traditional outlook of educated
Chinese, but theatre and music, food and drink, romance and
sex have been relished and hymned at large through most of
their history. To catch a glimpse of what pleasure means for
the Chinese, one need only consider them at table, in dalli-
ance, and at leisure – or to put it more plainly: enjoying food,
sex, and any pastime involving noise and crowds.

A satisfied stomach is one of the best preparations for life's
other pleasures, so the proper place to begin is food. And to
eat, one must take one's seat at table, as Woodrooffe relates:

> It is a matter of great moment at a Chinese banquet
> that guests and host should be seated simultaneously, so
> that no one should appear rude by being seated before
> another. It is no easy feat. The General leaned forward
> and began slowly to lower himself into his seat, keeping
> a watchful eye on the company. The others followed his
> movements closely and all was going well, when their
> host, suspecting that he might be seated first, bobbed
> up again. Immediately all the others straightened their
> knees, and the process started once more. There were

two more bobs until at last, with perfect timing, the company subsided with a unanimous sigh of relief.[1]

Westerners have learned to enjoy the exported simulacrum of oriental cuisine which appears in the Chinese restaurants of Western cities. But Chinese food in China has not always proved an instant attraction. Woodrooffe continues:

> In China cooking is considered an art no less than in France, though the Chinese palate differs considerably from that of the European. The use of sauces is understood but they are so highly spiced as to be almost inedible, while many of the dishes are tasteless and appear to be eaten merely because of their rarity, like the dormice in treacle or larks' tongues of the Roman emperors. But hot sauces and sea-slugs from the South Seas, the gruel of birds' nests from Southern China and the soup made from sharks' fins are included in a Chinese banquet for a set purpose. Apart from their rarity they are reputed to be powerful aphrodisiacs (though experts deny this quality in them) and the dinner is carefully planned as a whole. It finishes with sing-song girls who appear and sing amorous songs, so that the culminating effect of hot sauces, exotic dishes, rice wine and finally comely maidens in song should be to make those participating at the feast consider a visit to the Inner Chamber imperative.[2]

Christopher Isherwood proves his discernment in recognizing that Chinese pleasure in food is as much a matter of the eye as of the palate and stomach, and hints at the fact in his choice of simile:

> One's first sight of a table prepared for a Chinese meal hardly suggests the idea of eating, at all. It looks rather as if you were sitting down to a competition in watercolour painting. The chopsticks, lying side by side, resemble paint-brushes. The paints are represented by little dishes of sauces, red, green, and brown. The teabowls, with their lids, might well contain paint-water. There is even a kind of tiny paint-rag, on which the chopsticks can be wiped.

You begin the meal by wiping hands and face with hot moistened towels. (These towels are, perhaps, China's most brilliant contribution to the technique of material comfort; they should certainly be introduced into the West.) Then comes the food. It is served in no recognizable order of progression – fish does not necessarily follow soup, nor meat fish. Nor can the length of the meal be foreseen by the guest. His favourite dish may well appear at the very end, when he is too bloated even to taste it. *Hors-d'œuvre* delicacies remain in presence throughout – and this, too, is like painting; for the diners are perpetually mixing them in with their food, to obtain varying combinations of taste.

To-day we had shark's fin soup (one of the great soups of the world; quite equal to minestrone or borsch), lobster, chicken, rice, and fish. The drink, which was served in small metal teapots, resembled Korn or Bols. It was made from rose-petals and maize. . . . When a new dish comes in, the host makes a gesture towards it with his chopsticks, like a cavalry-commander pointing with his sabre to an enemy position, and the attack begins. This scramble, so informal yet so scrupulously polite, is the greatest charm of a Chinese meal; and even the most expert eater can hardly avoid making a certain amount of mess.[3]

It amazed Isherwood to find that the resources of life in China are so multiple and ambiguous. What is food in one context is a carpenter's materials in another – and vice versa: 'We stopped to get petrol near a restaurant where they were cooking bamboo in all its forms – including the strips used for making chairs. That, I thought, is so typical of this country. Nothing is specifically either eatable or uneatable. You could begin munching a hat, or bite a mouthful out of a wall; equally, you could build a hut with the food provided at lunch. Everything is everything.'[4]

Maritime provinces excel in fish dishes, central and southern areas use rice as their staple, and on the northern plains the staple is wheat, cooked into a variety of filled or plain dumplings either by steaming, boiling or frying. Peking has its roast duck with plum sauce and pancakes, while in Sichuan province the cuisine is hot and spicy, with 'pock-marked-face old woman doufu' among the tongue-scorching specialities. An ancient Buddhist tradition of exquisite vegetarian cookery flourishes. It caters also for meat-eaters who are temporarily on vegetarian fasts, by serving dishes of doufu miraculously contrived to look and taste exactly like fish, meat and poultry. But in the south, especially in Guangdong Province, the range of foodstuffs goes beyond what most Westerners can bring themselves to stomach, as Colin Thubron found:

I walked into the food market with a squeamish certainty of what was coming. Under its covered way the first stalls were pungent with roots and powdered spices. Sacks of medicinal tree-bark lay heaped up like firewood, and the air was drowsy with musk. But when I peered closer I saw that several of these piles were desiccated snakes – coiled skeletons and clouded skins – or smaller snakes dried rigid like sticks. I came upon a monkey skeleton, and four bears' paws. There were cellophane bags brimming with dried seahorses, and python skins folded up like linen.

In shallow bins among the fish-stalls, yellow-headed tortoises scrambled over one another's backs – many already overturned and dead – and strings of frogs dangled for sale in pendants of pulsing gullets and legs. The vendors described their wares as 'fresh', not 'alive'. They weighed and dismembered them as if they were vegetables. Throats were cut and limbs amputated at a casual stroke, turtles tossed about like small change.

Then I entered an arena resembling other countries' pet shops – but here it was a butcher's. From its banked cages rose the piping wails of hundreds of cats and kittens – mere scaffolds of fur-covered bones – which were huddled together in a congeries of ginger and white, or were tied to the cage-tops with gaily coloured string. Customers bought several at a time, the meat on them was so scant. They were weighed in mewing sacks and lugged away.

My revulsion, I knew, was hypocritical. When I

passed the huddled quails and pheasants I felt nearly
nothing, but the thrushes seemed pitiful and the tiered
death-cells of the dulled and hopeless mammals angered
me. The only dogs I saw had already been killed and
skinned, but six or seven racoons lay with their heads
buried in their legs, one still hopelessly suckling its
young. In another cage sat a monkey – monkey brains
are a delicacy – picking at its bars; in another was a por-
cupine, most of whose quills had already been pulled out.
And once I came across a deer lying on a crate, its head
tied up with newspapers from which the nostrils still
palpitated.[5]

An early Western encounter with Southern China's breadth
of diet is recorded by the assiduous diarist Peter Mundy, who
sailed with a four-ship British fleet to Canton in 1636: 'Snakes
and dogges flesh eaten for good meat in China. Here in the
Bazare or Markett among the other provisions there was a
snake to be sold, aboutt 4 or 5 foot long, alive, his Mouth
sowed uppe for biting, accompted good meat, and Dogges
Flesh allsoe, by report estimated a principall Dish.'[6]

Westerners might be charmed or repelled by Chinese food
and the manner in which it is eaten – on the repellent side
one might count the noisy slurping and shovelling, spitting
out and sucking in, dipping of chopsticks from many mouths
into one dish – but until the Chinese point of view on food
is understood, both the charm and the repulsion are inade-
quately based:

The question has often been asked as to what we eat.
The answer is that we eat all the edible things on this
earth. We eat crabs by preference, and often eat tree-bark
by necessity. Economic necessity is the mother of our
invention in food. We are too over-populated and famine
is too common for us not to eat everything we can lay
our hands on . . . we are undoubtedly the only truly
omnivorous animals on earth, and so long as our teeth
last, we should continue to occupy that position. . . .
All one can say is that we are very catholic in our
tastes, and that any rational man can take anything off
a Chinese table without any qualm of conscience. What

famine dictates is not for us human mortals to choose. There is nothing that a man will not eat when hard pressed by hunger. And no one is entitled to condemn until he knows what famine means. Some of us have been forced in times of famine to eat babies – and even this must be humanly rare – but, thank God, we do not eat them raw as the English eat their beef![7]

When Chinese people meet they do not say 'Hello!' but 'Have you eaten?' The memory of famine, and abiding interest in today's repast, combine to make this the only reasonable greeting between friends. And it is as culinary art – as *art* – that the Chinese think of food when famine is not the issue. The apparently cannibalistic author of the foregoing remarks, Lin Yutang, castigates the British for not taking food seriously. If a nation cares about food, he says, their language will show it; but the British call *cuisine* 'cooking' and a *chef* simply 'cook'; and the language has no word for *gourmet*, whom the British call a greedy-guts. 'The truth is,' says Lin, 'the English do not admit they have a stomach. No stomach is fit for conversation unless it is "sick" or "aching".'

Now you cannot develop a national culinary art unless you are willing to discuss it and exchange your opinions about it. Only in a society wherein people of culture and refinement inquire after the cook's health, instead of talking about the weather, can the art of *cuisine* be developed. No food is really enjoyed unless it is keenly anticipated, discussed, eaten and then commented upon. Preachers should not be afraid to condemn a bad steak from their pulpits and scholars should write essays on the culinary art as the Chinese scholars do. . . .

If there is anything we are serious about, it is neither religion nor learning, but food. We openly acclaim eating as one of the few joys of this human life.[8]

And what is the essence of Chinese culinary skill, the heart of their kitchen philosophy, the gustatory nub of their cuisine? It may be summed up in just two words, *texture* and *mixture*:

Two principles distinguish Chinese food from European cooking. One is that we eat food for its *texture*, the elastic or crisp effect it has on our teeth, as well as for fragrance, flavour and colour. Li Liweng said he was a slave to crabs, because they had that combination. . . . The idea of texture is seldom understood, but a great part of the popularity of bamboo-shoots is due to the fine resistance the young shoots give to our teeth. The appreciation of bamboo-shoots is probably the most typical example of our taste. Being not oily, it has a certain fairy-like 'fugitive' quality about it. But the most important principle is that it lends flavour to meat (especially pork) cooked with it, and, on the other hand, it receives the flavour of the pork itself. This is the second principle, that of mixing flavours. The whole culinary art of China depends on the art of mixture. While the Chinese recognize that many things, like fresh fish, must be cooked in their own juice, in general they mix flavours a great deal more than Western cooks do. No one, for instance, knows how cabbage tastes until he has tasted it when properly cooked with chicken, and the chicken flavour has gone into the cabbage and the cabbage flavour has gone into the chicken. From this principle of mixture, any number of fine and delicate combinations may be developed.[9]

Banqueting has always been a national pastime, and remains so in today's China; every 'work unit' in the People's Republic leaps at the least excuse for a feast, and periodically the government issues warnings about the expense thus incurred, because – nationwide – it runs into billions, recently exceeding the government's annual education expenditure. The first thing that happens to an official foreign visitor to China is a banquet of welcome, as the last is a banquet of farewell. The importance of food cannot escape the Western viewer of Chinese films, from any of which an audience is bound to emerge salivating.

The Chinese enjoy alcohol as much as other peoples do, although one rarely sees them drunk. They produce excellent

beers and liquors, the fiercest being *maotai*, a few small glasses
of which can utterly demolish a foreigner. But their favourite
beverage by far is tea. In connection with tea they display
all their refinement of taste and artistry: not in making an
elaborate ritual of it, as in Japan, but in enjoying fragrances
and tastes and varieties, and lubricating all social occasions by
means of the friendly refreshment it provides. And it sum-
mons forth the Chinese bent for connoisseurship:

> In the Wuyin year (1638) I travelled to the former capital
> Nanjing and headed immediately to pay a visit to Min
> Wenshui . . . [when he returned] I said 'I have long
> admired you and I refuse to leave before I have had a
> drink of your tea.' This pleased him and he went himself
> to the brazier to heat the water. The tea was shortly
> brewed and he led me into an inner room with clear
> windows and clean teapoys. His tea-service was of the
> most exquisite design with a teapot from near Yixing
> and about a dozen different types of china teacup from
> the imperial kilns of the 15th century. In the lamplight
> I took a look at the tea. In colour it was indistinguishable
> from the teacup itself and its fragrance was overpower-
> ing. I exclaimed in delight and asked: 'Where was this
> tea produced?' Wenshui replied: 'It is Langyuan tea from
> Sichuan.' I took another sip. 'Do not try to fool me,'
> I said, 'it has been processed in the same way as Langyuan
> tea but it has a different taste.' Wenshui concealed a
> smile. 'Do you know where it was produced?' he asked.
> I took another sip, and replied with a question: 'Why
> is it so like the tea from Luojie in Zhejiang?' His tongue
> shot out in astonishment. 'Extraordinary!' he said,
> 'Extraordinary!' I continued, 'Where does the water
> come from?' 'From the Hui Spring near Wuxi.' 'You
> are trying to fool me again. If this had come from Hui
> Spring it would have had to travel several hundred miles.
> Why has the water then lost none of its purity?' 'I dare
> not deceive you any more. It is in fact water from Hui
> Spring but it is taken from a new well. On a quiet
> night one waits for the spring to gush out for the first
> time, collects it immediately and pours it into a vat, the

bottom of which has been lined with mountain rocks. The boats only set sail when there is a good wind. In this way the water retains its purity and it is better than ordinary Hui Spring water, let alone water from elsewhere.' He rushed off and came back with another teapot from which he poured me a cup, saying, 'Try this.' 'The aroma is powerful, the taste full-bodied in the extreme. It must be spring tea. The tea I drank a moment ago was picked in the autumn.' Wenshui laughed and responded: 'In all my seventy years I have never met such a connoisseur of tea as yourself.' From that moment, we became friends.[10]

Where there are connoisseurs, there is of course art; as the foregoing shows, art in all the departments of growing, preparing, infusing, drinking and discussing tea. One old drawing shows a literatus, living in retirement, gazing out upon mountain scenery while his servants make tea; the caption tells us that he is 'preparing himself to enjoy his tea'.

There are special books about tea-drinking as there are special books about incense and wine and rocks for house decoration. More than any other human invention of this nature, the drinking of tea has coloured our life as a nation, and gives rise to the institution of tea-houses which are approximate equivalents of Western cafés for the common people. People drink tea in their homes and in the tea-houses, alone and in company, at committee meetings and at the settling of disputes. They drink tea before breakfast and at midnight. With a teapot, a Chinese is happy wherever he is. It is a universal habit, and it has no deleterious effect whatsoever, except in very rare cases, as in my native district where according to tradition some people have drunk themselves bankrupt. This is only possible with extremely costly tea, but the average tea is cheap, and the average tea in China is good enough for a prince. The best tea is mild and gives a 'back-flavour' which comes after a minute or two, when its chemical action has set in on the salivary glands. Such tea puts everybody in good humour.[11]

Tea originated in China. The British stole bushes and carried them to India, Ceylon and East Africa, starting the tea industries there. Most of the tea exported by the Chinese was of average or low grade; they knew it would be ruined by infusion in undistinguished water, or – worse – by the addition of milk, sugar or both; and they felt no compunctions. This is shown by a visitor to a Hankou tea factory

> where brick-tea is prepared for the Mongolian market. Bricks are made here of both green and black tea, but always from the commonest and cheapest; in fact, for the black tea the dust and sweepings of the establishment are used. The tea dust is first collected, and if it is not in a sufficiently fine powder, it is beaten with wooden sticks on a hot iron plate. It is then sifted through several sieves to separate, steamed over boiling water, after which it is immediately put into the moulds, the fine dust in the centre, and the coarse grains round the edges.
>
> These moulds are like those used for making ordinary clay bricks, but very much stronger, and of less depth, so that the cakes of tea when they come out are more like large tiles than bricks. The people who drink this tea like it black; wherefore about a teaspoonful of soot is put into each mould, to give it depth of colouring and gloss that attracts the Mongolian purchasers! . . . The Mongolians make their infusion by boiling. In this manner they extract all the strength, and as there is no delicate flavour to lose, they do not injure the taste.[12]

Tea might be for drinking, but tea-bricks had other uses in the meantime; with unsurprising results: 'These bricks are in some parts the current coin of the country: large transactions are settled for so many bricks of tea, while smaller payments are made by cutting pieces off the block as the Chinese cut fragments of silver. The infusion made from brick tea is coarse and nasty; it often has a musty taste owing to the damp confined in the cakes, which prevents their transport by sea.'[13]

In the stereotype of the Chinese before 1949 it was not gentlemanly sipping of tea, but depraved languishing in opium dens, that gave the foreigner his picture of the Chinaman at his pleasures. And it is true that opium use was very widespread until that time. Trade relations imposed upon China in the nineteenth century by Western nations, foremost among them Britain, consisted mainly in the exchange of opium for silk, tea, rhubarb and other commodities. The Imperial authorities and the Christian missionaries were equally opposed to opium's forced importation, and painted violent pictures of the harm it did. A.H. Smith described opium as 'more deadly to the Chinese than war, famine, and pestilence combined'[14] and G.T. Lay of the British and Foreign Bible Society gave a dramatic, famous and widely quoted description of 'the typical opium smoker' as having 'lank and shrivelled limbs, tottering gait, sallow visage, feeble voice, and death-boding glance of eye, proclaiming him the most forlorn creature that treads upon the ground'.

It is in this spirit that the notorious 'Resident of Peking', writing in 1912, somewhat prematurely applauded a change in Chinese habits:

> Opium smoking is nearly a thing of the past. Well would it be for China if nothing took its place. The first result of the campaign against opium was the introduction of morphia and morphine. Slaves of the opium habit, unable to procure the drug freely, took with alacrity to morphine injections. A large traffic in morphia and the appliances for injecting it grew, until it was made illegal, and with the active assistance of the foreign governments was quickly stamped out. . . .
>
> The crushing of the opium habit has given an enormous stimulus to the trade in foreign wines and spirits and tobacco. It would seem that the Chinese mean to substitute whisky for opium. It is a change considerably for the better.[15]

A famous episode in the joint effort of the missionaries and China's government to stamp out the opium trade was the dispatch of a passionate letter from Li Hongchang, the Viceroy of Chihli, to Queen Victoria, asking her to restrain her merchants so that China could 'escape from the thraldom of opium'.

But not all were persuaded by Li Hongchang's anti-opium rhetoric. G.E. Morrison, who travelled in Chinese dress (complete with pigtail pinned to his hat) by boat, foot and pony across the breadth of China in 1893, could not agree that either opium or the opium trade was harmful. Referring to Lay's portrait of 'lank and shrivelled' degradation, he wrote:

This fantastic description, paraded for years past for our sympathy, can only be applied to an infinitesimal number of the millions in China who smoke opium. It is a well-known fact that should a Chinese suffering from the extreme emaciation of disease be also in the habit of using the opium-pipe, it is the pipe and not the disease that in ninety-nine cases out of a hundred will be wrongly blamed as the cause of the emaciation.

During the year 1893 4,275 tons of Indian opium were imported into China. The Chinese, we are told, plead to us with 'outstretched necks' to cease the great wrong we are doing them in forcing them to buy our opium. But . . . it is extremely difficult for the traveller in China to believe that the Chinese are sincere in their condemnation of opium and the opium traffic. Li Hung Chang, in the well-known letter . . . still widely circulated and perennially cited, says, 'the poppy is certainly surreptitiously grown in some parts of China, notwithstanding the laws and frequent Imperial edicts prohibiting its cultivation'.

Surreptitiously grown in some parts of China! Why, from the time I left Hupeh till I reached the boundary of Burma, a distance of 1,700 miles, I never remember to have been out of sight of the poppy. Li Hung Chang continues, 'I earnestly hope that . . . all right-minded men of your country, will support the efforts China is now making to escape from the thraldom of opium.' And yet you are told in China that the largest growers of the poppy in China are the family of Li Hung Chang. . . .

Of the eighteen provinces of China four only, Kiangsu, Che-kiang, Fuh-kien, and Kuantung use Indian opium, the remaining fourteen provinces use exclusively home-grown opium. Native-grown opium has entirely driven the imported opium from the markets of the Yangtse Valley; no Indian opium, except an insignificant quantity, comes up the river even as far as Hankow. The Chinese do not want our opium – it competes with their own. . . .

Edicts are still issued against the use of opium. They are drawn up by Chinese philanthropists over a quiet pipe of opium, signed by opium-smoking officials, whose revenues are derived from the poppy, and posted near fields of poppy by the opium-smoking magistrates who own them.[16]

Morrison might have been right, and the Chinese, for all the protestations of their leaders, might willingly have grown, imported and smoked opium in large quantities. But was it not harmful nevertheless? A mission doctor reported the case of an elderly man who came to him for attention to an injured foot. He was such a splendid picture of robust old age that the doctor displayed him to his students, quizzing him the while for their benefit: 'I'll bet you don't drink, eh? Or smoke tobacco? Good!' – whereupon it transpired that the old gentleman attributed his excellent health to a regular use of opium for fifty years. Such stories were widely corroborated:

He told me he was between fifty and sixty years old, and had been a confirmed opium-smoker for twenty years and more, smoking regularly twice a day, once after each meal. He was as hale and hearty as need be, walking his thirty miles a day with a heavy pack on his back, for, with an eye to the main chance, he was going to combine with his official business a little peddling trade on his own account – a fresh proof that opium if not taken in large quantities is not so enervating after all. As for its effect on the mind, some of the cleverest Chinese are habitual smokers. I must say that I have never seen anything which bears the faintest resemblance to the horrors of opium-smoking described in books. This man told me that opium still gave him delicious dreams, but, said he regretfully, 'It's all folly, they never come true.'[17]

The old man gave no indication of what his delicious dreams might be, but it would only be natural if some of them were about women. 'Food, women and sex' are bracketed together by Lin Yutang as chief among the objects of Chinese interest, and in this he is supported by a classical tradition of erotic literature, including works like *The Golden Vase Plum* and *The Before Midnight Scholar*.

Youthfulness is the main desideratum in the Chinese conception of a beautiful woman:

> Every man has his own taste in women, and we Chinese are no exception to the rule. Some of us like little, plump, lively girls; others would rather have them tall and slender and elegant. But most of us in China have one preference in common: we have a weakness for youth, and if we had to describe our ideal of feminine beauty we should nearly all insist that it can only be found in girls of about 12 to 23. Once a woman gets beyond that age she soon begins to lose her attraction for us. Indeed, the women most celebrated for their beauty in our literature have as a rule died in the flower of their youth, and when you consider the wretched old age of so many once fashionable singing-girls, you have to admit that for such people an early death is a blessing.[18]

Other considerations aside, there is no doubt that among the reasons for this taste in nubility is the importance of children, especially sons. Mencius said, 'There are three ways of being a bad son: the most serious is to have no heir.'[19] Young women are acknowledged to be at the height of their fertility, and are more likely to produce robust babies; for this they are favoured in all societies that place a premium on children. If a man's wife produced no children or only daughters, he would take concubines, and thereby supply himself with sons enough to ensure the future observance of his family's ancestral rites:

> The old-fashioned Chinese idea was that a man was entitled to as many concubines as he could afford: good, solid, sensible Chinese logic. Sometimes a wife, to keep

her husband away from whorehouses, selected the concubines herself. Once when we were in Shanghai – where the doll-like whores with their tiny bound, jewelled feet were clothed in silks and satin – Mamma complimented a woman she met on her bevy of beautiful daughters. The woman said calmly, 'These aren't my daughters. They are my husband's concubines. I selected them myself.' The theory was, if he had diversion at home he would keep away from the cages in the red-light district. Mamma would never have done that. She hated the idea of concubines and she especially hated Papa's. She had never been able to bear him sons, to her shame, so he went outside for them. Knowing Papa, he would have had concubines anyway, but the difference was her status as number one wife would have been unquestioned. As it was, the office staff often referred to the concubine who gave my father five sons as 'number two lady' – humiliating to proud Mamma, who did not want any competition.

Virility was highly prized among Chinese men; it was quite commonplace for them to use aphrodisiacs like powdered rhinoceros horn on occasion. I doubt if Papa needed artificial stimulation. All his life he had great interest in women and sex. He had 18 acknowledged concubines and a total of 42 children by them. They are my half-brothers and half-sisters, for no child in China is ever considered illegitimate.[20]

The notorious Shanghai gangster Du Yueshang, who lived in a Renaissance-style mansion in the rue Wagner with a concubine on each floor, exemplifies the traditional Chinese attitude even in his departures from it:

Gaiety and noise possessed Tongfu Lane one morning in 1915. A red and gilded sedan chair, the dragon-and-phoenix-adorned kind hired on such occasions, brought a bride to Du Yueshang. Curtained off by the bridal veil, the young lady's high, powdered cheekbones and generous mouth did not show, nor the high and square forehead which, for beauty's sake, she had painfully scraped to a hairless smoothness, interrupted by the long

arc of her eyebrows. All these, unveiled, would have
been a revelation to the groom if he had been from a
good family and had had his marriage arranged for him,
for he would then not have ever seen the bride before
she came to him on the day of the wedding in her sedan
chair. But as it happened Du Yueshang knew this lady,
and had indeed chosen her for himself.

Sadly she was barren, and they had to adopt a boy.
She then languished, Du Yueshang often being in the bed
of another. . . .

When a man advances in the world, his sexual frontiers are not normally allowed to lag behind. There was
never a shortage of trembling virgins thrust forward
by the sycophancy of friends for his delectation. Not
long after the adoption of his son Du Yueshang took
two concubines, the gifts of friends, one at each end of
the year. They were both from Suzhou, that fount of
sing-song girls and nubile beauty, and they were both
aged fifteen, for Chinese men look for beauty only in
nymphets.[21]

The tradition of concubinage was ancient and imperial.
Marco Polo, not always detailed in his account of places and
practices in China, waxes loquacious when it comes to the
intimate aspects of imperial life. The Khan, he tells us,

has also very many other concubines, and I will tell you
in what way. It is true that there is a province in which
dwells a race of Tartars who are called Ungrat (and the
city likewise) who are very handsome and fair-skinned
people; and these women are very beautiful and adorned
with excellent manners. And every second year a hundred maidens, the most beautiful that are to be found
in all that race, are chosen and are brought to the great
Kaan as he may wish. The great Kaan sends his messengers to the said province that they may find him the
most beautiful girls according to the standard of beauty
which he gives them, 400, 500, more and less, as they
think right. And these girls are judged in this way.
When the messengers are come, they make all the girls
of the province come to them. And there are judges

deputed for this purpose, who seeing and considering all the parts of each separately, that is the hair, the face, and the eyebrows, the mouth, the lips, and the other limbs, that they may be harmonious and proportioned to the body, value some at 16 carats, others at 17, 18, 20, and more and less according as they are more and less beautiful. And if the great Kaan has charged them to bring those of the value of twenty-one, according to the number ordered them they bring them. And when they are come to his presence he has them valued again by other judges, and of them all he has thirty or forty who are valued at most carats chosen for his own room. And he has them kept by the elder ladies of the palace, one to each of the wives of the barons, who use diligent care in watching them; and makes them lie with them in one bed to know if she has good breath and sweet, and is clean, and sleeps quietly without snoring, and has no unpleasant scent anywhere, and to know if she is a virgin, and quite sound in all things. And when they have been carefully examined, those which are good and fair and sound in all their limbs are sent to wait on the lord in such way as I shall tell you. It is true that every three days and three nights six of these girls are sent to wait on the lord when he goes to rest and when he gets up, both in the room and in the bed and for all that he needs; and the great Kaan does with them what he pleases. And at the end of these three days and of three nights come the second six girls in exchange for these, and those depart. And so it goes all the year that every three days and three nights they are changed from six to six girls until the number of those hundred is completed, and then they begin again another turn. It is true that while one party remains in the chamber of the lord, the others stay in another room near there so that if the lord has need of anything extraordinary, as drink and food and other things, the girls who are in the lord's chamber order those in the other room what they must prepare, and they prepare it immediately. And so the lord is not waited upon by other persons but by the girls. And the other girls who were valued at less carats stay with the other women of the lord in the palace, and they teach them to sew and to cut out gloves and to do other genteel work. And when any gentleman is looking for wives, the great Kaan gives him one of them with a very great dowry, and in this way he finds them all husbands of good position.[22]

The Chinese have always mixed a curious prudery with matter-of-factness about sexual matters. 'You must know', Polo remarked, 'that the young ladies of the province of Cathay excel in modesty and the strict observance of decorum.' The same is largely true today. It is only in the big cities that some young people court freely as they do in the West; and only in Shanghai that one see couples embracing in public places – chiefly the Bund. In provincial towns and rural areas such behaviour is likely to be punished, a reflection of the conservative outlook general in contemporary China. Virginity is still expected in a bride, which is just as it was, according to Polo, in the days of the Khans:

If however anyone wishes to give a daughter in marriage, or she is asked for himself by another, the father offers the daughter to the future spouse as a virgin. . . . When the bonds also and agreements have been duly made between them and confirmed, the girl is taken for the testing of her virtue to the baths or stoves, where there will be the mothers and relations of herself and of the spouse, and on behalf of either party certain matrons specially deputed for this duty who will first examine the girl's virginity with a pigeon's egg. And if the women who shall be on behalf of the spouse are not satisfied with such a test, since a woman's natural parts can well be contracted by medicinal means, one matron of the aforesaid will cunningly insert a finger wrapped in white and fine linen into the natural parts and will break a little of the virginal vein so that the linen may be a little stained with virginal blood. For that blood is of such a nature and strength that its stain can be removed by no washing from cloth where it is fixed. And if it be removed it is a sign that she has been defiled, nor is that blood of her proper nature.

. . . And you ought to know that for the keeping of this virginity maidens always step so gently in the progress of their walk that one foot never goes before the other by more than a finger, because the privy parts of a virgin are very often opened if she take herself along too wantonly.[23]

The Tartars disdained these refinements; their wives and daughters rode on horseback with them, 'so that it is quite credible that their integrity might be somewhat affected', Polo primly remarks. But in Tibet the very reverse of the Chinese attitude was adopted. There, Polo tells us with relish,

No man of that country would on any consideration take to wife a girl who was a maid; for they say a wife is nothing worth unless she has been used to consort with men. And their custom is this, that when travellers come that way, the old women of the place get ready, and take their unmarried daughters or other girls related to them, and go to the strangers who are passing, and make over the young women to whomsoever will accept them; and the travellers take them accordingly and do their pleasure; after which the girls are restored to the old women who brought them, for they are not allowed to follow the strangers away from their home. In this manner people travelling that way, when they reach a village or hamlet or other inhabited place, shall find perhaps 20 or 30 girls at their disposal. And if the travellers lodge with those people they shall have as many young women as they could wish coming to court them! You must know too that the traveller is expected to give the girl who has been with him a ring or some other trifle, something in fact that she can show as a lover's token when she comes to be married. And it is for this in truth and for this alone that they follow that custom; for every girl is expected to obtain at least 20 such tokens in the way I have described before she can be married. And those who have most tokens, and so can show they have been most run after, are in the highest esteem, and most sought in marriage, because they say the charms of such an one are greatest. But after marriage these people hold

their wives very dear, and would consider it a great
villainy for a man to meddle with another's wife; and
thus though the wives have before marriage acted as you
have heard, they are kept with great care from light conduct afterwards.

Now I have related to you this marriage custom as
a good story to tell, and to show what a fine country
that is for young fellows to go to![24]

The other side of the coin here connoted – openness to
sexuality and its enjoyments – is captured in the pornography
of China. Like its other literary genres, China's classical
pornography is episodic and highly allusive, making plentiful use of quotation from earlier poetry and novels. But the
themes are perfectly familiar, as demonstrated by the most
famous of them, *The Golden Vase Plum*:

After they had laughed and joked with each other for
a while, Hsi-men Ch'ing reached into his sleeve and
pulled out a cylindrical silver pillbox that contained
breath-sweetening lozenges flavoured with osmanthus.
One at a time he proceeded to put these into the
woman's mouth on the tip of his tongue. The two of
them then fell to:

> *Hugging and embracing each other,*
> *Like snakes darting out their tongues.*
> *The sound of their sucking was audible.*

Dame Wang was so preocupied with serving food and
pouring wine that she could hardly concern herself with
what went on between them, and left them in her room
to enjoy themselves as they pleased.

In a little while, when they had both had enough wine
to:

> *Ignite the flames of desire,*

Hsi-men Ch'ing's lustful thoughts got the better of
him. Exposing the organ that lay between his loins, he
induced the woman to manipulate it with her slender
fingers. It so happens that ever since his youth Hsi-
men Ch'ing had frequented the streets and alleys of the

licensed quarter and patronized the women who dwelt there. About the base of his member he wore a clasp that had been:

> *Beaten out of silver, and*
> *Imbued with drugs,*

which had the effect of making that organ both large and long. It was:

> *Dark red, with black whiskers;*
> *Straight standing, firm, and hard;*

a fine object, indeed! There is a poem about its characteristics that testifies to this:

> *There is an object that has always been about six*
> *   inches long;*
> *Sometimes it is soft and at other times it is hard.*
> *When soft, like a drunkard it falls down either to*
> *   the east or to the west;*
> *When hard, like a mad monk it runs amok either*
> *   above or below. . . .*

It was not long before the woman had taken off her clothes and Hsi-men Ch'ing discovered, by both visual and tactile means, that her mount of Venus had been depilated of its pubic hair. It was:

> *Pale and fragrant,*
> *Plump to bursting,*
> *Soft and yielding. . . .*

To cut a long story short, from that day on, the woman slipped over to Dame Wang's teashop every day to keep her tryst with Hsi-men Ch'ing.[25]

The novel gets much more explicit, and does not omit the variations and elaborations that human ingenuity devises; but it never ceases to quote, reminding readers not just of the erotic writings that preceded it, but of the whole literary past, thus displaying its anonymous author's scholarship.

If the practices described in Chinese erotica are the same, so are the preoccupations, at least of male writers:

In reading such descriptions Noble Scent couldn't help thinking of her own connubial experience and drawing conclusions. 'Is it possible?' she wondered. 'Can such things be? My young husband's utensil was barely three inches long and no more than two fingers thick, and when we sported together, his outside limit was two hundred thrusts, then the cloud burst. He even used to boast of his vigour and endurance; and here I read about men capable of delivering at least ten times more than he. It seems hardly credible. . . .'[26]

Prompted to empirical research, Noble Scent decides to spy on the private life of a particularly muscular young farmer who rents land from her family, and who is having an affair with one of her maids:

The show was about to begin. First the couple removed all their clothes; then she sat down on the edge of the bed and he stepped up to her, drew her head and shoulders against his chest and let her play with his armament. And what armament! With a swift movement of her hand Noble Scent covered her mouth to stifle a tell-tale cry of joyous horror. What length! That was a horse of a very different colour from the modest two or three inches to which her Before Midnight Scholar had accustomed her; it was eight inches long or more, simply fantastic. And the thickness! Her tender lotus shoot fingers wouldn't even be able to encompass this mighty elephant's trunk. The couple meanwhile had completed the prologue and were putting on the main act. . . . And what a performance! Her amazement was aroused for a third time. What vigour, what endurance! Back and forth went the shuttle, not just a few hundred, but far more than a thousand times, and the extraordinary lover didn't show the least sign of exertion or fatigue. It was just like a novel.[27]

As Ovid says, *Cetera quis nescit?* – 'The rest, who does not know it?' Noble Scent of course gets hold of the young farmer, and tries out his endowments and stamina for herself.

Pulp Western literature has been responsible for promoting sensationalist views of 'oriental sexuality'.. These passages, typical of the pornographic classics of the Chinese tradition, put the record straight. Communist China bans these books, and assumes a mask of prudery in sexual matters; but it is a mask fast slipping as prostitution and homosexual 'tea parties' once more become common, and as karaoke bars proliferate, the young girls who work in them earning far more money than they could dream of otherwise. Pre-modern Chinese literature displays a common-sense acceptance of sex, and as in India and Japan – cultures better known for this attitude – discussion of it is frank. There are several venerable sex manuals in China, of which the most famous is a place, not a book: it is the Lama Temple in Peking, which possesses a large collection of erotic statuary once used to educate emperors' sons not just in the facts of life but their refinements. Visitors now see statues partly wrapped in yellowing scraps of newspaper.

After all that, one might well need another of China's pleasures: a bath. 'There is none', we are told by the indefatigable Polo, 'that does not go to the stove and have himself bathed at least three times the week, and in winter every day if they can do so; and every noble or rich man has his own stove at home at which he washes himself.'[28]

The institution of the bath house, as a place to relax and socialize as well as to get clean and warm, still flourishes. But it occasions much astonishment when a foreigner ventures in, as Colin Thubron found:

> I entered a hall lined with wooden beds. Its colours were those of school: buff and pale green. The cubicles smelt like school too – each one narrow as a plank, and each holding a locked cupboard. I was aware of eyes following me from numberless bunks – steam-drowsed eyes shaded by towels. Spectacles were being lifted and wiped and re-adjusted to focus the intrusion; confused murmurs of astonishment arose. I found a cubicle and slipped off my clothes. By now the whole hall was gazing at me. Swathed heads jostled and ogled along the tops of the

partitions. Opposite me sat an old man, his senile breasts
and stomach converging in three oil-smooth folds. When
he caught sight of me, his hand had been extended to
grasp a mug of tea, but now it remained outstretched
before him in meaningless semaphore, while he froze bolt
upright and stared. Could this foreign body be real –
white, hairy (comparatively) and mosquito-bitten?

I joined a shuffling queue, seized a towel from a pile
of others, and entered the bath chamber. In its white-
tiled hall some hundred men were soaping themselves
under showers or lying like drug-addicts in steamy pools.
Naked, they looked more than ever like a nation of boys.
They showed none of the accumulated muscle or flab of
the Westerner, nor the passive Russian bulk. Their skins
were creaseless and unblemished. There was something
lapidary, almost polished, about their hairless chests and
narrow shoulders. Their limbs were slender, unshaped.
Many looked malnourished.

The bath-ritual involved a slow self-broiling in three
connected tanks, each hotter than the last. I slid hesi-
tantly into the coolest of them, then submerged myself
until I presented no more than a small, dazed head, and
hoped for anonymity. All around, the heads of the pool's
other denizens gyrated to look at me – disembodied faces
whose eyes were all but closed. We were spaced like
prawns around the basin's sides, sitting feebly on an
underwater shelf.

Soon the steam-filled air induced a luxurious indolence. My head tilted back to stare unthinking at the
glass-panelled ceiling. My feet lifted sybaritically from
under me. Time stopped. Everything was blurred to a
ghost of itself. As for the others, even their eyeblinks
had slowed into torpid fluttering and their conversation
dwindled to sleep-talk.

I stared at those outside the water. Some men squatted
along the tiled pool-sides, soaping their armpits or
crutches with an odd, matter-of-fact delicacy as if flush-
ing out extra small fleas. Others scrubbed themselves
under the showers, chatting in staccato bursts, or scraped
at their feet with hunks of black pumice-stone. Among

them a few old men stood thin as storks. Their shoulder-
blades stuck out like those in famine posters. They
shuffled over the tiles with a terrible, pained caution
and lowered themselves into the baths as if into their
graves.

I remained for a long time plucking up courage to
slide over the lip of my bath into the deeper swelter of
the adjoining one. When I did, the water felt incandescent. For a moment I lay gasping against its tiles.
The steam ballooned about me while a new conclave of
heads turned to inspect. They murmured conspiratorially
together. But their lips were parted by seraphic smiles,
and their heads thrown back in a depersonalized ecstasy.
Everything here – even astonishment – had slowed to a
dream. . . .

In the bath beside me an old man was swimming
unconcernedly. He glanced at me and closed his eyes in
disbelief. Then we stared at each other out of our mutual
incomprehension. Through the steam he reminded me
of those photographs of Mao Zedong swimming the
Yangtze. Perhaps he wasn't really there. My eyes misted
over, probably in pain. His head was no more than two
feet from mine, but soon he became merely an expression
in the ether, like the smirk of the Cheshire Cat. There
was nothing to be heard but the slop and gurgle of
water. In the bath beyond, another old man was lying
with his legs splayed and his toes gripping the bath's
sides, like a woman in childbirth.

I don't know how long I lay immolated there, but
eventually I became alarmed by my own dizziness, and
lifted myself out. I was burnt raspberry pink from the
neck down. I walked with the raw delicacy of something
new-hatched. The warm tiles slid cold under my feet.
Near the door two masseurs in galoshes were scouring
men's chests and armpits with wooden blocks wrapped
in towels. The dirt was running off them in solid, black
tidemarks. I slunk past them, and out.

The dressing-room was like a morgue. Exhausted
bathers stretched inert under sheets, their heads covered,
their legs projecting limply. Some were asleep, others
had lapsed into limbo. From time to time a spate of

coughing or hawking announced their imminent resur-
rection. Then voices rose in confabulation, and a con-
vivial tinkling of teacups sounded.[29]

The steamy tranquillity of the baths seems a world away
from the main Chinese idea of fun, which is anything or anywhere that involves a large crowd and an enormous amount
of noise. It is the latter which the Chinese seem especially to
like. Parties, fairs, celebrations, weddings, theatrical performances, all take place in an immense din. Few writers on China
can resist discussing noise, which is an accompaniment not
merely to fun but every aspect of the daily round, including
the most mundane: 'I was told', wrote Gill, 'that in the early
days of Shanghai, the noises made by coolies and creaking
wheels became so great as to be at last utterly unendurable
to European nerves, and a regulation was made, which was
at first enforced with much difficulty, forbidding coolies to
groan, or wheels to creak, within the boundaries of the
Concession, and imposing fines for a breach of the rule.'[30]
Wheelbarrows appear rather often in Western reminiscences
of Chinese noise. Here Isherwood recalls: 'From the road outside came the continual pig-squeal of wheelbarrows going
past. To quote, all Chinese wheelbarrows squeak, because the
squeak is cheaper than the grease. Also, the boss can tell at
once if one of his coolies quits work.'[31]
     Theories about the Chinese love of – it even seems, need
for – noise abound. One is that it keeps off demons, who love
parties and celebrations as much as people do, and constantly
try to join in. Woodrooffe explains:

A demon hates a noise, but he is also incurably
inquisitive.
     At marriages and funerals, at festivals or family gather-
ings, even at the start of a journey, these malignant
creatures arrive unbidden in swarms. They gate-crash
weddings; throng the graveside at funerals; try and get
into the feast on someone's birthday, and jostle around
the station like a crowd greeting a film star, if precau-
tions are not taken. Therefore the celebrants on these
occasions annoy the delicate ear-drums of the unwanted

guests by a terrific gonging or heroic fusillade of fire-crackers. For this reason also, the wheelbarrow coolie is able to go his way unmolested as long as his wheel is making a hideous din.[32]

Another theory, owing to Acton, who prefers the aesthetic to the demonological possibilities, is that noise and cuisine are somehow linked:

> Was it that the vitality of this crowd pitched in a lower key than that of a crowd in Europe or America, required a higher pitch of sound to expand in? I had a theory that meat is the Western substitute for sound above a certain pitch: the meat we assimilate replaces the clash of gongs and tintinnabulation of cymbals, hence physically we can bear no more, our ears contract in misery at a Chinese theatre. The Chinese, being less carnivorous than we, enjoy what they call *je-nao*, of which 'hot din' is a literal translation. A hot din is an essential accompaniment to aimless amusement, and a spicy odour is characteristic of this humanity nurtured on rice. When I had lived for several years on Chinese cooking, the loud gongs, cymbals and *hu-ch'in* were sweetly soothing to my nerves. I had only to listen to them to recover my serenity on a sultry day, whereas a Western band affected me like a dirge. From the first I felt at home in a Chinese crowd of pleasure seekers, and rather than end the evening in a cinema or night club I preferred to take what Baudelaire calls 'a bath of multitude' and stroll where the throng was thickest.[33]

Whatever explains Chinese love of noise, it is certain that they regard it as decorative. Today one can see tiny, beautifully-made bamboo cages hanging outside Chinese houses, holding cicadas which stridulate loudly and endlessly in the heat of summer days. The fashion was started by an emperor:

> Among other things that Chien-Lung did for these temples, he imported from the palace of Jo Hol in Man-churia a quantity of a kind of tree cigala, by Europeans called wee-wees from the noise they make, by the

Chinese called Ta-tsu-chi-liao. They are the most curious insects, and make a clatter which is as if it were produced by the metal tongues of an accordion. They go on all day and drive one nearly distracted. Sometimes one can hardly hear oneself speak, but the Chinese delight in them, and my teacher told me the story of their introduction as if he had been speaking of an importation of nightingales. . . . The Chinese certainly find pleasure in what are to us very disagreeable noises. Fancy a flight of pigeons with Aeolian harps tied to their tails! The first time I heard it above my head I thought something dreadful must be going to happen. However, that fancy has a practical side to it, for it keeps off the hawks which abound at Peking.[34]

Among the many organized forms of noise in China – loudest must be the fire-cracker days of *Chun Jie*, the New Year Spring Festival, but any other ceremony requiring cacophony comes a close second – is opera. 'This evening we have seen our first Chinese opera,' wrote Isherwood.

The theatre was packed. Everyone in the audience was laughing, talking, shouting across the auditorium to greet his friends. People kept coming in and going out. Attendants ran round with hot face-towels and glasses of tea. It seemed nearly impossible to hear a single word from the stage: but no doubt this didn't matter, because the public knew the whole play by heart. As Auden remarked, it was like hearing Mass in an Italian church.
The performance was highly artificial and ritualistic – a mixture of song, ballet, fairy-story, and knock-about. The dresses were gorgeous: scarlet, orange, or green silk, embroidered with fantastic flowers and dragons. . . . The sleeves of their robes are cut so that they fall almost to the floor. The gestures made by the actors in flapping these sleeves, to express anger or contempt, are an important technical feature of drama, and are closely watched by connoisseurs in the audience. . . .
There is a certain amount of spoken dialogue, but the opera consists chiefly of sung recitative, within a five-note compass. The orchestra is seated upon the stage.

itself: there are several percussion instruments, a violin, and a sort of bagpipe. The singing is thin, reedy, nasalized; to western ears it startlingly resembles Donald Duck. We were quite unable to distinguish the gay from the tragic, or the bridge-passage from the climax. But the audience, despite its chatter, was evidently following the music with critical attention; for, at certain points, it broke into the kind of applause which, in Europe, greets a very pretty high C.

Our Chinese hosts did their best to explain the story. Some women flap their sleeves. 'The wives are despising her for not having a husband.' Lady Precious Stream utters some piercing, Disneyesque sounds. 'Now she is reconciling filial piety with her wifely duty.' A general is sent to kill the hero; they engage in a ballet-fight. The hero, to our surprise, is beaten. But he has won a moral victory, for the general repents and begs his forgiveness. The old Emperor, father of Lady Precious Stream, is deposed, and the hero takes the throne. His frumpish old mother is honoured; the villain is led out to execution. The old Emperor sulks a bit, but gives in at last with a good grace. Lady Precious Stream receives a little flag to show that she is now Wife Number One.[35]

There is no reference here to the musical performance itself, but no doubt, as the reporter of another occasion tells us, 'the musicians' band of cymbals, pipes, flutes and drums crashed out the most hideous din that mortal ears ever heard'.[36]

It seems hard at first to reconcile such a judgement with the following impressive anecdote: 'Confucius heard the Shao music in Qi and for three months after he did not notice the taste of food. "I never dreamed," he said, "that the joys of music could reach such heights." '[37]

There may be a great difference between sipping tea or floating in a hot bath, on the one hand, and being engulfed in the uproar of a Chinese opera on the other. But they all contribute to the 'art of all arts': 'In China,' Lin Yutang remarks, 'man knows a great deal about the art of all arts,

viz., the art of living.'[38] Its essence is captured by Shen Fu.
He recalls a visit with friends to West Mountain near Qingbo:

We reached a place where cassia flowers were most pro-
fuse and had a pot of pure tea, before climbing into the
sedan chairs and returning to the Pavilion of the Arriving
Cranes.

We found cups and plates already set out at the small
Pavilion of Descending Purity, east of Cassia Balcony.
Zhu Yi was a quiet man but fond of guests and fine wine.
We began playing the cassia drinking game and con-
tinued until everyone had drunk in round: by this time
it was the second watch.

'The moonlight is exquisite tonight,' I said, 'but if we
just go drunkenly to sleep, its beauty will be lost on us.
Where is there a high place with a good view, where
we could go to enjoy the moonlight? That's the only
way not to waste this beautiful evening.'

'We could climb up to Flying Crane Pavilion,' suggested Zhu Yi.

Xinglan has brought his lute,' said Yinke, 'and we
have yet to hear a tune. How about him playing for us
when we get there?'

We all went together, surrounded by the fragrance of
the cassias along a road bordered by a frosty forest. The
sky was empty and vast in the moonlight, and all was
silent. At the pavilion Xinglan played 'Three Variations
on the Plum Blossom' and it was as if we were immortals
floating in the air.[39]

7

GODS, GHOSTS
AND DEMONS

A pupil asked Confucius about the spirits of the dead
and the gods. Confucius replied, 'You are not yet
able to serve men, how can you serve their spirits?'
'May I ask about death?' 'You do not yet understand
life, how can you understand death?'

Confucius, *The Analects*, 11.12

The Chinese attitude to religion has long perplexed Westerners. When H.A. Giles roundly asserts that 'the Chinese
are emphatically not a religious people',[1] he is not saying
anything new: writers on China, most of whom were missionaries prior to his time, concur that the indigenous religions
of China – Confucianism and Daoism (Taoism) – are not
worthy of the name: 'Confucianism, of course, is not a religion at all, dealing as it does with the affairs of this life only;
and it will be seen that Taoism, in its true sense, has scarcely
a stronger claim.'[2]

Their opinions were given credence in the twentieth century
by the support of Chinese humanist voices, some of whom, like
Liang Qichao, are even more scathing about their native
religions: 'Taoism is the only religion indigenous to China . . .
but to include it in a Chinese history of religion is indeed a great
humiliation. Their activities have not benefited the nation at all.
Moreover, down through the centuries, they have repeatedly
misled the people by their pagan magic.'[3]

Therefore, when Buddhism entered China in approximately
the first century BC, it had little to contend with:

The ancient Chinese had very simple superstitions which
they rarely troubled themselves to rationalize into a

religious system. They never fully differentiated God from Heaven; they believed in the spirits; and they had some vague notion of retribution of good and evil. That was all. There was neither Hell, nor Paradise, nor a future life in the next world. But Buddhism came and changed all this.[4]

But acceptance of Buddhism as a religion is often tempered with caveats as to why the Chinese, even those who profess a belief in Buddhism, are not a religious people. For Giles a want of reverence is taken as indicative of a lack of faith: 'Crowds will laugh and talk, and buy and sell sweetmeats, in a Buddhist temple, before the very eyes of the most sacred images. So long as divine intervention is not required, an ordinary Chinaman is content to neglect his divinities; but no sooner does sickness or financial trouble come upon the family, then he will hurry off to propitiate the gods.'[5]

Simpson Cuthbertson speaks for many when he suggests that the habit of turning to all three systems in times of need is a reflection of the individual weaknesses of each:

A family mourning for a deceased member may call in the Buddhist priests to-day to pray for the soul of the deceased, and to-morrow the Tauist; or both may be called at the same time to perform the services they think needful for the dead. The explanation of this fact is to be found, probably, in a felt consciousness of some defect in them all. There is in the minds of the mass of the people such a want of confidence in the truth of the doctrines taught, or in the power of the deities worshipped, by these sects, that they adopt the whole, so that if they fail in one place, they may be more successful in another. They are like drowning men who catch at every straw that comes within reach.[6]

But even more common is the assertion that, while the common man is superstitious, the literatus does not have any religious feelings to satisfy: 'the educated people are indifferent to religion', claims Hu Shi. Their interests are seen to lie elsewhere, in Confucianism as an ethical system according to the observant and intrepid Lazarite missionary, Abbé Huc:

All Chinese are at the same time partisans of Confucius,
Lao-tze, and Buddha; or rather, they are nothing at all;
they reject all faith, all dogma, to live merely by their
more or less depraved and corrupted instincts. The literary classes only have retained a certain taste for the
classical books and moral precepts of Confucius, which
every one explains according to his own fancy, invoking
always the '*li*', or principle of rationalism, which has
become the only one generally recognised.[7]

The sinologist Derk Bodde concurs with this view: 'The
Chinese have been less concerned with the world of the supernatural than with the worlds of nature and man. They are
not a people for whom religious activities constitute an all-
important and absorbing part of life. . . . It is ethics . . . and
not religion of a formal, organized type that has provided the
spiritual basis of Chinese civilization.'[8]

Qian Duansheng believes Buddhism in China was valued
for its philosophy and art rather than as a religion in the true
sense: 'No great religion . . . has captivated the bulk of the
Chinese population. At its height . . . Buddhism was much
more in vogue than Christianity or Mohammedism at any
time. But the influence of Buddhism in China is more in the
realm of thought and fine arts than in that of belief.'[9]

And Bertrand Russell, an atheist, finds it easy to agree:

Chinese religion is curiously cheerful. When one arrives
at a temple, they give one a cigarette and a cup of
delicately fragrant tea. Then they show one around.
Buddhism, which one thinks of as ascetic, is here quite
gay. The saints have fat stomachs, and are depicted as
people who thoroughly enjoy life. No-one seems to
believe the religion, not even the priests. Nevertheless,
one sees many new rich temples.[10]

The situation in China has always been more complex than
that in the West where religion, whether Christianity,
Judaism or Islam, entails belief in a single deity and demands
fidelity. Even in Tang China, at the height of Buddhist
influence, it was common for a literatus to follow Confucian

tenets in his public life while, in his private life, openly expressing belief in Daoism or Buddhism. And although there were many cases of expedient faith – in trying to attract the patronage of an influential minister who showed an interest in Buddhism, for example – this does not mean that all professions of faith were insincere. Several Tang literati meditated, visited monasteries regularly and read sutras, although very few took orders.

A general religious zeal is confirmed by the early ninth-century depiction of what would happen if holy relics were brought to the capital, a depiction that could belong to medieval Christendom. The relics, in this case, are pieces of the finger-bone of the Buddha kept in the repository of the Famen Temple west of Xian. The memorialist is Han Yü, a vehement anti-Buddhist:

> Then would ensue a scorching of heads and burning of fingers; crowds would collect together, and tearing their clothes and scattering their money, would spend their time from morn to eve in imitation of Your Majesty's example passage [in earnestly worshipping at the feet of the Buddha]. The result would be that by and by young and old, seized with the same enthusiasm, would totally neglect the business of their lives; and should Your Majesty not prohibit it, they would be found flocking to the temples, ready to cut off an arm or slice their bodies as an offering to the god.[11]

Han Yü was exiled for his impertinence, but his Confucian argument against Buddhism – 'For Buddha was a barbarian. His language was not the language of China; his clothes were of an alien cut. He did not utter the maxims of our ancient rulers, nor conform to the customs which they have handed down' – was eagerly used as justification for action against the wealth and power of the monasteries only three decades later as the dynasty declined. In 844 thousands of monasteries were closed and tens of thousands of monks and nuns made to return to lay life (thus rejoining the ranks of the tax-payers). One of the first imperial edicts to be issued was a proscription of the worship of the finger-bone relics:

An Imperial Edict has forbidden offerings to the teeth of the Buddha. An edict was also issued saying that, whereas festivals had been held for the Buddha's finger bones in the monasteries at Mount Wutai, . . . and the Famen Temple . . . no offerings or pilgrimages to these places were to be permitted. Anyone presenting even as little as a single coin is to receive twenty strokes of the cane on his back.[12]

Social and economic documents found in the caves near Dunhuang in west China confirm the influence of Buddhism at this time. Most make at least a passing reference to Buddhism, if only because the copyist was a monk. Many of the contracts, for example, have monks or nuns as one of the parties or as a witness, and club circulars call their lay members to meetings at monastery gates. T.T. Meadows, writing in the mid-nineteenth century, therefore shows more insight than most in his answer to Abbé Huc and other like-minded writers:

If by 'want of religious feeling' they mean to assert that the Chinese have no longing for immortality; no cordial admiration of what is good and great; no unswerving and unshrinking devotion to those who have been good and great; no craving, no yearning of the soul, to reverence something High and Holy, then I differ from them entirely and emphatically contradict their assertion. The religious feeling, so understood, is as natural to man as hearing and sight; and I never yet heard of a nation or even a small tribe composed wholly of people deaf and blind. M. Huc himself dilates on the circumstance that China is covered with temples and monasteries, well or richly endowed; and, in spite of his after statement that they are the result of an 'old habit', I certainly adhere to the simple and obvious explanation that they are called into existence by strong religious feeling, however ill directed.[13]

Buddhism, however, did not displace Chinese deities. Buddha, his bodhisattvas, and the many denizens of the Buddhist heavens and hells, took their place alongside them, and spawned Chinese Daoist counterparts. By the Tang the

Chinese world view included a complex hierarchy of Daoist and Buddhist heavens and hells. These found their way into folklore and literature. One of the most popular episodes in Chinese opera is the story of Monkey – Xuanzang's legendary companion on the monk's pilgrimage to India – defeating the demon warriors of the Daoist pantheon. In desperation the Jade Emperor calls for assistance from the Buddha:

> The noise of the combat reached the Jade Emperor who in great consternation sent two messengers to the Western Region to see if Buddha could not come and help. When they had recounted Monkey's misdeeds and explained their mission, Buddha . . . called on his disciples Ānanda and Kāsýapa to follow him. Arriving in Heaven, they heard a fearful din and found Monkey beset by the thirty-six deities.[14]

The Buddha successfully imprisoned Monkey under a mountain, and then sat down for a banquet with the Jade Emperor.

The heavens and hells had a bureaucracy which mirrored that on earth:

> The popular Chinese conception of the other world is that it is run very largely on the same lines as life on earth. There are rewards and punishment, promotions and degradations, spells of happiness in rather earthly paradises, and sentences of expiation in very gruesome purgatories; re-births to pain and poverty, and to riches and honours. But none of these states are fixed and unchangeable; nothing is eternal but impermanence.[15]

The heavens and hells became more and more crowded as new spirits and demons were invented and local deities achieved eminence. This caused considerable logistic problems during major ceremonies when they all had to receive offerings. Kong Demao, a present-day descendant of Confucius, explains how their family steward circumvented this:

> Offering gruel to the ancestors and deities was an extremely finicky affair. The chapel alone contained hundreds of Buddhist and Daoist images: Guangong, the

God of War; Yuhuang Dadi, the Jade Emperor of
Heaven; Guanyin, the Goddess of Mercy; the Amitabha
Buddha; the Goddess of Childbearing . . . each deity had
to have a bowl of gruel placed before it. After the time-
consuming business of dishing it all out had been completed, it was put back in the pot and given to the chapel
attendant. When I was ten, the attendant was a smart
man named Chen who updated this method of presenting the offerings. He placed a huge dish of gruel in the
centre of the chapel for the gods to eat from in common,
and after a suitable period of time, took it home. I saw
him offer sacrifices like this several times and thought it
very novel and amusing. None of the ceremonial officers
censured him for the innovation.[16]

Much lower down in the hierarchy are the spirits of inani-
mate objects and the ubiquitous demons. Fortunately, these
creatures are easily deceived. The 'god of the stove' or kitchen
god, a heaven-sent spy, is given honey sweets by the family
at the end of each year, either in the hope that he will speak
'honeyed' words in his end-of-year report to the Heavenly
Emperor, or – the more popular explanation – so that his
mouth will be glued up, preventing him from speaking at all.
In Kong Demao's household he was considered a very lowly
deity:

The family ranked the Kitchen God far below the Yan-
sheng Duke and considered him inferior to the Duke in
terms of both wealth and power, so the masters of the
Kong Mansion never personally sacrificed to him, leaving
this to the servants. The room in which the image of
the Kitchen God was placed was dark and dismal. Since
he was not considered worthy enough to receive sacrifices in one of the Kong Mansion kitchens his portrait
was pasted up in a long-disused wood shed with black-
ened walls, full of soot and spiders' webs. But the ceremony was noisy and cheerful: there were always seven
or eight drummers and buglers along with a cushion
bearer and some footmen carrying sacrificial objects.
During the sacrifice, the servant in charge would give
directions to the god in a commanding tone, with no

hint of pleading, for 'the sage [Confucius] has the protection of heaven' and the Kitchen God was powerless to influence heaven against him. But in our time no-one paid much attention to these details; the main aim was to have fun, so my younger brother carried out the sacrifice in person.[17]

Demons are also easily misled:

The average demon is of low intellect; it can travel only in straight lines, it can reverse but cannot turn corners. In front of the door into every Chinese house, therefore, a light screen is placed. The householder can go round it into his dwelling, but the demon is baffled, and can only race backwards and forwards like an engine on its rails. Not content with wishing to enter every dwelling, the demon is sometimes in playful mood, and then is apt to amuse itself by sliding down the roof, as a small boy slides down the bannisters. To prevent this, the eaves of Chinese houses are curved, not with the idea of saving the demon from sliding off the edge, but so as to give him a nasty jolt as he is brought up with a jerk. The demon is also hideous. When a child has its first birthday, the most important in its life, it carries a small mirror on its forehead. When a demon rushes up to the child with soundless threats and curses, it catches sight of itself in the looking-glass and gets such a fright at the sudden apparition that it turns tail and flees.[18]

The spirits of mountains and rivers are not so easily avoided and must be placated with offerings. Barrow describes the ceremony on entering the Yellow River:

In the practical part of religion (which indeed may be considered nearly the whole) a Chinese is not less solicitous to avert a profitable evil, than to procure an eventual good; and of all evils personal danger is most apprehended. It was therefore deemed expedient that an oblation should be made in every vessel of the fleet to the genius of the river. The animals that were sacrificed . . . generally consisted of a fowl or a pig. . . .

The cups, the slaughtered animal, and several made-dishes remained on the forecastle, the Captain standing over them on one side, and a man with a gong in his hand on the other. On approaching the rapid part of the stream, at the signal given by the gong, the Captain took up the cups one by one . . . throwing their contents over the bow of the vessel into the river. The libation performed, a quantity of crackers and squibs and gilt tin foil were burnt, with uplifted hands, while the deep-sounding gong was incessantly struck with increasing violence as the vessels were swept along with the current. The victim and other dishes were then removed for the use of the Captain and crew, and the ceremony ended by 3 genuflexions and as many prostrations.[19]

Fengshui, the propitious placing of any man-made structure and especially houses, shrines and graves, was premised on the existence of such spirits, something the early missionaries to China failed to recognize at their cost, as Peter Fleming relates:

Further friction was created by their need for land on which to build their houses, churches and chapels. These tall edifices produced a disturbing impression, for they were held to invade the realms and to jeopardize the composure of the *feng-shui*. These were the spirits of wind and water, a nebulous but influential relic of the geomancy which had dominated Chinese beliefs before the advent of Buddhism; all that needs to be said about them here is that they were extremely temperamental and easily took umbrage if the delicate balance of their interests was upset. The spires of Christendom seemed only too likely to discommode them, and it became a common thing for local disasters to be blamed upon the missionaries, who in their teaching expressed views about the *feng-shui* which could hardly be called pro-pitiatory. The susceptibilities of these gremlins were often invoked more from a desire to obstruct the unwelcome foreigner than from any geomantic fervour; but once they were invoked the people felt strongly about them. 'Their disturbance by a church spire,' wrote a contemporary pamphleteer, 'is considered as much a grievance as the erection of a hideous tannery beside Westminster Abbey would be.' In a circular addressed to missionary societies the British Legation recommended that 'Chinese prejudice and superstitions should be more carefully considered in the forms and heights of the buildings erected'.[20]

The Chinese themselves were not above treating *fengshui* with a certain amount of irony. A well-known story tells of 'a high official named Song, whose families were all ardent supporters of *fengshui*: so much so that even the women read books on it'. When the official died his two sons each employed a geomancer to select the most suitable burial-site. Unfortunately, they chose different sites, and neither brother would concede to the other:

each set about making the grave on his own site, pitching marquees, arranging banners and making all necessary arrangements for the funeral. When the coffin arrived at the place where roads branched to the two graves, the two brothers, each leading his own little band of geomancers, bore down upon it with a view to gaining possession of the corpse. The struggle went on all day, and as neither gained advantage, the mourners and friends who had come to attend the funeral, crept away one by one, and the coolies carrying the coffin, after changing the poles from one shoulder to another until they were quite worn out, put the body down by the roadside and went home. It then became necessary to protect the coffin, whereupon the elder brother immediately set about building a hut close by. But no sooner had he begun than the younger brother followed his example; and when the elder built a second, and then a third, the younger followed suit . . . this went on for the space of three whole years by the end of which the place had become quite a little village.[21]

Fortunately, both brothers died shortly after and their widows co-operated to choose a new site. The author of this tale adds: '*Fengshui* may or may not be based upon sound principles . . . but to indulge such a morbid belief in it is utter folly. . . . Anyway, that two women should have thus quietly settled the matter is certainly worthy of record.'

The literati invariably took part in these ceremonies but there were always those who were more convinced of the efficacy of placating the people rather than the spirits: 'As for the appearance of spirits, I cannot see it. Nor can I know whether they accept the sacrifical offerings. This is because they are unfathomable and beyond comprehension: their obscurity is such that there is nothing to hold onto. The intent of the sages was only that the sacrifice must involve the *Dao*. It is not for spirits, but for men.'[22]

Confucius avoided the question of what happens to people after death and whether spirits exist, but his description of the use of ritual was vague enough to allow Xunzi's sceptical interpretation:

> How is it when people pray for rain and it rains? I say that there is no need to ask why. It is just like when it rains when no-one prays for it. When people try to prevent the sun or moon from being eclipsed, or when they pray for rain in a drought, or when they make a divination before deciding an important matter, they do so not because they believe they will get what they seek, but to use the ceremonies as an ornament. The ruler intends them to be an ornament, but the common people think they are supernatural.[23]

This was in the third century BC, when Daoism and theories of correlative cosmology – yin and yang and the five phases – were among the many schools which challenged Confucianism in popularity. The state 'religion' consisted of sacrifices to the ancestors and to certain major nature spirits, and the main 'deity' – 'Heaven' – was rarely depicted as an individual will. The Daoist idea that everything ultimately belongs to an undifferentiated oneness and that the world of forms – the world we see around us – is transient, entailed a singular lack of concern about death:

> When Zhuangzi's wife died, Huizi went to his house to give his condolences. To his surprise he found Zhuangzi

sitting with an upturned bowl on his knees to beat time as he sang.

'She lived with you, brought up your sons, grew old along with you,' said Huizi, 'that you should not mourn for her is bad enough, but to find you drumming and singing – this is going too far!'

'You misjudge me,' Zhuangzi replied. 'When she died, I was in despair. But soon, pondering on what had happened I told myself that in death no strange new fate befalls us. In the beginning we not only lack life, but form and substance. Then a time came when the substance evolved spirit, spirit evolved form, form evolved life. And now life in its turn has evolved death. She has passed from one phase to another like the sequence of spring and autumn, summer and winter. If someone is tired and has gone to lie down we do not pursue him with shouting and bawling. My wife has lain down to sleep in Eternity. To go about weeping and wailing would show that I knew nothing of nature's laws. This is why I have ceased mourning.[24]

Zhuangzi is similarly sanguine about his own death:

When Zhuangzi was dying his disciples wanted to give him a lavish funeral but he said, 'With heaven and earth for my inner and outer coffin, the sun and moon and the stars for my burial regalia and all the creatures of the earth to escort me to the grave, is there anything missing in this list of funeral goods?' The disciples replied, 'We are afraid that your body will be eaten by the carrion kite.' 'Above ground, I shall be food for kites; below, I shall be food for ants and mole crickets will eat me. You would rob the former to feed the latter. How come you like them better?'[25]

Also current at the time was the view that everything is composed of a substance called *qi*. It varies in quality, the purest ascending to form heaven, the basest descending to form the earth, with man containing a mixture of both. It was this view that informed the Daoist idea of immortality: there was no notion of an immortal soul, but a very long-lasting body filled with the purest *qi*. The First Emperor sought an elixir of immortality, and many others later died in this quest, as most concoctions involved the use of mercury.

The idea that everything is formed from the same stuff continued to form the basis of sceptical arguments against portents:

> That which is above and blue the world calls 'Heaven'. That which is below and yellow, the world calls 'Earth'. That which fills the space in between the world calls 'Primordial *qi*'. Cold and Heat, the world calls *yin* and *yang*. All of these, although they are immense, are no different in kind from fruits and gourds, abscesses and piles, and plants and trees. . . . Heaven and Earth are immense fruits, the Primordial *qi* is an immense abscess, *yin* and *yang* are immense trees. How can they then reward the beneficial or punish harmful acts? . . . You should trust only your own humanity and righteousness and stay within these principles, then it is simply a matter of life and death. How can you attribute existence and extinction, or success and failure, to fruits and gourds, abscesses and piles, and plants and trees?[26]

Although Buddhism rejected the idea of the individual soul, early Chinese commentators on Buddhist sutras frequently explained reincarnation by recourse to this idea. In pre-Buddhist China there were several 'souls' attached to an individual – although it is not clear that they are formed of anything other than *qi*. The several *po* join the body at the moment of conception while the *hun* are only attached at birth. After death it was variously believed that the *po* stay with the body and fade away as the body gradually decomposes, or go to live in the underworld of the Yellow Springs. The *hun* ascend and act as intermediaries between heaven and man: the sacrifices to the ancestors were to these. It was common for relations to climb to the roof-tops immediately after a person's death and call the *hun* to return to the body; in this way death could be reversed:

> The summoner of souls should take a suit of court robes formerly worn by the deceased. . . . he should then

climb on a ladder placed against the eaves to the front
and east. Then he should turn to the north, hold out
the clothing and call out three times in a loud voice:
'Hey, so-and-so, return!' Then he should pass down the
clothing to someone waiting below, who is to put it into
a box. This is then to be carried into the house by way
of the eastern steps.[27]

This was an ancient ritual and Mozi, in his essay against
the Confucianists written in the fifth century BC, failed to
understand that ritual was always important for its own sake:

When a parent dies, the Confucians lay out the corpse
for a long time before dressing it for burial. In this
time they clamber up onto the roof of the house, peer
down into the well, poke into the rat-holes, and examine
the washbasins, searching for the dead man. If they
imagine that they will really find the dead man in any
of these places, then they must be very stupid; while if
they know that he is not there but continue to search
for him, then they are guilty of great hypocrisy.[28]

From earliest times there had been shamans who summoned
souls, trying to frighten them with tales of other lands and
offering them inducements to return:

O soul return: in East thou canst not dwell.
There Titans live, a thousand cubits tall,
Who e'er upon the wandering spirit fall.
There ten successive suns thou mayst behold,
Their heat devouring stone, with bronze and gold.
The dwellers there are 'gainst these forces armed,
But never could thy soul escape unharmed.
Return, return, danger attends delay.

Return, O soul, in South thou canst not stay.
There live the Blackteeth and the Gaudybrows
Who murder strangers to fulfil their vows;
Men's flesh they sacrifice, their bones they grind;
There cobras move like grass beneath the wind.
There foxes huge a thousand miles hold sway,
And serpents with nine heads that dart and play;

Men they devour to fortify their pow'r.
Return, return; thou must not stay an hour.[29]

It was not only at death that the *hun* souls would leave the body: in popular fiction they frequently wander about during dreams or are forced out of the body as a result of trauma. After a long, hungry trek by foot, Du Fu reports that his host 'heats warm water to wash my tired feet and cuts paper charms to summon my wandering soul'.[30]

And, as if there were not enough spirits inhabiting the world of man, it was also held that these souls, if not given a proper burial, for example, could hang around, usually causing trouble. Some literati were dismissive of this notion:

> The dead do not become disembodied spirits; neither have they consciousness, nor do they injure anybody.
> . . . That which informs man at his birth is a vital fluid . . . and at death this vitality is extinguished, the body decays and becomes dust.
> . . . The number of persons who have died since the world began, old, middle-aged, and young, must run into thousands of millions, far exceeding the number of persons alive at the present day. If every one of these has become a disembodied spirit, there must be at least one to every yard as we walk along the road; and those who die now must suddenly find themselves face to face with vast crowds of spirits, filling every house and street.[31]

But, as Willoughby-Meade observes: 'The man in the street, a staunch ancestor-worshipper, has no doubts whatever about the existence and survival after death of souls of some sort; to him they are definite and often amazingly prosaic entities. The theories of the "high-brows" trouble him not at all.'[32]

And such creatures fill the pages of Chinese stories. Another popular subject of these is the 'fox fairy': the fox who takes on the form of a beautiful woman and seduces some unsuspecting young man; more rarely, it takes on the form of a man. Sitwell noted this gallimaufry of strange beings but failed to realize that belief in them had always existed side by side with both religious zeal and scepticism:

Not only does the Peking mind, even the most free-thinking, abound with portents, omens and magics, but many ghosts haunt it, together with will-o'-the-wisps and fairies. These ghosts are more harmful than ours, for they are perpetually, in order to gain their own freedom, luring and driving men to their death, or even, with true simplicity of plan, killing strangers by the shock of their materialisation. Continually the drowned thus rise on dark nights to misguide the feet of human beings and lead them into the water: while evil spirits exist who build up round men invisible rooms, thus walling them up alive, and others who urge them to hang themselves, actually holding the rope in position for their victims (one of these lives in a garden in the Legation Quarter!), or Demon Barbers come and shave off a man's hair while he is asleep, so that it will never grow again. Idols in temples can be possessed, and so can living people; these last often by dead relatives, who impose upon them their ways of speaking and tricks of manner. Of fairies, the fox-fairy is the most usual, and, though by nature intensely mischievous, aids mortals more than he injures them. . . . Against these ghosts and evil influences there are many remedies, such as biting the tip of the middle finger and smearing your intruders with the blood from it, or rubbing your hair very violently: while a mirror over your door will defeat spirits that want to enter it, then thrown awry in their orientation. A lion on the roof cornice is also said to be of some use.

Strict in their superstitions and superstitious observances, the Chinese have always been broad-minded where religion is concerned.[33]

An ambivalence in belief about ceremonies of ancestor-worship also persisted among the literati. Supposedly a method of asking the *hun* of the dead ancestors to intercede with heaven on man's behalf, ancestor-worship was seen as an 'ornament' to government by many. However, as the main Confucian ceremony, it was extensively and regularly practised in China. Some missionaries, sensing this ambivalence, petitioned Rome for it to be accepted as a non-religious practice, showing respect rather than reverence for the dead. But the more vociferous missionaries, unsettled by China's attitude to religion, won the day:

> The Chinese are not a naturally religious people. A vague piety is cultivated, but the frontiers of faith are ill-defined. A marzipan effect is produced by the superim-posal, on a basis of Shamanism and myth, of Buddhism, Taoism and Confucianism; the precepts of pre-Buddhist sages are still valid, and it is difficult to make out where the gods take over from the spirits, or to fit the philosophers in with the fertility rites. But in this amalgam the most important ingredient – regarded as such by everyone from the Emperor to the common thief – was ancestor-worship; and against this the nineteenth-century missionaries, following a lead originally given by Rome in the time of the great Emperor K'ang Hsi, set their faces.[34]

Matteo Ricci, the first Jesuit in China, who arrived in 1583, was not however the first Christian visitor. In 635 a Persian Nestorian built a temple in Xian and initiated twenty-one monks. By the end of the century there were several temples around China, the religion having received imperial support. But it remained a minor matter, and it was only in the seventeenth century that its existence was confirmed by discovery of the Nestorian stele, now in the 'Forest of Steles' in Xian:

> Here, too, stands the famous Nestorian tablet with its cross cut in the stone above the inscription. It records the imperial sanction for the 'most virtuous Alopun' and other monks to set up a religious establishment in the capital and to teach the pure doctrine. Prester John and his mystical Papal Embassy, those devoted Nestorian Christians, if Christians they can be called, and all the strange mediaeval half truths that were current about Cathay, come into one's mind as one stands before this tablet. It was set up in 781 AD, centuries before Marco Polo or Prester John, but how much more tangible a reminder of that remote groping contact between the East and West than anything else that is left in China.[35]

Missionary work over the past four centuries has not been much more successful, despite the optimism of its proponents. G.E. Morrison makes frequent ironic reference to missionary endeavours:

> During all the time I was in China, I met large numbers of missionaries of all classes, in many cities from Peking to Canton, and they unanimously expressed satisfaction at the progress they are making in China. Expressed succinctly, their harvest may be described as amounting to a fraction more than two Chinamen per missionary per annum. If, however, the paid ordained and unordained native helpers be added to the number of missionaries, you will find that the aggregate body converts nine-tenths of a Chinaman per worker per annum; but the missionaries deprecate their work being judged by statistics. There are 1,511 protestant missionaries labouring in the Empire; and, estimating their results from the statistics of previous years as published in the *Chinese Recorder*, we find that they gathered last year (1893) into the fold 3,127 Chinese – not all of whom it is feared are genuine Christians – at a cost of £350,000, a sum equal to the combined incomes of the ten chief London hospitals.[36]

China at this time 'was swarming with missionaries' of many denominations, a fact that some used to their advantage: 'The Chinese "Rice Christian", those spurious Christians who become converted in return for being provided with rice, are just those who profit by these differences of opinion, and who, with timely lapses from grace, are said to succeed in being converted in turn by all the missions from the Augustins to the Quakers.'[37]

The country has also been home to several other religions, although they have all been associated with foreign communities. Manicheanism was the religion of the Uighur community in the Tang capital but disappeared with the massacre of this community in the ninth century. This was not a religious persecution, but a result of the Uighur soldiers rising against the Chinese to the west. Even the clampdown on Buddhism in 844 was carried out, in large part, for practical rather than dogmatic reasons: the monasteries were tax havens and constituted a considerable economic power, while many people were ordained simply to avoid paying tax, thus depriving the state of considerable income. The Qianlong emperor rejected George III's request that his missionaries be allowed to propagate their religion freely, but fifty years later an imperial rescript tolerating Christianity was issued: 'I do not understand the lines of distinction between the religious ceremonies of the various nations; but virtuous Chinese will by no means be punished on account of their religion. No matter whether they worship images or do not worship images, there are no prohibitions against them if, when practising their creed, their conduct is good.'[38]

It is only under Communism that religious believers have been persecuted consistently and specifically for their beliefs – despite the fact that the Chinese constitution permits freedom of religion – and Christian martyrs are now not unknown.

Zoroastrianism also came along the Silk Road at about the same time as Manicheanism, and became popular enough to necessitate the establishment of a government office to oversee its affairs and to manage the five Zoroastrian temples in Xian. It also faded after the Tang. Islam was probably introduced by Arab merchants and is the religion of the Hui people who still live in China. The mosque in Xian serves a community of over a quarter of a million Muslims and a stele gives the date of foundation as 742, although the present building is of more recent construction. Their religion is, suggests Morrison, 'a thinly diluted Mohammedanism' which 'excites the scorn of the true believer from India'.

The dilution of religion over time has been cause for far more consternation among the Jewish community, who have long debated whether the Jews of Kaifeng are worthy of the name. The considerable foreign Jewish community of Shanghai founded a 'Society for the Rescue of the Chinese Jews' in 1900. A 1933 guidebook to China gave the history of the community and claimed it had more or less died out:

Kaifeng is noted as the location of a now extinct Jewish colony, which has attracted a great deal of attention from students of history. . . . When the great Jesuit missionary, Matteo Ricci, was in Peking, he was visited by one of the Kaifeng Jews, who was familiar with the tenets of his religion and told of a large congregation of Jews with a synagogue in Hangchow, as well as large Jewish populations in other provinces. . . . it is evident that the Jewish community at Kaifeng was at one time large and supported a fine synagogue. As late as the first part of the eighteenth century the colony was still vigorous and the members distinguishable from their neighbors by their Hebraic features. . . . A letter from European co-religionists was sent to the Kaifeng Jews, and the reply received in 1870 told a pathetic story of the colony's plight. The teachers were all dead and no one remained who could read Hebrew. . . . 'Daily with tears in our eyes we call on the Holy Name; if we could but again procure ministers, and put our house of prayer in order, our religion would have firm support.' . . . The Kaifeng Jews are now indistinguishable from their Chinese neighbours, with whom they have intermarried, though a few persist in calling themselves Jews. Only in abstinence from Pork do they exhibit any knowledge of the beliefs of their religion. The synagogue itself has disappeared, but its site and a number of important relics have been preserved.[39]

Like all foreign religions other than Buddhism, it remained the faith of the foreigner and did not succeed in displacing the multitude of Chinese beliefs.

It is perhaps only travellers in this century less encumbered with their own religious beliefs who have been able to view the religious practices of the Chinese with equanimity. Bertrand Russell, with his delight at the fat Buddha, was travelling without any religious baggage. Others, despite their contrary beliefs, have enjoyed the tranquillity of Buddhist temples. Acton, for example, said of those in the hills west of Peking:

I had seldom, if ever, found such peace in Christian places of worship: the Crucifix alone recalls scenes of agony, and death and tears are always present. But here the smiling Buddhas and Lohans tranquillized the minds, and their smiles pervaded each temple. Impatience, the most marked characteristic of all modern modes of thought and the curse of all our lives, was banished by the light of Buddha's smile. The ascendancy of inward culture and of love to others – Buddha's meditation under the Bo-tree – was reflected, with subtle variations, in each haven of peace, and there seemed no doubt that Buddha had grasped the solution of the great mystery of sorrow and had learnt its causes and its cure.[40]

Ann Bridge was similarly enthusiastic:

Nothing is stranger to the new-comer to China than this custom of Temple authorities of throwing open their sacred precincts to European visitors. A courtyard, or two, or three, according to their needs, is let off to each party. . . . But they are not confined to their hired apart-ment – freely they stroll about the terraces, among the shrines and the pavilions, where the wealth and tribute of centuries is accumulated in buildings, in treasures, or a stylised beauty and formal grace peculiarly Chinese, saluted with grave courtesy as they go by the black-robed monks. And in and around the whole temple, in spring, the fruit blossom flows like a tide, surging up in waves of exquisite pale colour against the ancient walls, spring-ing like flowery fountains in the paved courtyards. . . . Strange music of the blossoming tree – ancient wisdom that brings in the spring to worship within its holy places![41]

William Empson took delight in the faces of the Buddha, describing a sculpture from the Yungang caves in central China: 'my example from Yun-Kang, almost winking as it is, gets, I think, with these simple means, an extra-ordinary effect both of secure hold on strength and peace and of the humorous goodwill of complete understanding'.[42]

In their aesthetic delight in religion, these Western literati come closer to their Chinese counterparts. And if others remain perplexed they are not without hope of enlightenment.

Chan Buddhism (Zen) – a Chinese development – is meant, after all, to enlighten through bemusing or startling its adherents out of their conventional views:

> Shide was sweeping the ground one day when the abbot was passing by and asked him: 'You are called a foundling, because you were found by Fenggan. What is your real name? And where do you live?' Shide put down the broom and stood with his hands crossed. When the question was repeated he picked up the broom and resumed his sweeping. At the sight of this Hanshan beat his own breast and repeated: 'Good heavens! Good heavens!' Shide was quite amazed. 'Why are you doing that?' he asked. Hanshan replied: 'Don't you know, when a man dies in the east house the west house neighbours should show their sympathy by groaning.' Both burst out laughing, danced, cried, and left.[43]

8

RITES AND FESTIVALS

> Lin Fang asked about the basis of the rites. Confucius said, 'A great question indeed! With the rites it is better to err on the side of frugality than on the side of extravagance; in mourning, it is better that there be deep sorrow than a minute attention to the detail of the ritual.'
>
> Confucius, *The Analects*, 3.4

> When Confucius went inside the Grand Temple he asked about everything. Someone remarked, 'Who said that this man understood the rites?' Confucius, on hearing of this, said, 'The asking of questions is itself the correct rite.'
>
> Confucius, *The Analects*, 3.15

Ritual is a central tenet of Confucian life, constituting the proper way in which ceremonies of all kinds should be performed. As the expression of the central virtue *ren* – humanity or benevolence – it was an essential component of moral life: 'The Chinese are so ceremonious among themselves, and so punctilious with regard to etiquette, that the omission of the most minute point established by the court of ceremonies is considered as a criminal offence,' records John Barrow.[1] The rites regulated the most basic behaviour:

If the mat was not straight, Confucius did not sit on it.[2]

When in bed he did not lie like a corpse, nor did he sit in the formal manner of a guest when at home.[3]

The order and regularity in serving and removing the dinner was wonderfully exact, and every function of the ceremony performed with such silence and solemnity as in some measure to resemble the celebration of a religious mystery.[4]

The rites also, of course, governed the most important ceremonies of state. Barrow continues: 'The sober pomp of Asiatic grandeur is exhibited only at certain fixed festivals; of which the principal is the anniversary of the Emperor's birth-day, the commencement of a new year, the ceremonial of holding the plough, and the reception of foreign ambassadors.'[5]

And it was probably in the rules of behaviour developed for the early ceremonies of divination and ancestor-worship in the second millennium BC that the rites have their basis. By the time of Confucius they were important both as an expression of the legitimacy of the ruler – the 'ornament' of government, as Xunzi called them – and, more generally, of moral behaviour.

The former role was taken seriously. One of the most important ceremonies was the sacrifice to Mount Tai in Shandong recorded in the ancient texts as having been performed by the first ruler of the Zhou dynasty. When the First Emperor came to replicate the ceremony in order to assert his legitimacy as a sage ruler he is said to have been subjected to a great buffeting of wind and rain on his descent: the mountain was expressing its opposition. Nevertheless, he conferred ministerial rank on the trees under which he and his retinue took shelter.

Yuan Shikai, president of China after the fall of the last dynasty in 1911, sought to consolidate his pretensions by sacrificing at the Temple of Heaven in Peking, an honour reserved for emperors:

In his sublime egotism, but with a full knowledge of what is latent in the Chinese mind, the late Yuan Shih-k'ai promised his people that if they recognized him as emperor he would go to the Temple of Heaven and sacrifice. . . . But often led to enthusiasm by similar 'concessions' of usurpers, the people were unmoved by Yuan's appeal to their religious superstitions . . . and seemed to doubt if the Supreme Being would receive the customary homage from the commoner from Honan, who had assumed the vice-regency.[6]

The ploughing ceremony, mentioned by Barrow, was performed in the spring and, in more recent centuries, at the Temple of Heaven in Peking:

> Here also, it was the custom for the emperor to take off his royal robes, assume the role of a peasant, follow an imperial-yellow plough, drawn by an ox draped in yellow and also led by an official draped in yellow garments; he plowed nine furrows and the princes followed him and scattered the seeds, while imperial choristers chanted anthems in praise of husbandry. It is said that this spectacular ceremony dates from the Emperor Shun, who flourished in 2200 BC, and being a practical farmer, was particularly concerned with agriculture, which has always held a place of importance and dignity in China.[7]

Another of the ceremonies listed by Barrow, the emperor's birthday, is described by Marco Polo in the thirteenth century:

> Now, on his birthday, the Great Kaan dresses in the best of his robes, all wrought with beaten gold; and full 12,000 Barons and Knights on that day come forth dressed in robes of the same colour, and precisely like those of the Great Kaan, except that they are not so costly; but still they are all of the same colour as his, and are also of silk and gold. Every man so clothed has also a girdle of gold; and this as well as the dress is given him by the Sovereign. And I will aver that there are some of these suits decked with so many pearls and precious stones that a single suit shall be worth full 10,000 golden bezants.
>
> On his birthday also, all the Tartars in the world, and all the countries and governments that owe allegiance to the Kaan, offer him great presents according to their several ability, and as prescription or orders have fixed the amount.
>
> . . . On this day likewise all the Idolaters, all the Saracens, and all the Christians and other descriptions of

people make great and solemn devotions, with much chaunting and lighting of lamps and burning of incense, each to the God whom He doth worship, praying that He would save the Emperor, and grant him long life and health and happiness.

And thus, as I have related, is celebrated the joyous feast of the Kaan's birthday.[8]

But ceremonies had another function, as noted by Sitwell:

The people of Peking love spectacles, and, in the time of the Emperors, constant ceremonies were staged for them to enjoy. The Emperor might pass on his way to the Summer Palace, or to sacrifice at the Altar of Heaven, and there would be a procession to watch. Or, for instance, on the sixth day of the sixth month, the Imperial Elephants were taken down to the moat outside the Tartar City to be washed, and all Peking made holiday for the occasion. Then the inexorable Chinese calendar always imposed upon the rich certain details of costume, recurring at regular dates in the year, to which the populace could look forward. Thus the nobles of the Court, and those officials entitled to wear them . . . adorned themselves, on the first day of the Eleventh Month, with sables, known here as 'jackets turned inside out', and discarded them with equal punctuality, in favour of silver-fox furs, on the ninth day of the First Month. . . . But all these free spectacles have now vanished from the scene, leaving the loafer (of whom, as in all great cities, there are considerable numbers) disconsolate. . . . Only religion is left him for the comfort of his eye, if not of his soul. He has less to look at, but looks at it just as much.[9]

The 'sombre pomp' and 'solemnity' of the state rituals, however, stood in marked contrast to the noise and bustle of most ceremonies:

And then there were always the fairs, perpetual fairs. . . . The crowds, stopping to give alms before they enter, are pouring into the courts – at other times deserted – of the temple of the day. According to their means, they buy sweets and apples, and silks and antiques, and badly cured furs, and paper lanterns, and Western hats and, even, chickens and small, grunting, black-and-tan pigs, squealing and rocking on their short legs. The background of arches and painted eaves and tiled roofs, of decaying shrines and old trees, sets off the animated bustle of the jostling, pushing groups, always with an undercurrent of small children hitting and running beneath their elbows, while the sun flickers over them its flat, golden light, as though a boy were playing with a piece of mirror.[10]

And in the absence of these there was always a funeral or wedding: '. . . though the extreme pomp of weddings and funerals had been officially discouraged by the Republic, the demand for it in the hearts of the people is strong enough to defeat any quantity of government decrees'.[11]

The Republic was not the first time voices had been raised against the expense of such ceremonies. Mozi, a philosopher of some influence but little humour who lived not long after Confucius, devoted a chapter of his book to this cause. His main argument was against the elaborate funerals of rulers and officials:

They must have inner and outer coffins, three layers of embroidered hide, jades and jewels; and when these have been provided, they still require spears, swords, tripods, baskets, vessels, basins, embroideries, silks, countless horse bridles, carriages, horses, waiting women, and musicians. On top of this they demand roads and approaches to the grave going this way and that, and a mound as round and high as a hill. All of this interferes with the daily labours of the people and wastes their wealth to an incalculable degree. Such is the uselessness of elaborate burials.[12]

The First Emperor, even though like the followers of Mozi he abhorred much of Confucianism, spared no expense on his own burial. His grave-mound, a rammed-earth hill over 4,500 feet in circumference, has not yet been excavated but its splendours are recorded by Sima Qian:

As soon as the First Emperor became king of Qin excavations and building had been started at Mount Li, while after he won the empire more than seven hundred thousand conscripts from all parts of China worked there. They dug through three subterranean streams; they poured molten copper for the outer coffin, and the tomb was filled with models of palaces, pavilions and offices, as well as fine vessels, precious stones and rarities. Artisans were ordered to fix up crossbows so that a thief breaking in would be shot. All the country's streams, the Yellow River and the Yangtse were reproduced in quicksilver and by some mechanical means made to flow into a miniature ocean. The heavenly constellations were shown above and the regions of the earth below. The candles were made of whale-oil to ensure their burning for the longest possible time.

The Second Emperor decreed, 'It is not right to send away those of my father's ladies who had no sons.' Accordingly all these were ordered to follow the First Emperor to the grave. After the internment someone pointed out that the artisans who had made the mechanical contrivances might disclose all the treasure that was in the tomb; therefore after the burial and sealing up of the treasures, the middle and outer gates were shut to imprison all the artisans and labourers, so that not one came out. Trees and grass were planted over the mausoleum to make it look like a hill.[13]

In reaction to these excesses of the First Emperor – of which his burial with its enormous cost in human life was seen to be indicative – Emperor Wen of the succeeding Han dynasty sought to present himself in a very different light. His Testamentary Edict is a model of Confucian humility:

I, who am without virtue, have had no means to bring succour to the people. If, having passed away, I were to inflict upon them deep mourning and prolonged lamentation, exposing them to the cold and heat of successive seasons, grieving the fathers and sons of the people and blighting the desires of young and old, causing them to diminish their food and drink and to interrupt the sacrifices to the ancestors and spirits, I would only deepen my lack of virtue.

Let the officials and the people of the empire be instructed that, whenever this order shall reach them, they shall take part in lamentations for three days, after which they shall remove their mourning garments.

As for those who shall take part in the actual funeral proceedings and lamentations, they need not wear the customary unhemmed robes, and their headbands and sashes should not exceed three inches in width. There shall be no display of chariots or weapons, nor shall men and women be summoned from among the people to wail and lament in the palace. . . . After the coffin has been lowered into the grave, deep mourning shall be worn for fifteen days, then all mourning clothes shall be removed.[14]

But his example was not widely emulated; funerals have continued to be costly and showy affairs:

The funeral of a Chinaman is naturally the most momentous event in his career, as is evidenced by the proverb 'The most important thing in life is to be buried well'; and the ceremonial is extraordinarily elaborate and complicated for all ranks of society. There are certain imperial roads across which a corpse must not be borne, lest it imperil the health of the Son of Heaven – a fact impressed on English minds by the misunderstanding which, many years ago, nearly brought about an act of war, when Chinese authorities barred the passage of the funeral cortège which bore ashore of a little middy from an English man-of-war.

When a man dies, all the external paraphernalia of his house (lamps, doorsteps, signs, etc.), normally red, are changed to white, the mourning colour of China. The family wails around the coffin seated on the floor for seven days, during which time, since cooking is forbidden, they are dependent on the kindness of neighbours for their rice. Sackcloth is worn, or white garments (and in some provinces blue), and mourners may not shave or cut their nails till after the interment. The ceremonies connected with death recur every seventh day for seven periods, a curious parallel with Jewish ceremonial. One of the earliest and most peculiar of the rites is 'the buying of water'. The eldest son, accompanied by a musician playing funeral dirges on an out-of-tune instrument, visits a pool of water, throws in cash to appease the spirit who dwells there, and carries away a bowl of water with which to wash the corpse. Water in the house is never used for the purpose. The date of the interment is decided, not by sanitary conditions, or the convenience of the family, but solely by the dictum of an augur, whose business it is to find a lucky day for the soul to depart to its last rest. He also sets forth the nature and number of the religious rites, as, for example, in a native novel quoted by Mr Dyer Ball in his admirable article on Chinese funerals: 'During the forty-nine days . . . a hundred and eight Buddhist *bonzes* should perform in the Main Hall the High Confession Mass, to ford the souls of departed relatives across the abyss of suffering. . . . That, in addition an altar should be erected in the Tower of Heavenly Fragrance, where nine times nine virtuous Taoist priests should for nineteen days offer up prayer for absolution from punishment, and purification from retribution; and that after these services . . . fifteen additional *bonzes*, and fifteen renowned Taoist priests should confront the altar and perform meritorious deeds every seven days.'

When the auger has settled dates and arrangements, and also what persons it will be 'lucky' to have at the funeral, the ceremony proceeds. The procession to the grave is always headed by hideous figures, to frighten away evil spirits, and includes, besides mourners and servitors, priests, both Buddhist and Taoist, and other persons, a large number of paper gifts to burn at the grave. Custom does not require a man to wear mourning for his wife and children; it is a matter of choice.[15]

Even today's Communist government, which has also decried the expense, has been unsuccessful in curbing the lavish ceremonies. An essential part of the procedure is the burning of paper models of all the possessions needed by the dead person in his next life. Arthur Miller records the skill of a craftsman who used to make these:

The Chinese artistry with papier-mâché continues to amaze me. After the Lomans' refrigerator, impossible to tell from porcelain, they have made two football helmets modeled after the one I brought from the States. . . . An eighty-year-old master of papier-mâché has supervised these constructions. He is now retired but his students did this work for us. He has made whole banquet tables complete with dishes and glasses and loaded with food, all of papier-mâché, which can be lifted in toto on one hand and carried off the stage.

He learned the technique as a young man in prerevolutionary times in order to construct funerary objects. In the case of a wealthy man, the artist would be brought to the house and be permitted to simply walk through it slowly, never taking out a tape measure, but under cover of his voluminous sleeves, pressing measuring marks onto pieces of paper with his thumbnail. He would then hurry back to his shop, construct the *entire house*, including all the rooms and important pieces of furniture, which would be set afire at the funeral. The destruction of his work finally was too painful for our expert, and it led him to the theatre, where his creations were preserved and used.[16]

The procession – the public part of the funeral – is described by many travellers. Archie Bell was in Peking for Yuan Shikai's funeral:

Outriders, brilliantly costumed, galloped along the avenue, which was closely guarded by soldiers, standing shoulder to shoulder. Then came a big Chinese band playing (in deference to European custom) Chopin's 'Funeral March'. Then dignitaries of the army and navy, each in full uniform and surrounded by their staffs. Then hundreds of the government officials in full evening dress, the diplomatic corps in full dress togs and plumes, then more Chinese officials in native costumes. There was another band playing Chopin, then hundreds of officials and the 'parade' threatened to become tiresome, but finally an enormous Chinese band, dressed in yellow silk robes, came along, fairly shaking the stones of the wall with metal cymbals, drums (draped in black crepe), flutes that shrieked horribly, stringed instruments that sounded like the moaning of lost souls, and triangle metal affairs that resembled the tumtum of bronze bells.[17]

After this came men carrying paper money for the necessities of Yuan's after-life, then came the coffin, 'the size of an ordinary living-room in an American house', carried by eighty-two bearers. Finally the mourning family, the wreaths loaded on carts, and clothing and food for the next world.

A funeral ceremony continued at the graveside:

When the procession reaches the grave they wait for the hour fixed by the fortune-teller before lowering the coffin into it. As soon as the grave is filled up with earth an offering is made to the dead man – rice, meat, and cakes are placed on the ground, incense and candles are lighted, and a quantity of paper money is burnt for his use in the spirit-world. The tablet on which the name of the dead man has been written is then placed in front of the grave. The mourners all kneel while the eldest son solemnly says, 'Let the bones and flesh return to the earth, and spirit enter the tablet.' It then becomes an ancestral tablet. The eldest son carefully takes it home after the funeral, and it is kept in a place of honour for five generations. At the end of a year the grandchildren go out of mourning – that is, they no longer wear white threads plaited in with their hair and white top-knots on their caps. After twenty-seven months, which the Chinese call three years, all the family go out of deep mourning; now they wear blue in their hair and on their hats, for blue is slight mourning in China.

Weeping and wailing, they kneel down, and offer food before the dead man's picture, then they take off their badges of mourning and burn them all. After this, if it has not been done before, they take away the picture and the table and screen, and put the ancestral tablet in its niche, and after that they worship and make offerings before the tablet, and not before the picture. This tablet is of carved wood, about nine inches long, and three or four wide; it is often gilded. It belongs to the eldest son, and after his death it will be handed on to his eldest son. There is another ancestral tablet, on which are written, not only the name of the father, but of the grandfather, great-grandfather, great-great-grandfather, and sometimes of the great-great-great-grandfather too.

Dutiful sons worship before these tablets very regularly. On the first and fifteenth days of each month they light candles and incense before them, and on certain other festivals they invite their dead ancestors to pay them a visit. They light lamps before the tablets, and place a bowl of rice and a bowl of vegetables before each; then, bowing low, they say, 'Please, Ancestors, come and eat of your descendants' rice!' After a little while they take the food away and eat it themselves.[18]

One aspect of the ceremonies associated with death took Western observers by surprise: 'A Chinaman, come to annouce to you the death of a beloved parent or brother, laughs heartily as he tells you – you might think he was overflowing with joy, but he is really sick and sore at heart, and is laughing to deceive the spirits.'[19]

Also an occasion for fairs and 'feast-making' was the *Qingming* – Clear Bright – festival, when everyone would go to sweep the graves of their ancestors. It offered the opportunity for picnics and drinking: but there was also a darker side:

During the Clear-Bright festival of spring
Peach blossoms and the flowering plum smile;
But from long-forgotten graves on the heath
Come sounds of lamentation.
Thunder disturbs heaven and earth,
Disquieting ground-sliding snakes and sky-coiling
    dragons;
Rain lashes the open fields

And trees and grass bend underneath its fall.
The long-dead entreat our sacrifice,
Fearing to fade ignobly from memory;
But it is difficult now to tell one from another
Under the overgrown neglected gravemounds of long
    ago.[20]

This was only one of the occasions on which the ancestors
would be honoured: as Kong Demao explains, the ritual calendar, especially for a family with a long lineage, was full:

But the Clear and Bright Festival was not the only occasion for a visit to the Forest of Confucius. Frequently
we went to offer sacrifices to my father, grandfather,
great-grandfather and even great-great-grandfather and
their relatives. Sacrifices were offered on their birthdays,
the anniversaries of their deaths, the anniversary of the
birth of Confucius, the Clear and Bright Festival, the
first day of the tenth lunar month and on many other
fixed dates. Besides this we also had to worship at the
Family Temple, the Worship the Shadows Hall, the Hall
for Cherishing Ancestral Kindness, and the Requite
Ancestral Kindness Hall. There was a huge, thick book
inside the manager's office which recorded the dates of
the births and deaths of clan members, a wooden board
was hung up in front of the Great Hall and at the beginning of each month a list of the dates, places (Temple
or Forest of Confucius) and names of those to be worshipped in the coming month were posted. It was rather
like a list of homework assignments.[21]

Among the most important of ceremonies is, of course, the
wedding, also a traditionally large and expensive occasion:

The Kong and Sun families held long discussions on their
wedding arrangements, and finally decided to hold a
wedding which combined the old and new. The bride
wore a modern-day white gauze gown and high-heeled
shoes specially made in Beijing, but Decheng wore a
traditional long gown and mandarin jacket of silk woven
with large circular patterns. It was an old-fashioned ceremony performed with the couple kneeling. Large-scale

construction was carried out in the Mansion before the wedding, and every wall from the Main Gate to the rear of the Inner Apartments was freshly whitewashed. Other changes were made as well. In the past, two door gods had always been painted on the Main Gate, but for this occasion they were done away with and the gate painted a plain red. Gold dragons on a blue background that had once decorated the roofs were replaced with cloud designs. A stage with seats for the audience on either side was put up outside the Main Gate along with a scarlet decorative archway and red palace lanterns. A pinewood pole was erected in the gateway ready to be hung with strings of firecrackers. The newlyweds were going to live at the Houtang Building in the Inner Apartments, and thus the path between it and the main gate was decorated with coloured marquees supplied by the Kong Mansion's own tentmakers. They were beautiful: the four sides were decorated with coloured glass pictures of five little boys (the 'Five Happinesses') bearing the written character 'longevity', and the roofs were woven of red and green cloth strips. Inside were huge traditional silk congratulatory messages in gold appliqué sent by friends, relatives and officials. These messages alone took twenty factory workers an entire day to hang.

The procession was very long: those in front were already inside the Kong Mansion before those in the rear had even left the Shunxian Hall. It was also a synthesis of old and new. In accordance with tradition, five complete operatic orchestras led the procession, while the official insignia – fans, parasols, golden melons, hatchets, and the 'heaven facing stool' – brought up the rear.[22]

In the evening three operas were staged, one in the streets outside for general entertainment, and the banquet 'began in the morning and was still going on at midnight'.

Food always plays a central part in any ritual or ceremony: eating, after all, is considered a ceremony in itself. Each ceremony has its special foods: for New Year, for example, large quantities of small steamed pork dumplings are taken round to friends and neighbours.

The New Year is perhaps the most important festival in the Chinese year. It is calculated according to the lunar calendar and therefore falls at the end of January or the beginning of February. Originally it was one of five 'beginnings of the year', but it is now the only one still widely observed. Marco Polo gives an account of the celebrations in thirteenth-century Peking:

> It is the custom that on this occasion the Kaan and all his subjects should be clothed entirely in white; so, that day, everybody is in white, men and women, great and small. And this is done in order that they may thrive all through the year, for they deem that white clothing is lucky. On that day also all the people of all the provinces and governments and kingdoms and countries that own allegiance to the Kaan bring him great presents of gold and silver, and pearls and gems, and rich textures of divers kinds. And this they do that the Emperor throughout the year may have abundance of treasure and enjoyment without care. And the people also make presents to each other of white things, and embrace and kiss and make merry, and wish each other happiness and good luck for the coming year. On that day, I can assure you, among the customary presents there shall be offered to the Kaan from various quarters more than 100,000 white horses, beautiful animals, and richly caparisoned.[23]

More mundane matters were described by Abbé Huc:

> The last days of the year are ordinarily, with the Chinese, days of anger and of mutual annoyance; for having at this period made up their accounts, they are vehemently engaged in getting them in; and every Chinese being at once creditor and debtor, every Chinese is just now hunting his debtors and being hunted by his creditors. He who has just returned from his neighbor's house, which he has been throwing into utter confusion by his clamorous demands for what that neighbor owes him, finds

his own house turned inside out by an uproarious credi-
tor, and so the thing goes round. The whole town is
a scene of vociferation, disputation, and fighting. On
the last day of the year disorder attains its height; people
rush in all directions with anything they can scratch
together, to raise money upon, at the broker's or pawn-
broker's, the shops of which tradespeople are absolutely
besieged throughout the day with profferers of clothes,
bedding, furniture, cooking utensils, and movables of
every description. . . . This species of anarchy continues
until midnight then calm resumes its sway. No-one, after
the twelfth hour has struck, can claim a debt, or even
make the slightest allusion to it. You now only hear the
words of peace and good-will; everybody fraternizes
with everybody. Those who were just before on the
point of twisting their neighbor's neck, now twine their
friendly arms about it.[24]

Sitwell remarks another vital component of the festival –
the fire-cracker – exploded to scare the spirits:

In Shanghai the temperature was down in unfathomable
regions below zero – a change for us after the tropics
– but this seemed only to impart a greater zest to the
celebrations. The first night the noise, reaching these tall
New York-like towers from the direction of the Chinese
town, was prolonged and often indefinable; but the
sound of fire-crackers, at least, could be distinguished,
and must, no doubt, have been pleasing to the spirits of
the dead, as well, I fancy, as to the great majority of the
living. They were ricocheting in all directions, and with
many modulations of sound, so that, had I been the
possessor of a properly trained ear, I should, in all prob-
ability, have been able to differentiate between the bang
and hiss of the numerous varieties cited by Tun Lich'en
as to be bought in the shops, and to distinguish Small
Boxes, Flower Pots, Lanterns of Heaven and Earth, Fire
and Smoke Poles, Silver Flowers, Peonies Strung on a
Thread, Lotus Sprinkled with Water, Golden Plates,
Falling Moons, Grape Arbours, Flags of Fire, Double-
Kicking Feet, Ten Explosions Flying to Heaven, Fire

Devils Noisily Splitting Apart, Eight-Cornered Rockets, and Bombs for Attacking the City of Hsien Yang, one from another.[25]

And he also describes the pleasure of the residents of Shanghai watching the street entertainers the following day:

> Knot after knot, group after group, of Chinese, in European clothes and caps, in nondescript rags, or in their own quilted, padded winter robes, topped with fur caps, waited, laughing and talking, round the numerous attractions, until the wide pavement had become a mile-long stage, for actors, acrobats, mountebanks and charletans of various descriptions. The scene must somewhat have resembled a less elaborate Venetian carnival, save that here there was no architectural framework, and that this grey blanket of cloud above us was substituted for the blue, autumnal, transparent sky of Italy. . . . The noise was immense, actors and female impersonators, singers, clowns and ventriloquists, all ranted and vociferated: conjurors shouted as loud as they could. . . . This was my first experience of a Chinese Fair, and . . . none remains more vividly in my memory than this New Year pavement fair at Shanghai.[26]

The traditional almanac is replete with important days to celebrate, and each locality has its own special festivals. Many of these are now no longer observed, while the major festivals are celebrated in more or less the same way throughout China. But there are exceptions: Reginald Johnston describes the Lantern Festival – falling on the fifteenth day after New Year – in the north-eastern port of Weihaiwei:

> So far as Weihaiwei is concerned the Feast of Lanterns may be regarded as pre-eminently the holiday season for children. During several days before and after the fifteenth of the first month bands of young village boys dress up in strange garments and go about day and night acting queer little plays, partly in dumb show and partly in speech, dance and song. Some of them wear the terrifying masks of wild beasts, such as lions, a few assume the white beards of old men, and many are

attired in girls' clothing. The children perform their parts
with great vivacity and go through their masquerades,
dances and chorus-singing in a manner that would do
credit to juvenile performers at a provincial English
pantomime.[27]

The next festival in the Weihaiwei calendar is the 'Awakening of the Torpid Insects' and, inevitably, food plays a major
part:

in many villages it is customary to rise before dawn and
cook a kind of dumpling, which as it 'rises' is supposed
to assist Nature in her work of awakening the sluggish
or dormant vitality of animals and of vegetation. The
presiding deity of this festival is, naturally enough, the
Sun, and it is to him that the dumplings are offered.
Similar offerings are made by the Emperor himself in
his capacity of High Priest. It is believed that if on the
evening of this day children wash their faces in a kind
of soup made from a certain shrub (*Lycium chinense*) they
will never be ill and never grow old.[28]

The Dragon Boat Festival, originating in Hunan Province,
an area known for its rivers and lakes, is strongly linked with
water: it now commemorates the suicide of Qu Yuan. An
absence of water, conclude Cable and French, does not deter
the desert-dwellers of west China from enjoying the occasion:

All over China there is a special and traditional way
of celebrating each festival, and even in far-away Gobi
oases the pasteboard cow is dragged forth at the birth
of spring, and each time his anniversary comes the old
dragon curls and twirls through the sandy streets of
dusty villages. Moon cakes appear at the full moon of
the eighth month, and on the correct day the Boat
Festival is remembered.
    This fifth day of the fifth moon demands special
recognition. In happier climes it is the Dragon-boat
festival, but Gobi folk have never seen a boat, so must
find some other way of merry-making than sailing small
river craft, and therefore celebrate the event with a theatrical performance.[29]

Shen Congwen describes the ceremonies in Hunan, scene of events they commemorate:

> On the Dragon Boat festival in the fifth month, women and children put on new clothes and paint the character for 'king' on their foreheads with a mixture of realgar and yellow wine. Fish and meat are eaten by every family. The whole town sits down to lunch round about eleven, then the doors are locked and they go out to watch the boat-race. . . . The dragon boats are longer and narrower than ordinary sampans, with curved ends and sides painted with vermilion stripes. They are stored in dry caves by the river for the rest of the year. Each boat seats twelve to eighteen oarsmen, a cox and two men to beat drums and gongs. Each rower has a short oar, and the beat of the drum regulates their speed while the red-turbaned cox in the stern signals with two small flags the course to take. Generally, the drum and gong are in the middle, and when the race reaches a critical stage they raise a din like thunder which, added to the roar of cheers and boos on the banks, reminds you of some epic river battle of old.[30]

The festival held on the seventh day of the seventh lunar month commemorates a love affair between the Herdsman and the Weaving Maid – the constellations of Aquila and Vega:

> The Weaver-girl, daughter of the Sun-god . . . was so constantly busied with her loom that her father became worried at her close habits and thought that by marrying her to a neighbour, who herded cattle on the banks of the Silver Stream of Heaven (the Milky Way), she might awake to a brighter manner of living.
>
> No sooner did the maiden become wife than her habits and character utterly changed for the worse. She became not only very merry and lively, but quite forsook loom and needle, giving up her nights and days to play and idleness; no silly lover could have been more foolish than she. The Sun-king, in great wrath at all this, concluded that the husband was the cause of it, and determined to

separate the couple. So he ordered him to remove to the other side of the river of stars, and told him that hereafter they should only meet once a year, on the seventh night of the seventh month. To make a bridge over the flood of stars, the Sun-king called myriads of magpies, who thereupon flew together, and, making a bridge, supported the poor lover on their wings and backs as if on a roadway of solid land. So, bidding his weeping wife farewell, the lover-husband sorrowfully crossed the River of Heaven, and all the magpies instantly flew away.[31]

Unfortunately, if it rains their annual reunion is not possible because the river is full to the brim and 'one extra drop causes a flood which sweeps away even the bird bridge'.

The Moon Festival is celebrated about a month later, traditionally regarded as the middle of autumn, although as Amy Tan's heroine recalls, the weather at that time of year is not always autumnal:

In 1918, the year that I was four, the Moon Festival arrived during an autumn in Wushi that was unusually hot, terribly hot. When I awoke that morning, the fifteenth day of the eighth month, the straw mat covering my bed was already sticky. Everything in the room smelled of wet grass simmering in the heat. . . . That day, instead of dressing me in a light cotton jacket and loose trousers, Amah brought out a heavy yellow silk jacket and skirt outlined with black bands.

'No time to play today,' said Amah, opening the lined jacket. 'Your mother has made you new tiger clothes for the Moon Festival. . . .' She lifted me into the pants. 'Very important day, and now you are a big girl, so you can go to the ceremony.'

'What is a ceremony?' I asked as Amah slipped the jacket over my cotton undergarments.

'It is a proper way to behave. You do this and that, so that the gods do not punish you,' said Amah as she fastened my frog clasps.

'What kind of punishment?' I asked boldly.

'Too many questions!' cried Amah. 'You do not need to understand. Just behave, follow your mother's example. Light the incense, make an offering to the moon, bow your head. Do not shame me, Ying-ying.'[32]

But the main part of the festival was held in the cool of the evening when everyone could view the full moon and ask a wish of the Moon Lady. It was also common for people to climb hills with lanterns in the shape of hares – one of the creatures said to live in the moon.

The last festival before the onset of winter is held on the ninth day of the ninth month and is traditionally commemorated by picnicking on the hills and enjoying the late autumn chrysanthemums. In Hangzhou:

> Nearly eighty different varieties were grown in the neighbourhood. Everyone bought them on that day and rooms in the taverns were transformed into bowers of chrysanthemums. The townspeople went picnicking on the hillsides, taking with them pomegranates, chestnuts, apricots, pineapples, and pies and cakes decorated with little lions or little figures made of flour scented with musk.[33]

Like most of the festivals, this one had its origins in the times when men's lives were dictated by the seasons. It is the last festival before the winter deadness covers the land, and the pomegranates, symbols of fertility in China because of their numerous seeds, are a reminder of the spring. For many, especially women, it was a time of melancholy as distant loved-ones were recalled:

> Fine mist turns to dense clouds.
> This day of sorrows seems endless;
> Camphor-smoke breathes from the mouth
> Of the golden censer shaped like a beast.
> It is the ninth day of the ninth month;
> Restless on my ornate pillow
> In the night's middle reaches
> I feel a chillness steal through the gauze curtains.
> In the eastern hedged garden

We drank wine as yellow dusk gathered;
Its fragrance stays with me still.
Do not say my spirits fails me;
Yet when the screen trembles in the west wind
I feel more frail than the chrysanthemum.[34]

9

SONS OF HEAVEN

Guide them by edicts, keep them in line with punishments, and the common people will avoid the punishment but will have no sense of shame. Guide them by virtue, keep them in line with the rites, and they will, besides having a sense of shame, reform themselves.

Confucius, *The Analects*, 2.3

How true is the saying that after a state has been ruled for a hundred years by good men it is possible to overcome cruelty and dispense with killing.

Confucius, *The Analects*, 13.10

When the king of the state of Zhou marched east at the end of the second millennium BC and defeated the Shang dynasty he claimed that Heaven had given him its mandate to rule. This was not given unconditionally: to retain it, the Zhou would have to rule justly and humanely over their people. If they became tyrants, then, just as the Mandate of Heaven had been removed from the last king of the Shang, so would the Zhou lose their power: 'Heaven sees with the eyes of its people and hears with the ears of its people.'[1] *The Book of History* records the accession of the first Zhou ruler:

Heaven has removed the Shang's mandate. There are many former wise kings of Shang in Heaven, and for a while the later kings managed their mandate. But in the end wise and good men lived in misery. Leading their wives and with their children in their arms, lamenting and calling to Heaven, they fled to where no-one could come to seize them. Heaven had pity on the people of the four quarters, and looking with affection and giving its mandate, it employed the zealous leaders of the Zhou.[2]

Five hundred years later Confucius inherited and developed this theory of kingship. The ruler was to be as a father whose example of virtue would control the people more effectively than laws and punishments: 'In administering government what need is there to kill? Just desire the good yourself and the people will be good. The virtue of the gentleman is like the wind and that of the little man like the grass: when the wind blows the grass is sure to bend.'[3]

Mencius extended this theme; he lived in a time of great political unrest in which the Zhou retained power only in name:

> The appearance of a true king has never been longer over-due than today nor have the people suffered more under a tyrannical government than today. It is easy to provide food for the hungry and drink for the thirsty. Confucius said, 'The influence of virtue spreads faster than an order transmitted through posting stations.' At the present time if a country of ten thousand chariots were to prac-tise benevolent government the people would rejoice as if they had been released from hanging by the heels. It is only at this time when one can, with half the effort, achieve twice as much as the ancients.[4]

But it was to be another two hundred years before the empire was pacified, and the state which achieved this was guided by a very different philosophy from Confucianism.

The state of Qin in the west of China had started reforms before the time of Confucius and these were continued under King Xiao in the fourth century BC when the hereditary nobles were suppressed and a new social order instituted based on military merit. The originator of these measures, Lord Shang, was charged with sedition after the king's death in 338 BC and killed. But later historians recognized the efficacy of his laws: 'By the end of ten years of Lord Shang's ministry, the Qin people were acquiescent. Nothing lost on the road was picked up and pocketed, the hills were free of bandits, every household was comfortably off, men fought bravely on the battlefield but avoided picking fights when at home, and the cities and villages were well governed.'[5]

King Zheng was only thirteen when he came to the throne of Qin in 246 BC, but he continued the legalist reforms started by Lord Shang under the counsel of the minister Li Si. At the heart of the system was the absolute power of the king: all feudal privileges were abolished, and control was maintained by the strict enforcement of laws with harsh punishments for transgressors. Agriculture was encouraged in order to provide grain to feed the army, and the only merit was military merit.

Li Si had been a pupil of the Confucian philosopher Xunzi, who was not impressed by Qin when he visited it in about 264 BC:

> the Qin rulers employ their people harshly, terrorize them with authority, embitter them with hardship, coax them with rewards, and cow them with punishments. They see to it that if people hope to gain any benefit from their superiors, they can only do so by achieving distinction in battle. They oppress the people before using them and make them win some distinction before granting them any benefit.[6]

But Li Si was not persuaded: 'The Qin have been victorious for four generations. Their army is omnipotent and their might intimidates all the kings within the four seas. They have not accomplished this by humanity and righteousness, but by conducting their affairs according to what is most useful and expedient.'[7]

Xunzi could only counter with the argument that it was all very well to gain power by these means but they could not ensure its continuance:

> Rites are the highest expression of the hierarchical order, the basis for strengthening the state, the means by which to create authority, the key to achievement and fame. By proceeding in accordance with the rites, a king will gain possession of the world; by ignoring them, he will bring destruction to the heart of his kingdom. Strong armour and sharp weapons are not sufficient to assure

victory; high walls and deep moats are not sufficient to guarantee defence; harsh orders and numerous punishments are not sufficient to assure authority. What follows the way of the rites will advance; what follows any other way will fail.[8]

In 221 BC the new statecraft seemed to have rendered obsolete this Confucian humanity and righteousness: King Zheng defeated the last of the independent states and acclaimed himself ruler of the empire. A new order demanded a new title – the Zhou rulers had merely been called 'kings':

'Insignificant as I am,' King Zheng said, 'I have raised troops to punish the rebellious princes, and with the aid of the sacred power of our ancestors all six kings have been punished as they deserved, so that at last the empire is pacified. Now unless we create the dignity of a new title, how can we record our achievements for posterity? Pray discuss the question of our title.'

The prime minister Wang Guan, the Grand Counsellor Feng Jie and the Chief Steward Li Si replied: 'In the past the Five Emperors ruled over a hundred square miles of territory, beyond which there were barons and barbarians. The distant barons were free to pay homage or not as they pleased; the emperor had no control over them. Now Your Majesty has raised forces to punish tyrants, subjugating all the lands within the Four Seas; your provinces are everywhere and the law codes have been unified. This is something never achieved before, which not even the Five Emperors could match. We have therefore consulted learned men and, as long ago there were the Heavenly Sovereign, Earthly Sovereign and Supreme Sovereign, of whom the last named was paramount, we presume to suggest the exalted title Supreme Sovereign. Your Majesty's commands should be called "edicts", your orders "decrees"; and you should refer to yourself as "our royal self".'

The king then announced, ' "Supreme" may be omitted but "Sovereign" will be adopted along with the ancient title of "Emperor". Let me be called Sovereign Emperor.'[9]

But Xunzi was proved right. The First Emperor died in 210 BC and his son was unable to retain power. Within a few years the empire disintegrated. Historians ascribe the first revolt to a peasant, Chen She, who was called for corvee duty in the capital. Realizing that he would arrive late because of the inclement weather, he decided he had nothing to lose by taking up arms: he would have been put to death on reaching the capital anyway. By 206 BC the empire had been united again under the leadership of another peasant, Liu Bang, who became the Han emperor Gaozu. Determined to distance themselves from the tyranny of the Qin, the Han set about restoring a Confucian heritage. Xunzi's vision was vindicated as Han historians ascribed the Qin's fall to its lack of humanity and righteousness:

> The empire of Qin was at this time by no means small or weak. Its base at Yongzhou, a stronghold within the pass, was the same as before. The humble position of Chen She could not compare with the Lords of Qi, Yan, Zhao, Han, Wei Song and Zhongshan. The improvised weapons from hoes and branches could not match the sharpness of spears and battle-pikes. His small band of conscripts was nothing beside the nine armies. His stratagems and methods of warfare were far inferior to those of men of earlier times. Yet Chen She succeeded where they had failed. Why was this, when in ability, size, power and strength his forces came nowhere near the eastern kingdoms that had formerly opposed Qin? Qin began with an insignificant amount of territory yet reached the power of a great state, and for a hundred years it made all the other lords pay homage. It became master of the whole empire and established itself within the pass, yet when a single commoner rose in opposition, its ancestral temples toppled, its ruler died by the hands of men, and it was derided by the world. Why? Because it failed to rule with humanity and righteousness and to realize that the power to attack and the power to retain what one has thereby won are not the same.[10]

The Han dynasty reclaimed the Mandate of Heaven, but their Confucian rule utilized much of the Legalist legacy. A bureaucracy largely replaced feudal lords and, over the next thousand years, the method of recruitment by merit, first by recommendation and later by a competitive examination system, provided officials to govern the empire.

The emperor's power was meant to be kept in check by the criticism of his ministers, although this was a risky undertaking and thus criticism was usually couched in literary and historical allusions, often taken from *The Book of Odes*. Traditionally, these folksongs had been compiled to bring intelligence of the people's mood: the idea being that songs expressed their feelings. The emperor continued to send out ministers among the people, a fact noted by Marco Polo in his description of Kublai Khan's rule almost 1,500 years later:

> Now you must know that the Emperor sends his Messengers over all his Lands and Kingdoms and Provinces, to ascertain from his officers if the people are afflicted by any dearth through unfavourable seasons, or storms or locusts, or other like calamity; and from those who have suffered in this way no taxes are exacted for that year; nay more, he causes them to be supplied with corn of his own for food and seed. Now this is undoubtedly a great bounty on his part. And when winter comes, he causes inquiry to be made as to those who have lost their cattle, whether by murrain or other mishap, and such persons not only go scot free, but get presents of cattle. And thus, as I tell you, the Lord every year helps and fosters the people subject to him.[11]

Periodically the emperor would also go on 'tours of inspection'. These were dreaded by local officials and those who were expected to provide provisions for his retinue.

China's modern Communist rulers, despite the rejection of Confucianism and the imperial system, today use the same word from classical Chinese to describe their 'tours of inspection'. No doubt they hope to gain legitimacy among the people for the continuation of their power, in just the same way as did the emperors of old.

Mao Zedong was not averse to this use of traditional methods of statecraft, as Hugh Trevor-Roper noticed in 1968:

Today Peking is once again the capital of the Middle Kingdom, Chairman Mao, like the Son of Heaven, is to live for ten thousand years. The Europeans are again outer barbarians, whom the self-sufficient Celestial Empire has no need to know. The usages of international diplomacy, of the comity of nations, have been rejected; and foreign embassies provide the means not of negotiation but of tribute: of the enforced kowtow, of the sacked legation, and of periodic humiliation of a vast, impervious, conformist bureaucracy. Such is the revenge of history on those who ignore it.[12]

This was written at the height of the Cultural Revolution and Trevor-Roper saw parallels with the late, isolationist Qing. But Mao preferred to see himself as resembling the First Emperor: a progressive who discarded the old, feudal practices of Confucianism to bring in a new order, in line with Marxism's interpretation of history.

The emperors of the Qin and the Qing shared totalitarianism in common with Mao, and were equally feared and hated. Matteo Ricci, in the sixteenth century, noted that the people lived in terror of the Wanli emperor and that he, in turn, seemed 'as if in the land of his greatest enemy who wishes to kill him', his life 'a reflection of hell'. Yuan Shikai, president of the new republic of China from 1911, sought to join the ranks of these feared and hated men; within a few years he had started calling himself emperor:

No doubt, Yuan was a monster. Sometimes in the news despatches that reached us in America we were led to think of him as a progressive president of a great republic that was striving to forget the traditions of old empire. We were asked to think of him as a noble personage who came to the aid of his country in times of stress. It was acknowledged, even by his bitterest enemies – and they seemed to be numbered by the tens of thousands – that he was a powerful man. He was thought to be the only man, after the Manchu dynasty had been overthrown, who should be president, because it was thought that he was the only man who could unite the various political factions. He held China together in a fashion, until vain ambition rose to the surface and the country beheld the real Yuan.[13]

Sitwell observes a general disillusionment with their rulers among the Chinese in the Republican period:

I do not believe that either Emperor or Republic, or any General, was ever popular in Peking. It must be remembered that the former Emperors of the Manchu Dynasty were never 'Chinese Emperors', as they are often loosely called, but Emperors *of* China; originally they had belonged to one more of the several foreign dynasties, ruling over savage tribes, which had imposed themselves by force (and the Chinese, though tolerant, despise both foreigner and force) for a term of two or three centuries upon a peaceful people; while, on the other hand, the Republic was a new idea (and the majority of Chinese are by nature violently opposed to new ideas).[14]

But his explanation, that they were hated because they were either foreign or new, is not entirely satisfactory. Even the emperors of the dynasty regarded as the apogee of Chinese culture, the Tang, were 'foreigners': they came from the peoples of the north-west. But they became so assimilated and, more importantly, they ruled over so peaceful and prosperous an empire, that their 'foreignness' was overlooked. Nevertheless, the first Tang emperors felt they needed some help to legitimize their rule. Their surname was 'Li' and they thus claimed that they were descendants of the Daoist Laozi, who had the same surname.

Mao was unique in looking back only as far as the Qin: but he was restricted by Marxist historiography and the need to denounce the old even as he was using its methods to legitimize his reign. Most emperors have looked for their exemplars to the mythical Sage Emperors: among them the Yellow Emperor, Yao, Shun and Yu. These are the legendary founders of Chinese civilization: they controlled the floods, invented agriculture, the wheel, the compass and sericulture, and everything else on which traditional Chinese culture is founded. More importantly, they fought and defeated demons who threatened the stability and prosperity of their rule. The

Chinese have always euhemerized their gods and the Yellow Emperor accordingly has a 'tomb' at the foot of Mount Qiao in Shaanxi Province at which later, historical emperors have sacrificed and there are 'historical records' of the reigns of Yao and Shun in *The Book of History*: 'Looking into the distant past, we find that Emperor Yao . . . was reverent, intelligent, accomplished and mild. He was sincerely respectful and modest. His glory penetrated to the four corners of the empire, ascended to Heaven above, and descended to earth below. . . . The population were well nourished and prosperous and therefore the kingdom was harmonious.'[15]

Confucius was clear about the duties of the ruler towards the people:

Zikong asked Confucius about government. He replied, 'Give them enough food, sufficient arms and sufficient reason to make them trust you.' Zikong said, 'If one had to give up one of these three, which should one give up first?' 'Give up arms.' 'And if one had to give up one of the remaining two . . .?' 'Give up food. Death has been with us since the beginning of time but when there is no trust the people will have nothing to stand on.'[16]

And his perception explains Sitwell's observation: emperors were accepted, foreigners or Chinese, if they showed themselves capable of rule by maintaining stability and more or less left the people alone to manage their own lives. Colquhoun was unusual among observers of imperial China in understanding something of this:

The great fact to be noted, as between the Chinese and their Government, is the almost unexampled liberty which the people enjoy, and the infinitesimally small part which Government plays in the scheme of national life. It is the more necessary to emphasise this, that a contrary opinion is not uncommon among those who are unacquainted with the country. The Chinese have perfect freedom of industry and trade, of locomotion, of amusement, and of religion, and whatever may be required for regulation or protection is not supplied by Act of Parliament or by any kind of Government interference, but by voluntary associations; of these the Government takes no cognisance, though it may sometimes come into collision with them – never to the disadvantage of the popular institution.[17]

The Chinese imperial bureaucracy was never extensive enough to rule the grass-roots of society. It depended heavily on local gentry and village-level organizations. Totalitarianism, with its tentacles reaching down into every household, has only been made possible with the increased communications of the modern era.

The rulers of China have always been isolated: few people had contact with them, even ambassadors accompanying foreign embassies were not assured of an audience:

> The prime minister of the king of the Alechan told us that a sight of the Emperor is not easily obtained. One year, when his master was ill, he was obliged to take his place at Peking, in the ceremony of the temple of the ancestors, and he then hoped to see the Old Buddha, on his way down the peristyle, but he was altogether mistaken in his expectation. As minister, the mere representative of his monarch, he was placed on the third file, so that, when the Emperor passed, he saw absolutely nothing at all. 'Those who are in the first line,' he said, 'if they are cautiously dextrous, may manage to get a glimpse of the yellow robe of the son of heaven; but they must take heed not to lift up their heads, for such an audacity would be considered a great crime, and be punished very severely.'[18]

Matteo Ricci himself never met the Wanli emperor, despite his long residence at the court of Peking, and an account of the next emperor is intended more to flatter the French king to whom it is addressed than to offer a truthful depiction of the Kangxi emperor:

> The Jesuits, whom Your Majesty sent [to China] some years ago, were astonished to discover at the ends of the earth something that hitherto they had seen only in France: namely, a Prince who, like you, sire, combines a genius that is both sublime and practical and with a

heart worthy of his empire, who is master of himself and of his subjects and is equally adored by his people and respected by his neighbours. . . . A Prince, in short, uniting in his person most of the great qualities that heroes have, who could be the most accomplished monarch to reign on this earth for a long time were it not that his reign coincided with that of Your Majesty.[19]

Marco Polo was equally complimentary about Kublai Khan, emperor of China from 1257 to 1294:

Now am I come to the part of our Book in which I shall tell you of the great and wonderful magnificence of the Great Kaan now reigning, by name CUBLAY KAAN; *Kaan* being a title which signifieth 'The Great Lord of Lords', of Emperor. And of a surety he hath good right to such a title, for all men know for a certain truth that he is the most potent man, as regards forces and lands and treasure, that existeth in the world, or ever hath existed from the time of our First Father Adam until this day. All this I will make clear to you for truth, in this book of ours, so that every one shall be fain to acknowledge that he is the greatest Lord that is now in the world, or ever hath been. And now ye shall hear how and wherefore.[20]

Those on the Macartney Embassy reported favourably on the Qianlong emperor's etiquette: 'His manner was dignified, but affable and condescending; and his reception of us was very gracious and satisfactory.'[21] And on the pomp and ceremony of the court: 'Thus I have seen Solomon in all his glory. I use this expression as the scene recalled a puppet show of that name which I recollect to have seen in my childhood and which made so strong an impression that I thought it the highest pitch of human felicity and greatness.'[22]

Chinese historians have not been so kind. The official history of a dynasty was always written by its successor dynasty who had assumed the Mandate. In order to legitimize their own usurpation of power, the last emperor of any dynasty was invariably portrayed as weak, evil or both. In contrast, founding emperors were depicted as strong, capable and moral rulers.

The women who have gained power in Chinese history have been vilified. Empress Wu reigned in her own right from 690 to 705, although she had considerable power during the reigns of the two preceding emperors. A few years after her death another woman briefly held power, albeit indirectly – Empress Wei. The attitude of many to this period is summed up by a Song historian who describes it as 'the calamity of the empresses Wu and Wei'. The truth is probably more complicated: a tenth-century stele unearthed in Sichuan Province is inscribed: 'in time of natural disaster, floor or drought, those prayers of the soldiers and the people who come here, at this temple of the Celestial Empress Wu, will certainly be answered'.

History has been similarly robust in its criticisms of the Dowager Empress Cixi, who, in effect, was ruler of China from 1884, in its last imperial decades. Willard Straight saw a 'nice-looking little old lady with a Roman nose, brown and neat',[23] but Reginald Johnston concurred with the Chinese view, and sought to refute her Western supporters by laying the responsibility for all China's ills on her shoulders in true Chinese fashion:

Had the 'Great' empress-dowager been the statesmanlike, wise and patriotic ruler some of her Western admirers declare her to have been, there is far more than a mere possibility that there would have been no China-Japan war in 1894, no necessity to alienate ports and concessions to Foreign Powers in 1898, no opposition on the part of court and government to measures of reform, no imperial association with any such movement as that of the Boxers, no siege of the Legations, no indemnities, no revolution, no 'republic', no collapse of law and order, no loss of Mongolia, Turkestan, Tibet, Jehol, and Manchuria. All 'unequal treaties' might have been abrogated by mutual agreement long ago without any detriment to her friendly relations with other countries, and China might now be taking a leading part in the great task of saving humanity from the economic, nationalistic and other perils in which the whole world is involved to-day.[24]

Lady Susan Townley found the image of the cruel and ruthless autocrat difficult to reconcile with 'this friendly little woman with the brown face of a kindly Italian peasant',[25] but if Princess Der Ling's records are to be believed, Cixi was a woman of formidable character and self-assurance:

> I have often thought that I am the most clever woman that ever lived, and others cannot compare with me. Although I have heard much about Queen Victoria . . . and read a part of her life which someone has translated into Chinese, still I don't think her life was half so interesting and eventful as mine. . . . England is one of the great powers of the world, but this has not been brought about by Queen Victoria's absolute rule. She had the able men of parliament back of her at all times and of course they discussed everything until the best result was obtained, then she would sign the necessary documents and really had nothing to say about the policy of the country. Now look at me. I have 400,000,000 people, all dependent on my judgement. . . .[26]

And she sees her reign in very different terms from Johnston, while accepting that her judgement failed in the case of the Boxers:

> I have been very successful so far, but I never dreamt that the Boxer movement would end with such serious results for China. That is the only mistake I have made in my life. I should have issued an Edict at once to stop the Boxers practising their belief, but both Prince Tuan and Duke Lan told me that they firmly believed that the Boxers were sent by heaven to enable China to get rid of all the undesirable and hated foreigners. Of course they meant mostly missionaries.[27]

Johnston was prepared to accept that she was shrewd, although this was used to further her deceit; women were easy targets:

But if she loved flattery she was shrewd enough to know that others loved it too, and her knowledge of human nature was sound enough to enable her to turn the heads of many of the Legation ladies who attended her receptions. She hated them all, but it amused her to observe how readily they absorbed her loving assurances of esteem. She entertained parties of foreign ladies several times before, as well as after, the siege of the Legations; and it is on record that on one of those occasions she murmured gently to each of the wives of the foreign plenipotentiaries, 'We are all of one family', and sent them home full of admiration for her grace and charm and rejoicing in tangible tokens of her affectionate regard. Very soon afterwards, as an American missionary observed, she was issuing edicts ordering her troops to slaughter all the foreigners within reach, so that only the Chinese and Manchu contingents of the 'one family' might be left surviving.[28]

But whatever the true version, and there have been many to chose from, she was a ruler of China when the ways of humanity and benevolence had fallen into disuse and imperial power was no longer checked.

As a woman, however, her legitimacy was always in question. This had also been a problem for Empress Wu, who had responded by producing a Buddhist document which foretold that Maitreya, the future Buddha, would appear in female form to rule the world. The document was, needless to say, forged by supportive monks. Cixi claimed to be the reincarnation of Guanyin, a very popular boddhisattva who, in China, became associated with an indigenous female deity, a Goddess of Mercy:

> I have said that the empress-dowager loved to pose as the 'Goddess of Mercy' . . . for she believed, and was encouraged by the court to believe, that she was actually an incarnation of that boddhisattva. Thereby hangs a tale which we may, if we choose, regard as a tragic one. It happened that in 1908 the empress-dowager was not the only avatar of the boddhisattva Kuan-Yin then existing in China. Every Dalai Lama is – according to Lamaistic

doctrine – an incarnation of that divine being, and the Dalai Lama had recently arrived at the sacred mountain of Wu-t'ai in the Chinese province of Shansi.

. . . Shortly afterwards – in September – the incarnate Kuan-Yin from Tibet processed at the invitation of the court from Wu-t'ai to Peking, where he was accorded a state-reception by the incarnate Kuan-Yin of China. For a short time, therefore, there were two Kuan-Yins living in Peking at the same time. Within a few weeks, however, there were no longer two but only one, that one being the Dalai Lama. His rival, the empress-dowager, was dead. In her death the lama fraternity in Peking, and many of the Peking populace, found a strik-ing illustration of the well-known fact that if two 'Living Buddhas' or two incarnations of the same boddhisattva are rash enough to manifest themselves simultaneously in the same locality, one of them must perforce withdraw to another world to await in patience the result of one more revolution of the wheel of metempsychosis.[29]

Mao perhaps ought to have considered how Cixi met her end before taking on himself the mantle of the hated First Emperor: it is dangerous to rewrite history in China, for tradi-tional explanations have a habit of rising, inexorably, to the surface. The First Emperor is viewed as standing outside the tradition of rule by virtue and has always been hated: 'he failed to rule with humanity and righteousness and to realize that the power to attack and the power to retain what one has thereby won are not the same'. In a country steeped in history, the Communist leaders ignore it at their peril.

10

COMMUNIST CHINA

There is little to choose between overshooting the
mark and falling short.

Confucius, *The Analects*, 11.16

Even so rigid a faith as Communism, if for the sake
of convenience it had temporarily to be accepted,
would find itself powerless to alter the national
character: on the contrary, the national character
would very soon modify Communism to suit itself,
or even assimilate it, as it has always assimilated
foreign conquerors.

Osbert Sitwell, *Escape with Me!*, p. 202

On 1 October 1949 Mao Zedong stood with his comrades on
the high balcony of Tiananmen, the Gate of Heavenly Peace
at the entrance to the Forbidden City, and in his high reedy
voice, eerily captured on the remote newsreels of the time,
proclaimed the birth of the People's Republic of China. Ever
since then China has been a matter of unfinished, and rapidly
changing, business.

A great deal of the traditional China described in preceding chapters survives under the red banners and the rhetoric
of Communism; but in many respects it is of course an entirely
new country. In less than a century, from the revolution
of 1911 which disposed of the last imperial dynasty, China
has developed from a pre-industrial to a modern society –
although in many rural areas one might still fancy oneself
two thousand years adrift in time. The change has been painful, even brutal: scores of millions have died in the upheavals,
struggles, campaigns and disasters that have characterized
New China since its inception. And the horrifying suppression

of the democracy movement in Tiananmen Square on 4 June 1989 shows that there is struggle still to come.

The exact flavour of Communist China is given by Mao Zedong's account of 'democratic dictatorship', that useful concept employed by most regimes describing themselves as Communist:

'You are dictatorial'.

My dear sirs, what you say is correct. That is just what we are. All the experiences of the Chinese people, accumulated in the course of successive decades, tell us to carry out a people's democratic dictatorship. This means that the reactionaries must be deprived of the right to voice their opinions; only the people have that right. Who are the 'people'? At the present stage in China, they are the working class, the peasantry, the petty bourgeoisie, and the national bourgeoisie.

Under the leadership of the working class and the Communist Party, these classes unite to create their own state and elect their own government so as to enforce their dictatorship over the henchmen of imperialism – the landlord class and bureaucratic capitalist class as well as the reactionary clique of the Kuomintang which represents those classes and their accomplices. The people's government will suppress such persons. It will only allow them to behave themselves properly. It will not allow them to speak or act wildly. Should they do so, they will be instantly curbed and punished. The democratic system is to be carried out within the ranks of the people, giving them freedom of speech, assembly and association. The right to vote is given only to the people, not the reactionaries.

These two things, democracy for the people, and dictatorship for the reactionaries when combined, constitute the people's democratic dictatorship. . . .

Why must things be done in this way? Everyone is very clear on this point. If things were not done like this, the revolution would fail, and people would suffer, and the state would perish.

'Don't you want to abolish state power?'

Yes, we want to but not at the present time. We cannot afford to abolish state power just now. Why not? Because imperialism still exists, because, internally, revolutionaries still exist and classes still exist.[1]

China has had a succession of elaborately drafted constitutions since 1949, all paying lip-service to political and human rights and asserting the power of the 'people' (whether qualified, as above, or not). But in fact the Party is supreme, and in the Party the old comrades of the pre-1949 struggle, especially of the celebrated 'Long March' of 1934–5, are yet more supreme; and among them one man – more recently, Deng Xiaoping; but for a long time, although not without interruptions, Mao Zedong – is the most supreme, as Thubron shows:

The dead catalyst of China's past vision and terror lies in a vast mausoleum in Tiananmen Square. Several times a week a serpent of pilgrims, four abreast, wraps itself quarterway around the square, curls beneath the granite Monument to the People's Heroes and approaches the tomb of Mao in sudden quiet. They are dowdy in green and blue, and most have come in from the provinces. They number many thousands.

Whatever may have happened since Mao's death, the poetry of Revolution still sings around his tomb. Massed sculptures of Struggle and Plenty rear to either side in a surge of soldiery and sheaf-waving land-girls. The Little Red Book is held aloft. Yet even here, like some ineradicable disease, tradition has leaked in. The 120-foot Monument to the People's Heroes resembles nothing so much as a Confucian memorial stele, the terraces of the mausoleum mimic those of the emperors' halls and its yellow roof-friezes are haunted by the saffron canopies of the Forbidden City. As the pilgrims trickled under the dwarfing colonnades, their tread slowed to a shuffle and their caps were cautiously doffed. What they were feeling as we entered the cenotaph of their dead god and tormentor, I could not tell. I tried to listen to their muttered conversations, as if they might yield up some posthumous key. But the only remarks I caught were about children and train-tickets.

We entered a hall where a marble colossus of Mao gazed at us from behind a bank of flowers. Our feet turned silent on the crimson carpet. Two military policemen with fixed bayonets and fiercely polished boots (the only ones I ever saw) stood rigid to either side. Then we passed into the mausoleum.

It was airy and spacious, lit evenly from pale lights in the coffered ceiling. Somewhere a fan whirred. In the centre, roped off all around, the crystal coffin looked small, almost temporary. Here was none of the violently illumined, claustrophobic theatre of Lenin's tomb in Red Square, but a simple lying-in-state. The crowd bifurcated round it and was forbidden to stop walking. We were in its presence for barely half a minute.

The embalmed body lay stiff and shapeless under its mantle, only the head exposed. I did not feel as if I were looking at anything that had been a man. Nestled in its jowls and double chin, the face held a sheen like discoloured ivory. Its eyes were closed, the hair swept back from the high forehead, thin and barely greyed. All that distinguished it were the wide convexities of the cheeks, and a faint, ashy discolouration which spread around the nose and upper lip. Otherwise it presented a heaped enigma. And those who passed by on either side were expressionless too, hurried on by plain-clothes security men. The whole uneasy ceremony seemed to have no heart at all, as if this corpse now belonged only to the terribleness of history. China was already moving away from it. I told myself: this man wreaked havoc and change on a quarter of mankind. Yet I passed in and out of that awesome presence as if through a void. He looked altogether smaller than that. It was strange.[2]

China's Communist Party came into existence in Shanghai in 1921. It was supported by the Soviet Union from then until 1960 when Mao and Moscow quarrelled. Its first twenty-five years were precarious; civil war with the Kuomintang Party under Chiang Kaishek alternated with uneasy alliances between them, first to oppose the northern warlords (1926–7) and later, from 1937 onwards, to fight the Japanese.

But in 1934–5 the Kuomintang nearly annihilated the Communists, who saved themselves only by a long and desperate escape through China's remoter provinces. This ignominious scramble for survival was transformed into heroic legend by the Party, a version of history accepted by such Western apologists for the Party as Edgar Snow and Harrison Salisbury. The latter describes it thus:

> Each revolution is carried out under its own legend. The American was fought with Valley Forge engraved in the hearts of the patriots, that ordeal from which George Washington and his men came forth steeled for victory.
>
> The French stormed the Bastille and in Petrograd in 1917 it was the Winter Palace. There were only seven prisoners in the Bastille; the Bolsheviks walked into a Winter Palace defended only by a handful of teenagers and some women. Never mind. These became the symbols of revolution.
>
> China's Long March of 1934 was no symbol. It was a great human epic which tested the will, courage, and the strength of the men and women of the Chinese Red Army. It was not a 'march' in the conventional sense, not a military campaign, not a victory. It was a triumph of human survival, a deadly, endless retreat from the claws of Chiang Kaishek; a battle that again and again came within a hair's breadth of defeat and disaster. It was fought without a plan. . . . In the end, it won China for Mao Zedong and his Communists.[3]

The Long March ended in the north-west of China, in Yanan, where the Communists established a base and made it a soviet state. Leaving the Kuomintang to conduct the bulk of the fighting against Japan, they bided their time and built their strength, waiting until the Japanese were defeated; and then they resumed the civil war with the Kuomintang, whom they routed in just three years.

This does not mean that the Communists were inactive against the Japanese. They kept up a guerrilla war against them, using techniques that proved successful later in North

Vietnam's war against the United States. Agnes Smedley reports what Communist army commanders told her:

> They sketched battle scenes, explaining how they avoided frontal engagements with a powerfully equipped enemy but instead prepared the whole battle region to serve in the lines or right behind them; how they attacked the enemy's flanks or rear, cut up his columns and destroyed their segments, and disrupted his lines of communication. . . . Of the civilian population they said: 'We move about among the people as freely as fish swimming in the ocean. By organizing and training the people we automatically eliminate traitors. We rest in the hearts of the people.'[4]

These techniques were equally effective against the Kuomintang after Japan's defeat. The Communists had a far more effective propaganda machine than their rivals, and while the civil war raged they succeeded in giving a favourable impression in those parts of the country they captured. Good report among the people proved a more powerful weapon than guns and grenades.

Yanan was the model for what China as a whole was intended to become when war was over. Visiting Western journalists were charmed by what they found there:

> Tang Cheng-kuo is only twenty-five, but she is the director of 1,500 amazons in the Women's Self-Defense Corps of Nankuo Hsien in Chin-Cha-Chi. She had been called to Yanan for special political training, so that I was able to have long talks with her about the activities of her Central Hopei amazons.
>
> There was nothing hard about Tang Cheng-kuo. She was a smallish girl with a shock of bobbed hair framing a triangular face, with regular teeth and steady brown eyes. Dressed simply in tunic and trousers – faded but clean, with her sleeves rolled and a portrait of Mao Tze-tung on a tiny celluloid badge pinned over her heart, she spoke quietly, in crisp, almost military accents. She was a very self-possessed young woman.

'Only about 800 of our girls are what you might call fighters,' she said. 'They are recruited from the unmarried or childless women in our villages, between the ages of eighteen and twenty-five. We are armed, trained in the use of rifle, grenade, and mine, and given a knowledge of military tactics. Sometimes we engage the enemy alone as a unit, but mostly we work in co-ordination with the guerrillas and the Paluchun regulars.'

The older women were trained in intelligence activities, taught how to take care of the wounded, and given courses in what might be called the household duties of an army. During battle they were stretcher-bearers and food and ammunition porters, and upon occasion they fought.

Nor were Tang Cheng-kuo's amazons the only ones in Chin-Cha-Chi – there were thousands more like them organized in local units having little connection with one another. These groups were not, of course, regarded as mobile units, their work being principally to defend their villages and their homes. During quiet periods they stood sentry at village entrances or guarded road crossings, checking the credentials of all passers-by. On the arrival of Japs, the girls joined with the guerrillas, the militiamen, and the regulars in giving battle. They ambushed Jap transport, sniped at Jap columns, grenaded them from walls and rooftops when the enemy entered the villages.

She continued briskly, with gestures of her very expressive hands.

'Every year, usually around March 8th – International Women's Day – we hold general manoeuvres. The girls gather from all the Hsien villages, bringing their weapons and enough food for ten days. The meeting place is secret, of course, and is changed from year to year. The last meeting over which I presided before coming to Yanan was held within four miles of the nearest enemy strong point and only ten miles from the Peiping-Hankow Railway.

'We try usually to work out some practical problem. On this occasion our problem was to destroy commu-

nications between the Jap strong points at Peilu and
Ankuo, about two miles apart. And, if need be, we were
to be prepared to fight, too. First I sent out scouts to
find out how many Japs there were in each of the strong
points. This information they got from the villagers near
by. The scouts went out in pairs, one staying on watch
while the other returned with a report.'

I offered her a cigarette. She refused it. 'I never
smoke,' she said smilingly – and I suspected that what
she really meant was, 'I have no time or thought for such
things.'[5]

Although drilling and skirmishing were a necessary preparation for the real enemy – the Kuomintang – Yanan's Communists did not neglect other aspects of preparation for the
coming Utopia. They established a university, Yanan Daxue
or 'Yanda' for short; its classes and dormitories occupied caves
in the Yanan hillsides where the Communists lived. The university's curriculum was wholly devoted to practical subjects:

Most of Yanan University's thirteen hundred students
are married. However, school regulations forbid husbands and wives to live together, except on Saturday
nights when special 'Guest Caves' are made available by
the school authorities.

'Keeping them apart during the week not only enables
boys and girls to study better, with fewer distractions,
but at the same time sweetens love between married
couples,' I was told by Chow Yang, the president of the
university. When I questioned the students about this
rule they would not discuss it.

Children live in the women's dormitories with their
mothers, who form labor exchange brigades through
which the mothers take their turns, by groups, in caring
for the children. This seemed to work out satisfactorily
and everyone appeared quite happy about it. The girls
apparently felt that they might have their cake and eat
it too – that is to say, they could have a husband and
a family, and still obtain an education. The education

they got at Yanda (the popular name for Yanan University) was wholly a practical one, so that Yanda is hardly a university in the Western sense. 'The principal characteristic of our new educational program,' Chow Yang explained, 'is that it is based firmly upon practical realities. Until last year we modelled our curriculi upon those of foreign institutions, placing too much emphasis upon such studies as the classics, philosophy, and abstract sciences. We paid too much respect to foreign forms in literature and art and neglected native Chinese forms. As a result, our students left Yanda wholly unfit to meet the urgent demands of wartime environment.

'Today our students spend at least three months of the year obtaining practical experience – the equivalent of your laboratory work. A student in banking works in a bank. A student of law is attached to a law court. A student of practical science gains appropriate experience in a factory. A student of administration takes employment in a Government office.'

Students also participate in the Production Movement. Last year they were already 60% self-sufficient in food, having cultivated and harvested their own fields of wheat, millet and vegetables and raised their own meat on the hoof.[6]

A diet of practicalities might have taken the place of philosophy and classics, but the arts of music and drama were not entirely neglected. Named after China's greatest twentieth-century writer, Lu Xun, there existed in Yanan a revolutionary college to provide musicians and actors to entertain, instruct and encourage the masses:

Connected with Yanda is the Lu Hsun College of Arts and Literature, popularly called Lu I. There are about three hundred students of music and drama at Lu I, which occupies an abandoned Catholic church about three miles from the city. The church proper is used as an auditorium for student meetings, dramatic performances, and such, while the old converts' resident quarters have been turned into dormitories. The boys and girls are chiefly from the frontline areas. After two years they are sent back to the various fronts to organize dramatic plays, musical entertainments, and the like. The sexes were dressed alike, in simple trousers and belted blouse. Their interest in one another seemed to be confined to that required for enthusiastic co-operation in their studies.

The place was a bedlam. A high soprano practised scales while a drummer rapped out an intricate figure. A few yards away a student with the face of an esthete seemed quite undisturbed as he played his battered 'cello. In a dormitory cell a lusty-voiced girl from Honan sang a plaintive folksong to the accompaniment of a dozen Chinese fiddles played by her room-mates. In the courtyard three plays were being rehearsed – war plays whose simple plots were based upon true incidents such as an heroic deed or a Japanese atrocity. They were simply but powerfully told, and told in a language understandable by the peasant and the soldier about whom they were written, and for whom they were to be performed. Later these same students would troop from village to village, performing for the *laopaishing* – the peasantry. . . .

The Communists take their culture seriously. Artists, writers, musicians, educators, dramatists, and newspapermen meet regularly, to discuss their problems frankly and criticize each other and their work. There were about forty present at the meeting I attended. Most of those who came from Shanghai were as far from the peasant folklore of hinterland China as James Joyce is from Confucius. Under war conditions, away from Shanghai, the literati resembled fish out of water. It was almost impossible for them not to look down upon the ignorant peasants, the workers and soldiers, who retorted by rejecting them. Without a public, they wrote, painted, and made music for themselves, ignoring the common folk below their cultural and intellectual level. If the peasant failed to appreciate good literature and art, that was his misfortune. Art could not debase itself by talking down to the masses. Far-seeing Mao Tze-tung observed this and decided that it was no good. Calling a meeting of all cultural workers, he flayed them for their high and mighty airs, warned them of retrogression and decay if they persisted. They must adjust themselves to new conditions, a new society – a society unlike the feudal Shanghai aristocracy of intellectuals, students and wealthy patrons, but a new democratic society created by and for the peasant, the worker, and the soldier.

'For this you must go to the people, must strive to understand them before you can ever hope to have them understand you,' he continued. 'You must study their dialects as mediums of expression. You must study their sentiments, their local customs and habits for content. You must learn to love them for what they are, not for what you think they should be.'

This was wartime, he pointed out, and it was the duty of the cultural worker to contribute his talents to the war effort. For this he must not try to introduce new and bewildering forms of expression but must work with the familiar forms accepted by the people themselves. The people's traditional music, art, literature, and drama must serve as basic moulds for new wartime content. New forms must be rooted in these and evolve from them.

Yanan's literati took Mao Tze-tung's words to heart with amazingly good results.[7]

The early years of the People's Republic were a period of mixed fortunes for China's new leaders. The Soviet Union gave money and practical help, but the Korean War was a drain. In China itself the masses in general approved of the new dynasty in the Forbidden City – the Party, although opening the main palaces to public view, had given itself luxurious quarters around the Central Southern Lake in the Forbidden City's western park – because many abuses had been removed, and a new hopeful spirit was abroad. But there were straws in the wind: terrible scenes of bloodshed and bullying had occurred in the land reform campaign, in which landlords were beaten, humiliated, and turned out of their property or killed; and even before 1949 intellectuals had been persecuted in Yanan and other areas as they were 'liberated', because Mao Zedong distrusted and disliked them.

A five-year plan was announced, co-operatives were organized, counter-revolutionaries were arrested and punished. Mao Zedong announced that all was proceeding so well that it was time for anyone and everyone to voice their feelings openly about how matters stood in New China: 'Let a hundred flowers bloom,' he said, inviting open debate. Such an outburst of criticism followed that the Party leadership, alarmed, had to clamp down, claiming that the Hundred Flowers call had been a ploy to flush out 'bad elements'. There followed a harsh campaign of 'rectification' in which hundreds of thousands, mainly intellectuals, were branded 'Rightists' and punished by exile to the remote countryside or incarceration in the growing gulag of labour camps:

> By the mid-1950s the intellectuals seemed to have won the leadership's confidence. Bracketed until then as part of the bourgeoisie, their social status was reclassified during the Hundred Flowers campaign by Zhou Enlai. 'The overwhelming majority of the intellectuals', he said, 'have become government workers in the service of socialism and are already part of the working class.' . . . But Mao took a more critical view as the wave of scholarly criticism broke over the Party during the campaign. Most intellectuals, he concluded, had not yet managed to shed their 'bourgeois world outlook . . . and unite with the workers and peasants'.
>
> As many as 200,000 intellectuals were labelled as 'Rightists' in the reaction to the Hundred Flowers, prevented from teaching or writing, and sent to work for long periods in the countryside.[8]

Very few of those who thus suffered ever fully recovered; after release from prison or return from exile they kept their Rightist stigma with all its handicaps, and were liable to fresh persecution when any new campaign started. They could not hope for promotion at work or preferment in the Party. When the Cultural Revolution started, the Hundred Flowers survivors were instantly resubmerged in nightmare.

A personal account of suffering in the Hundred Flowers campaign is included in B. Michael Frolic's anthology of voices from China's experience under Communism. As with all the accounts Frolic collected, the identity of the speaker remains concealed:

> It was 1957 and the Party launched the Hundred Flowers campaign, which was supposed to provide an open forum to discuss and evaluate the Party's performance and policies since Liberation. It was a good idea in theory: get criticism out in the open so that mistakes could be corrected, so that inadequate Party members and cadres would be rooted out and Party policy would be reaffirmed after a period of criticism. In my naïveté and through political miscalculation, I made the blunder of my life. I wasn't careful enough and acted recklessly. What happened was that I actually had believed the Party wanted honest criticism of its policies. And I had plenty of criticisms. Several times over the years we economists and planners had found ourselves restricted in our work by Party officials who mindlessly applied Marxist-Leninist theory to situations way beyond their understanding. Not every Party member had good character and only a few possessed enough expertise to understand our work. Often while we were trying to work out complicated statistical or planning concepts and policies, we would have to listen to endless political talk and empty phrases about the correct political line. I suppose that was one reason why I had hesitated from making a strong bid up till then to become a Party member. A part of me had always resisted the prospect of having to become a political organizer. Old Lin knew I felt this way, although we never talked about it openly. I figured he was my weathervane. I'd follow his actions whatever the campaign, since he would always know what to do.
>
> Well, I followed old Lin, right to my doom. Here's what happened. At the beginning of the campaign we all kept our mouths shut to see what it was all about. Even a political amateur like myself knew that was the

thing to do. But then, as public criticism of the Party
and of particular Party members mounted in intensity,
we let up our guard and plunged into the fray. Lin
himself led the attack on Party cadres in the ministry
who had been arrogant in dealing with lower-level Party
cadres and who had tried to substitute the wrong
political line for correct knowledge. Lin gave a speech
denouncing three of these officials, calling them rem-
nants of the Gao-Rao clique and people in need of serious
re-education by the masses. The gist of his criticism
spilled out into the press, and suddenly our school was
awash with debate and wall posters. Most of them
repeated Lin's attack: 'Down with the evil clique that has
betrayed the Party line.' Meetings were held to discuss
the criticisms, and Lin encouraged me to let myself
follow the correct political line.

So I did, but only privately to my girlfriend. We
talked about the campaign and what it meant. I said that
I agreed with Lin's criticism. The Party secretary was
right in exposing arrogant and corrupt Party members.
The Party was not perfect; it had made countless mistakes. Why should Party members not be called into
account just like ordinary citizens? Some Party policies
needed changing, and why not seize the chance now?
Even the Party was involved in this criticism. If the
Party leads such criticism of itself, then should we not
follow? To hold back and say nothing when we were
expected to join in the campaign might be seen as a lack
of faith in the Party. We talked a lot about these
things, but only to each other. We both hesitated to
take a public stance, even though our own Party
secretary, Lin, had committed himself on behalf of the
school.[9]

And then there happened something that has become all too
familiar in Communist China, where child has learned to
betray parent, friend to turn on friend, and lover to sacrifice
lover to the cause:

Well, the tide suddenly changed and she turned me in.
It was the blackest time of my life. She turned me in

without blinking an eye and we never spoke to each other again.

It happened like this. Lin had been spearheading the attack when a small item appeared in the press warning about 'those who cover up their own errors by attacking others.' A few days later a poster appeared at the school: 'All Party members must undergo self-criticism. It is not enough to criticize others.' Then there were more and they were more specific. Lin was accused of being 'a fox who could no longer hide his tail'; 'a white-eyed wolf'; and 'a cat who weeps over the death of a rat' (that is, one who doesn't say what he means).

Give sly old Lin credit for cunning. As soon as he saw what was happening, he changed course and began to admit all his mistakes. This saved his neck because somehow he managed to deflect the attack on himself to others. I was one of them. Lin admitted that he had made mistakes and that he had not criticized himself for his own arrogance and failings. But no one knocked him down for what he had said about the Party cadres. He wriggled off the hook without suffering a damning blow to his career. But others like myself weren't so lucky. If the big fish get away, then you settle for shrimp. So it was with me. The old Chinese proverb 'Beat the mule to terrify the horse' fitted my case perfectly. Old Lin jumped to the attack and suddenly there was earnest talk about 'those rightists who presume to destroy the Party by their words and deeds.' Who was the next target? I wondered, and there I was walking along the corridors when I saw my name on the wall, along with four others accused of being 'secret counter-revolutionaries in their hearts and deeds', 'stinking fish who must not be allowed to pollute our school any more.'

It was like a stab of ice in my heart. How could it be? Why me? What had I done? The answers came swiftly enough at my general meeting in which I had to stand at attention and hear my girlfriend in a clear confident voice tell the whole hall that I had secretly opposed the Party and had tried to enlist her co-operation in this effort. She said I had spoken maliciously of specific individuals, including Lin, and was plotting to restore the old pre-Communist government. She said that at first she thought she could persuade me to come forward and admit my mistakes, but now she realized I was too dangerous and had to be exposed. She looked straight ahead while reciting these lies. Her accusation, together with Lin's testimony that I was a secret rightist, sealed my fate.

They 'struggled' me and criticized me for several weeks. At first I just denied their accusations and refused to say anything else. I was enraged at her perfidy, at Lin's slippery behaviour, and at all the rest of them who unhesitatingly joined the hue and cry against me. It wasn't fair and I had become a convenient target, a handy scapegoat to get the rest off the hook. They dragged out my past and accused me of having a reactionary class background because my father had been a landlord under the Kuomintang. I said that I hadn't seen my family for eight years and that I came north to serve the revolution as a good cadre. But Lin and his toadies fabricated all kinds of accusations and my girlfriend sealed my fate. True, I had been politically naive, but I never consciously opposed the Party. I had assumed that the Party's request for criticism was legitimate and had confided my inner-most thoughts to someone I had trusted. Now my career was in ashes. Try as I might, I could not prevent them from putting the rightist hat on my head. The more I protested, the worse it became.[10]

There followed the usual fate of the victims in this and later campaigns: ostracism, deportation to a labour camp, 're-education', and highly qualified rehabilitation – if, with such stigma attached, it could be so called:

For several weeks I stayed at the school, took meals by myself, and underwent struggle and criticism. I was forced to confess to a number of rightist crimes, which included 'trying to undermine the Party's authority at the school'; and 'plotting with others to restore Kuomintang supremacy.' I wrote a confession that took weeks to finish, and then they sent me to Hulin, an isolated farm for cadres in the northeast, 100 kilometres from the Soviet border. There must have been a thousand of us there. Conditions were primitive, the work harsh. We spent most of our time in the forests, planting, tending, and cutting trees. It was tough work and when we weren't on the job we would be in political study sessions. All of us were being re-educated, and some had been at Hulin from before the Hundred Flowers campaign. What a group we were! Some had been high-level cadres in Peking; many were Party members; all had stumbled and fallen at a critical time in their careers; all of us felt the injustice of what happened and our own powerlessness in the face of Party policy.

Most of my time at Hulin was spent outdoors or in rewording my confession. You see, they had trouble with this confession because, except for my father's landlord status, there was no other concrete flaw in my record. So they made me invent conspiracies and put words in my mouth. I finally just wrote what they told me to, and then things began to get better. Within a few months I was told 'your political attitude has improved,' and then I was released after having spent nearly two years there. Actually the last year wasn't so bad. The work had toughened me up, and I had grown used to the political re-education sessions. They taught me a lot. I was no longer a political simpleton. I had learned how to mask my true feelings and how to repeat the correct phrases when required. Still I was a 'broken reed,' someone who had a black mark on his record, and I knew that I could never expect much for my career again.[11]

The exhausting effect of political campaigns prevented the advance in economic strength and military development for which the Communist leadership longed. Losing patience, Mao initiated the madcap scheme of the 'Great Leap Forward' in 1958, an attempt to accelerate economic growth through collectivization of agriculture and industry. It ran until 1961 and resulted in disaster. As a result Mao fell from power; and it was to regain control of the Party that in 1966 he launched that even greater fiasco, the Cultural Revolution.

The Great Leap Forward was meant to propel China to Britain's 1958 level of industrial output in just fifteen years, and thereby usher in Utopia. On 1 September 1958 the journal *Red Flag* proudly predicted:

> After a period following the Transition to Ownership by the Whole People, the Productive Forces of Society will be expanded even more greatly; the Products of Society will be extremely Abundant; Communist Ideology, Consciousness and Moral Character of the entire people will be raised immensely, and Education will be Universal and raised to a Higher Level.[12]

The people, said Mao, would 'stride towards Communism with such speed that one day would equal twenty years'.

In 1958 the Party announced that steel production was to double in a single year. A yield of 10.7 million tons of steel was to be produced by means of the workers 'emancipating their minds, breaking with conventions, and carrying on a large-scale campaign of mass steel-making.' Accordingly workers in every kind of trade halted their own work in order to build blast furnaces wherever they could – in streets, courtyards, kitchens and fields. Because there was not enough equipment available for the building of standard furnaces, new methods of steel-making were proposed, including a method of 'stewing' steel in earthenware pots of the kind used for cooking. Anything made of iron or steel was contributed by every family – knives, axes, spades, window frames, camp beds, and so on. School hours were limited to the morning; in the afternoon children went out 'gleaning' coal for steel-making. Ideological enthusiasm was at fever pitch. . . . In the schools a show was put on each week in which long rows of teachers formed a Chinese dragon, exemplifying the strength of the People's Republic, and they danced along, overhauling two sorry figures dressed in Western clothes and representing the United States and Britain.[13]

The disastrous and predictable consequence was shortages and mass starvation which resulted, according to conservative estimates, in twenty million deaths.

The internecine Party warfare which followed the Great Leap Forward saw Mao lose his standing as Great Helmsman for a time, only to regain it in the way he knew best: by political in-fighting. At this he was a master. He was a soldier, not a statesman, and seemed only to flourish when he had enemies to defeat. Mao's public reason for launching the Cultural Revolution was the need to purge the Party of 'capitalist roaders'. For this phrase read 'Mao's opponents in the Party'.

> When the Cultural Revolution began strong adjectives were used to describe it. The Chinese press called it 'unprecedented' and 'earth-shaking', and indeed, as events proved, it well deserves both epithets in respect of its folly, destructiveness and savagery. It plunged a billion people into meaningless political struggles, and in doing so called forth some of the lowest and most corrupt aspects of human nature. It was a terrible time for the Chinese people and the human spirit.
>
> The Cultural Revolution was a vivid manifestation of the character of Mao and the Communist Party. To this day its shadow lies long and dark over China. It blighted lives and left deep scars; it stole from millions their chance of a normal childhood and education, of family life, of improvement and progress in material and personal respects. In short, it traumatized and embittered practically all the Chinese people. Until the Beijing Massacre of 4 June 1989 and its attendant circumstances, the Cultural Revolution was, among the many horrors of the Communist Party's 'New China', the worst.[14]

Nothing can substitute for the voices of those who actually lived through these events. To begin with, of course, practically everyone enthusiastically responded to Mao's call for permanent revolution, and waved the Little Red Book aloft in joy:

When the cultural revolution began, I was twenty-three years old, a third-year chemistry student at Amoy University. . . . I had a natural aptitude for my studies and was doing well. My political record was clean and I was an active member of the Youth League. I had fallen in love with a classmate, and we planned to get married as soon as I graduated and the state assigned me a job. That was still a year off, however, so in the meantime I was indulging myself in the pleasures and excitement of youth. . . . When the first big character poster appeared in Peking, we didn't really know what to do. Peking seemed a long way off, and so we waited cautiously for the provincial Party leadership to respond. Who could have predicted that a few months later we would be toppling these leaders and dragging the powerful Ye Fei and his wife out to face mass public criticism in the streets of Fuzhou?

All classes were stopped, and the university was in confusion. What was going on in Peking? What were we supposed to do? Who were the targets? Who would take the lead and strike the first blow? The safest course was to attack the most visible targets – the teachers, especially those who had a known class background. Party and Youth League members put up big character posters like those in Peking, using the same words and themes. We attacked a few professors and lecturers who should have been criticized long ago, either for their poor attitudes or their zealous worship of foreign things. Some posters merely observed that 'Professor Wang has more books published outside China on his bookshelves than Chinese books,' and then asked the question 'Why?' Others referred to 'Jiang, who has never mentioned Chairman Mao's Thought in any of his lectures,' and added that this poster was a 'solemn warning to Jiang to change his ways at once or face the wrath of the masses.' Another poster referred to 'the dozens of teachers who have been hiding their reactionary backgrounds from the masses who want to criticize them.'

Between June and November 1966, we locked up almost every university department head, deputy department head, professor, and lecturer. Every day we rounded them up and read them quotations from the works of Chairman Mao. We marched them off to the student dining halls to eat the same food that the students had to eat. No more fancy meals for them in the special professors' dining halls. No more getting fat on meat and fish while students were eating grain and leftovers. Every day they had to clean the lavatories and carry out the night soil. At night we made them write confessions 'asking Chairman Mao for punishment.' If we didn't like what they wrote, we made them do it again and again until they clearly showed how they had demeaned the Party and Chairman Mao in their lectures, how they had ignored socialism, and how they had deliberately spread the bourgeois life-style at the university. Once every three days we had a small struggle meeting, maybe with a few hundred persons, and once a week we mobilized a large struggle meeting with over a thousand people in attendance. That's when we really gave it to them. By that time, covered with honest dirt and night soil, fancy clothes and leather shoes looking no better than a peasant's clothing, their once-proud voices stilled by the fierce criticism of the assembled masses, they were a sorry spectacle indeed.

Most of them deserved their fate. Chairman Mao was right when he warned us always to be on guard against intellectuals. You can't trust intellectuals. They resist the Party line, become arrogant, develop a bourgeois way of thinking, and worship foreign things. Take old Wang, for example. When the Red Guards went to his place and took it apart, it was full of fancy scrolls and feudal Chinese art. Must have been worth a fortune. We dug out foreign coins and books, and you should have seen the furniture! He had closets full of leather shoes, fancy clothes, and junk like that. He even had a servant living in that apartment doing the cooking and cleaning. How can a socialist society tolerate people like that teaching the young? True, he was a leading specialist in physics and we needed his skills, but was it worth the cost, to keep this rotten way of life? Students who took Wang's classes never liked him. He treated us with contempt and barely noticed us. All he ever did was show up to lecture and then leave abruptly. We could never talk with him, never ask questions. There were many others who were arrogant like that. Old Jiang taught mathematics as if feudalism had never left China. We had to repeat theorems and equations endlessly; examinations were thrust upon us without warning; we could never talk out in class. It was just the way education used to be in the time of the Manchus. We tolerated Jiang because he was a good mathematician, but was it worth perpetuating a feudal relationship in order to learn mathematics?[15]

In Peking itself, at the hub of affairs, where thousands of Red Guards from all over the country assembled in Tiananmen Square to cheer Mao, both the excitement and the subsequent disillusion began earlier. A journalist who started as a participant but changed into an increasingly worried observer explains what happened in the capital:

The posters were imaginative and colorful, and required considerable skill in execution. Since we were a group of intellectuals who were gifted with words (and many of us were also skilful practitioners of ink and brush), we had some of the best posters in the city. At the beginning, the poster writing seemed to be spontaneous, but as the Cultural Revolution developed, especially when two factions, the Red Flag and the Red Alliance, were locked in mortal combat, the poster war was well-planned and sophisticated. To write a good poster you first planned it out on typing paper. You decided the target and the tone of the poster. It was essential to decide the tone, how high to go. This was called *ding diaozi* (setting the tune). We'd compile a list of X's crimes and then decide what he should be; a 'contradiction among the people,' a 'counter-revolutionary element,' a 'three anti-element,' and so on. If the target was a cadre, we usually called him 'a capitalist roader,' but we also had other labels, such as 'royalist,' 'opportunist,' or 'a refuge for ghosts, freaks and monsters.' Two or three of us planned the poster, and then we got the best character writer to write out the text of the poster. Every faction had its own *xiucai*, a scholar who had great command of the Chinese language and of Mao's writings. We used Chinese brushes, paper and ink from the office, finished the poster, and then sought out the proper spot to paste it up. Some of the posters were true works of art, both in appearance to the eye and in content. Too bad they have all been destroyed.

In the beginning we criticized the top leaders in the bureau. That wasn't so difficult since Emperor Fang and Mao were universally disliked, and while Director Fu was all right for a high cadre, he still had his faults and it wasn't hard to find reasons for criticizing him. But once the outside work team came and took over the campaign, things began to change. It was clear that they were going to deflect criticism from the top Party people in the bureau. Indeed, it seemed that the targets of our criticism were actually colluding with' the work team. Quite a few of us backed away at that point, saying, 'It's another Hundred Flowers campaign designed to put us off our guard.' I was one of those, and instead of hanging around the bureau I went out on the streets to learn what was going on in Peking. It was my way of doing *chuan lian* (exchanging revolutionary experience with the Red Guards). I went to the centre of the city to Wangfujing and bought Red Guard newspapers for 2 cents a copy. They were publishing all sorts of stuff, including policy documents that had been stolen from government offices and the unpublished texts of Chairman Mao's speeches. You could spend days reading these newspapers and the thousands of wall posters. You could also bump into victims of Red Guard zeal, young men with their stove-pipe pants cut off at the knees, girls with their braids chopped off, and half-bald young men who had received a 'flying haircut' by a group of Red Guards. Later you would see groups of people wearing 'hats' and 'signs' being paraded around by the Red Guards. Things had changed on Peking's streets. My favourite restaurants had been shut down, as had the second-hand book stores. Chairman Mao's picture was everywhere, and his sayings blanketed Peking almost as deeply as the dust that blows in from the Gobi. People didn't linger on the side walks or in the shops, and now they always seemed to be on their way to some meeting. A rag-tag element had appeared, mainly young folk who were either Red Guards who had themselves been sent to the countryside but didn't want to leave, or 'black youth' (those who had earlier been sent down to live in the countryside but had returned illegally and were now hanging around Peking doing nothing except 'making revolution').

In the bureau the political struggles began in earnest after the work teams had been repudiated by Chairman Mao. The bureau soon split into two factions – the more radical Red Flag and the larger Red Alliance. Both claimed to be true supporters of Chairman Mao's revolutionary line, and they fought for months before Red Flag finally took over the bureau. Then we had a 'red terror' for over two years because the Red Flag faction wasn't content just to root out the true class enemies and those who had subverted Chairman Mao's line. Now the Red Flag became a bunch of extremists, attacking anybody who stood in their way – innocent and guilty, it didn't matter. It was a terrible time for those whom the Red Flag targeted as enemies and counter-revolutionaries. Of course, many deserved their fate – they deserved to be struggled, criticized, and sent down to do physical labor. There were basic ideological differences that had to be resolved, and not a few of us had been influenced by Liu Shaoqi's revisionist and bourgeois way of thinking. But a lot of the violence and the loss of life – for example, three cadres committed suicide because they couldn't endure the red terror of violent criticism and struggles – came not because the Red Flag faction was genuinely engaged in applying Chairman Mao's Thought, but because individual members of that group had become involved in power struggles while being misled by some clever conspiratorial elements. The notorious '516 group' was behind all this. '516' was a national conspiracy against Mao by a group on the extreme left who used the revolution for acquiring personal power. They duped

a lot of people and it took intervention from the very
highest places, Zhou Enlai himself, to expose and crush
them. Later, when the extremists had been removed
from power, we realized how we had all been duped.[16]

The '516 Group', better known as the 'Gang of Four', was
led by Mao's wife, Jiang Qing. It was blamed for the excesses
of the Cultural Revolution in order to protect Mao's reputation. The Cultural Revolution lasted from 1966 until 1976,
when Mao died; in his last years he was bedridden and feeble,
and obsessed with the history of imperial palace intrigues, so
it is probable that the struggle he had started was being continued by those around him in their efforts to settle the
succession.

Revolutions consume their own makers, of course, but they
hurt many others besides, and the Cultural Revolution was
no different. Many in China found themselves at the rough
end of a bitter process. The chief victims were those beaten
to death, or exiled and starved in the countryside, or deprived
of education, or terrorized and humiliated by rampaging Red
Guards. The greatest victim was China itself: the plunge into
anarchy wasted a whole generation, and put the country into
reverse. Not surprisingly, China now calls the Cultural Revolution 'The Ten Year Calamity'.

When Deng Xiaoping came to power in 1979 there was
a brief flurry of democratic hope. 'Democracy Wall' with its
'Big Character Posters' appeared in Peking, openly discussing
the Party's failings and criticizing the Cultural Revolution's
years of turmoil. The hero of the hour was a young worker,
Wei Jingsheng, who founded a magazine, *Explorations*, and
in it called eloquently for democracy. Unnerved, the Party
imprisoned Wei and moved Democracy Wall to a remote
suburb, shortly afterwards dismantling it altogether.

But this seemed a hiccup; there followed a decade of
what appeared to be quiet political liberalization to accompany the improving economic situation, itself the result of
adoption of Western economic practices. Most visitors and
commentators began to wax optimistic about China's future:
they foresaw increasing openness and democracy; China

seemed to be joining the world at last. The savage crackdown in Tiananmen Square in June 1989 therefore came as an appalling shock to many, although in the light of precedents it should not have done so. It showed that although the members of the Party gerontocracy in the Forbidden City were prepared to allow market forces into the economy, they were not in the slightest prepared to loosen their grip on political power.

What explains the fastness of the Party leaders' grip on power is their revolutionary history and its dream – in which at some point in the more arduous stretches of their biographies these old men almost certainly believed. They after all are the people who – in the 1930s and 1940s, when the future was yet to be, and still shone bright – had told the masses stories about revolutionary ardour and heroism of the following kind, which they had themselves wished were true:

[Chao I-man] had come to Harbin some months before. Here she had set up another 'family'. The other member of the 'family' was Tsao, secretary of the Federation of Trade Unions of Manchuria. Chao I-man was his secretary. In order to cover their revolutionary activities, they called themselves man and wife to better cope with the enemy's investigations.

In the last two years I-man had not lived a single quiet day. Shortly after her return to Shanghai, her child had contracted pleurisy and grew thinner and thinner. At first she had thought of taking him to Szechuan to be cared for by her Second Sister. But then she heard that Second Sister was also busy doing revolutionary work. Among other things, I-man heard that once when Second Sister was transporting arms for a peasants' uprising, she was detected by the enemy and only escaped by rolling down a steep mountainside with the weapons in her arms. How could I-man add to her sister's burdens at such a time!

Then she had a bit of luck, for she was transferred to the Central Headquarters, where she made the acquaintance of her husband Chen Ta-pang's sister. After some discussion they decided to take the child to Wuhan to Chen Ta-pang's brother's home. But as soon as she reached Hankow her whereabouts was discovered by enemy agents who started to shadow her and attempted to arrest her. She had to leave her child in a hurry and run away in the midst of a storm. She did not even have time to kiss him goodbye.

She returned to Shanghai and during all the time she was there she worked in the Central Headquarters, sometimes disguised as a school teacher and sometimes as a rich merchant's wife. Dangerous situations trained her nerves and made them particularly sensitive. When she heard a car honking she would instinctively look out of the window; and the sound of a cough or the ringing of a bell would keep her vigilant for a long while. For two years she slept without taking off her clothes or stockings. Every moment she was prepared to flee or to deal with searches or interrogations. This was a battle: keep alert when you're asleep; be ready to go to the enemy's prison when you are sitting down to dinner; have your answers ready for a court trial when you are going to contact a comrade. . . .[17]

But even revolutionary vigilance is sometimes not enough. Heroine Chao I-man was arrested, tried, and condemned to death; and she was carried off to meet it in an open cart:

The singing rang in the ears of the people and soared to the clear blue sky. The cart drove outside the Little North Gate and stopped. Chao I-man looked towards the east. The sun had just climbed above the mountain top, its bloody rays lighting up her face, lighting up all her body. She staggered down from the cart, but when two of the enemy agents made to take hold of her she struggled free, refusing to be stained by their dirty hands.

Chao I-man moved forward a couple of steps, the gentle morning breeze stirring her dishevelled hair. She took another glance at the green earth. Soon the 'green curtains' would rise on sorghum fields and from there the comrades would shoot at the enemy. . . .

At this moment gunfire sounded. Chao I-man lurched forward, but did not fall. With all her strength she shouted, 'Long live the Communist Party of China!' and the disorderly shots failed to drown this stubborn voice. . . .

With bullets and bayonets the villains took away Chao I-man's life. She was only thirty-one when she fell. But the value of a life is not judged by the length of its existence. The moment it was above the horizon, this young life showed the blinding radiance and fiery vigour of the morning sun of summer![18]

For what did Chao I-man die? One of contemporary China's most distinguished dissidents, who suffered repeatedly in the various campaigns described above but kept his courage and his convictions throughout, is Liu Binyan; and he deserves the last word:

I gave up my youth for the Communist Party in its struggle to seize state power. And now a handful of tyrants have betrayed the Party, turning themselves into the enemy of the people in the real sense of the word. My generation has thrown itself into the struggle led by the Communist Party in the hope that our children will lead a better life, and now it is precisely the best and brightest of their generation who have died at the butchers' hands, or are fugitives fleeing from arrest.

Looking forward now, I do not indulge in sentiment. The price that has been wrested from the Chinese people was inevitable, I suppose. We greeted the founding of this new state with wild acclaim in 1949; we submitted so docilely to its rule from the fifties right through to the seventies. What is there for me to say? But the Chinese people have now changed. They will not tolerate this state any longer. The handful of octogenarians and the privileged bureaucratic clique whom they represent will neither change their ways nor hand over power. Thus they are doomed to destruction. Yes, the people will pay a bloody price, but in the end they will shake off this monstrous thing that is draining them of their life's blood.[19]

CHRONOLOGY

The following is intended as a guide only. The early dates are approximate and only the main dynasties are given.

c. 1600–1066 BC	SHANG	
1066–221 BC	ZHOU	Western Zhou (1066–771 BC)
		Eastern Zhou (770–256 BC)
		Spring and Autumn Period (722–475 BC)
		Warring States (475–221 BC)
221–206 BC	QIN	
206 BC–AD 220	HAN	Western (Former) Han (206 BC–AD 23)
		Eastern (Later) Han (25–220)
220–65	THREE KINGDOMS	
265–581	PERIOD OF DISUNION	
581–618	SUI	
618–907	TANG	
907–60	PERIOD OF DISUNION	
960–1279	SONG	Northern Song (960–1127)
		Southern Song (1127–1279)
1279–1368	YUAN	
1368–1644	MING	
1644–1911	QING	
1912–49	THE REPUBLIC OF CHINA	
1949–	THE PEOPLE'S REPUBLIC OF CHINA	

NOTES

Many of the translations from the Chinese are our own. Where this is the case we have merely given the author and the translated title of the work, followed by the romanized Chinese title. All works are published in London unless otherwise stated.

1. POINTS OF ENTRY: PEKING AND SHANGHAI

1. Harold Acton, *Memoirs of an Aesthete*, 1948, p. 276.
2. Ibid., pp. 276–7.
3. Harold Acton, *Peonies and Ponies*, 1941, p. 160.
4. Marco Polo, *The Book of Ser Marco Polo, the Venetian*, trans. Henry Yule, 1871, Vol. 1, pp. 331–2.
5. S.T. Coleridge, 'Kubla Khan', lines 1–11.
6. A.B. Freeman-Mitford, *The Attaché at Peking*, 1900, pp. 61–2.
7. Osbert Sitwell, *Escape With Me!*, 1939, pp. 177–8.
8. Ibid., p. 267.
9. Ann Bridge, *Peking Picnic*, 1932, p. 68.
10. Pierre Teilhard de Chardin, *Letters from a Traveller*, 1962, p. 106.
11. Freeman-Mitford, op. cit., pp. 62–3.
12. Ibid., p. 63.
13. Ibid., p. 64.
14. W.H. Auden and Christopher Isherwood, *Journey to a War*, 1934, p. 76.
15. C.A.S. Williams, *Outlines of Chinese Symbolism and Art Motives*, Shanghai, 1941, p. 26.
16. Bridge, op. cit., pp. 24–5.
17. Peter Quennell, *A Superficial Journey Through Tokyo and Peking*, 1932, pp. 171–2.
18. Jin Shoushen, *Beijing Legends*, Beijing, 1982, pp. 128–31.
19. Ibid., p. 131.
20. Reginald E. Johnston, *Twilight in the Forbidden City*, 1934, p. 174.
21. Sitwell, op. cit., pp. 271–2.
22. Pierre Loti, *Les Derniers jours de Pékin*, Paris, 1902, p. 283.
23. Simone de Beauvoir, *The Long March*, 1958, p. 67.
24. Somerset Maugham, *On a Chinese Screen*, 1922, pp. 33–4.
25. Ibid., pp. 34–5.
26. Paraphrase of Jin Shoushen, *Beijing Legends*, op. cit., pp. 101–4.
27. Bertrand Russell, *Autobiography*, 1978, p. 362.

28. Acton, *Memoirs of an Aesthete*, p. 285.
29. Thomas Woodrooffe, *River of Golden Sand*, 1936, pp. 16–17.
30. Auden and Isherwood, op. cit., pp. 237–8.
31. Mao Tun, *Midnight*, Beijing, 1979, pp. 8–10.
32. Acton, *Memoirs of an Aesthete*, pp. 286–7.
33. Russell, op. cit., p. 262.
34. Acton, *Memoirs of an Aesthete*, p. 290.
35. Ibid., p. 291.
36. Pan Ling, *Old Shanghai: Gangsters in Paradise*, Hong Kong, 1984, p. 39.
37. Tsai Chin, *Daughter of Shanghai*, 1988, pp. 34–5.
38. Lytton Strachey, *Eminent Victorians*, pp. 229–30.
39. Vicki Baum, *Shanghai '37*, reprinted Hong Kong, 1986, preface by H.J. Lethbridge, pp. ix–x.
40. Auden and Isherwood, op. cit., pp. 239–40.
41. J.G. Ballard, *Empire of the Sun*, 1985, p. 56.
42. Woodrooffe, op. cit., pp. 29–30.
43. Acton, *Memoirs of an Aesthete*, pp. 292–4.
44. Pan Ling, *In Search of Old Shanghai*, Hong Kong, 1982, p. 1.

2. MUTUAL PERCEPTIONS

1. Graham Peck, *Through the Great Wall*, 1945, pp. 132–3.
2. Anon. ('A Resident of Peking'), *China As It Really Is*, 1912, pp. 110–11, 112.
3. Thomas Woodrooffe, *River of Golden Sand*, 1936, pp. 174–5.
4. Peter Fleming, *The Siege at Peking*, 1962, pp. 46–7.
5. Ibid., p. 47.
6. William Gill, *The River of Golden Sand*, 1883, pp. 87–8.
7. W.H. Auden and Christopher Isherwood, *Journey to a War*, 1934, pp. 149–50.
8. Fleming, op. cit., p. 42.
9. Quoted ibid., p. 38.
10. Gill, op. cit. p. 22.
11. Ibid., pp. 45–6.
12. Ibid., pp. 7–8.
13. Ibid., pp. 85–6.
14. Ibid., p. 86.
15. A.B. Freeman-Mitford, *The Attaché at Peking*, 1900, pp. 168–9.
16. E. McCormack, *Audacious Angles on China*, Appleton, New York, 1924, pp. 78, 79.
17. J.R. Chitty, *Things Seen in China*, 1912, p. 162.
18. Gill, op. cit., p. 129.
19. Ibid., pp. 155–6.
20. Freeman-Mitford, op. cit., p. 64.
21. G.E. Morrison, *An Australian in China*, 1895, pp. 100–1.
22. W. Somerset Maugham, *On a Chinese Screen*, 1922, pp. 180–1.

23. Morrison, op. cit., pp. 101–2.
24. Freeman-Mitford, op. cit., pp. 190–9.
25. Lin Yutang, *My Country and My People*, 1936, p. 158.
26. Ibid., p. 159.
27. Ibid., pp. 159–60.
28. Quoted ibid., p. 160.
29. Ibid., p. 161.
30. Lu Xun, *The True Story of Ah Q*, trans. Yang Hsien-yi and Gladys Yang, Beijing, 1953, pp. 15–18.

3. RIVERS AND ROUTES

1. Mildred Cable and Francesca French, *The Gobi Desert*, 1942, p. 19.
2. Ibid., pp. 19–20.
3. Osbert Sitwell, *Escape With Me!*, 1939, p.ix.
4. After Szuma Chien (Sima Qian), *Selections from Records of the Historian*, trans. Yang Hsien-yi and Gladys Yang, Beijing, 1979, pp. 410–11.
5. M. Aurel Stein, *Ruins of Desert Cathay*, 1912, Vol. 2, p. 63.
6. Marco Polo, *The Book of Ser Marco Polo, the Venetian*, trans. Henry Yule, 1871, Vol. 1, p. 184.
7. Stein, op. cit., Vol. 2., p. 31.
8. Ibid., Vol. 2, p. 169.
9. Ibid., Vol. 2, p. 172.
10. Harold Acton, *Memoirs of an Aesthete*, 1948, p. 366.
11. Fa Hien, *A Record of Buddhistic Kingdoms*, trans. James Legge, Oxford, 1886, p. 12.
12. *History of the Zhou Dynasty (Zhoushu)*, chapter 50.
13. Cable and French, op. cit., pp. 15–16.
14. Zhang Xianliang, *Getting Used to Dying*, 1991, p. 261.
15. Bai Juyi, 'Song of Never Ending Sorrow' ('Chang hen ge'), lines 36–42.
16. Shen Fu, *Six Records of a Floating Life (Fu sheng liu ji)*, chapter 2.
17. W.H. Auden and Christopher Isherwood, *Journey to a War*, 1934, pp. 129–30.
18. Langdon Warner, *The Long Old Road in China*, 1927, p. 52.
19. Ibid., pp. 54–5.
20. *Ennin's Diary. The Record of a Pilgrimage to China*, trans. E. Reischauer, New York, 1955, p. 314.
21. Auden and Isherwood, op. cit., p. 130.
22. Pierre Teilhard de Chardin, *Letters from a Traveller*, 1962, p. 90.
23. Ibid., pp. 87–8.
24. Lin Qing, *Traces of a Wild Swan on the Snow (Hong xue yin yuan)*.
25. Lord Macartney, quoted in Aubrey Singer, *The Lion and the Dragon*, 1992, p. 21.
26. Li Daoyuan, *Commentary on the Classic of Water (Shuijingzhu)*, trans. James H. Hargett in *On the Road in Twelfth Century China*, Stuttgart, 1989, p. 14.

27. G.E. Morrison, *An Australian in China*, 1895, p. 19.
28. John Barrow, *Travels in China*, 1806, p. 542.
29. Fan Chengda, *The Canluan Record* (*Canluan lu*), 16–17th days.
30. P. Hanan, *The Chinese Vernacular Story*, 1981, p. 189.
31. Liu Zongyuan, *The Tale of Red Li* (*Li ji zhuan*).
32. William Gill, *The River of Golden Sand*, 1883, p. 19.
33. Zhang Jiuling, 'Record of Opening the Road over the Great Yü Pass' ('Kai da yu ling lu ji').
34. Auden and Isherwood, op. cit., p. 199.
35. Fan Chengda, op. cit., 26th day.
36. Acton, op. cit., pp. 294–5.
37. Noël Coward, *Autobiography*, 1992 edition, p. 218.
38. Paul Theroux, *Riding the Iron Rooster*, 1988, p. 140.
39. Ibid., pp. 364–5.

4. THE POET IN THE LANDSCAPE

1. Pierre Teilhard de Chardin, *Letters from a Traveller*, 1962, p. 74.
2. Ann Bridge, *Peking Picnic*, 1932, pp. 82–4.
3. Harold Acton, *Memoirs of an Aesthete*, 1948, p. 280.
4. Ann Bridge, op. cit., p. 183.
5. Han Yü, translated in A. Waley, *The Secret History of the Mongols*, 1963, pp. 167–8.
6. Liu Zongyuan, 'Prison Mountain' ('Qiu shan fu').
7. Han Yü, 'Memorial of acknowledgement as Prefect of Chaozhou' ('Chao zhou ci shi xian shang bao').
8. Liu Zongyuan, 'Record of Flat Iron Lake' ('Gu mu tan ji').
9. Liu Zongyuan, 'Preface to the Poem "Fool's Stream" ' ('Yu xi shi xu').
10. Qu Yuan *et al.*, *The Songs of the South*, trans. David Hawkes, Harmondsworth, 1985, pp. 254–5.
11. Liu Zongyuan, 'Rain and Wind at Miluo River' (Mi luo yu feng').
12. Liu Zongyuan, 'Mourning Qu Yuan' ('Diao Qu Yuan').
13. Asia Watch, *Anthems of Defeat: Crackdown in Hunan Province*, New York, 1992, p. 193.
14. Su Shi, 'The Qu Yuan Temple' ('Qu Yuan miao fu')
15. Mencius, 5a.7.
16. Tao Yuanming, 'Returning to my Country Home', Poem 1 ('Gui yuan tian ju').
17. *History of the Han Dynasty* (*Hanshu*), 62:17b–21b.
18. Ibid.
19. Zhuangzi, Chapter 17.
20. Jia Dao, 'Searching for the hermit but not finding him' ('Xun yin zhe bu yu')
21. Shen Fu, *Six Records of a Floating Life* (*Fu sheng liu ji*), chapter 2.
22. Tsao Hsueh-chin and Kao Ngo, *A Dream of Red Mansions*, trans. Yang Hsien-yi and Gladys Yang, Beijing, 1978, Vol. 1, pp. 227–9.

23. Ibid., p. 233.
24. Ibid., p. 235.
25. Sir William Temple, 'Of Gardening', in *The Works of Sir William Temple*, 1770, pp. 229–30.
26. Lord Macartney's journal, quoted in John Barrow, *Travels in China*, 1806, pp. 128–30.
27. Barrow, ibid., p. 123.
28. Tom Stoppard, *Arcadia*, 1993, p. 12.
29. Laozi, *The Way and the Power* (*Dao de jing*), chapter 80.
30. Ji Cheng, 'Treatise on Gardening' ('Yuan ye'), trans. Osvald Sirén, *Gardens of China*, New York, 1949, p. 14.
31. Shen Fu, op. cit.
32. Colin Thubron, *Behind the Wall*, 1987, pp. 134–7.
33. Marco Polo, *The Book of Ser Marco Polo, the Venetian*, trans. Henry Yule, 1871, Vol. 2, p. 162.
34. Archie Bell, *The Spell of China*, 1917, pp. 165–7.
35. Bertrand Russell, *Autobiography*, 1969, p. 359.
36. A.C. Graham, *Poems of the West Lake*, 1990, p. 19.
37. Ibid., p. 23.
38. Thubron, op. cit., p. 163.

5. LITERATURE AND LITERATI

1. Szuma Chien, *Selections from Records of the Historian*, trans. Yang Hsien-yi and Gladys Yang, Beijing, 1979, pp. 177–8.
2. H.A. Giles, *A History of Chinese Literature*, New York, 1901, p. 7.
3. Liu Hsieh, *The Literary Mind and the Carving of Dragons*, trans. Vincent Yu-ching Shih, Hong Kong, 1983, p. 3.
4. Lu Chih, 'Essay on Literature', trans. Shih-Hsiang Chen in *Anthology of Chinese Literature*, ed. Cyril Birch, New York, 1965, pp. 204, 207.
5. 'Li Qingzhao's Preface to *Records on Metal and Stone*', trans. Stephen Owen in *Remembrances: The Experience of the Past in Classical Chinese Literature*, Cambridge, Ma., 1986, pp. 82, 84–5.
6. Tsao Hsueh-chin and Kao Ngo, *A Dream of Red Mansions*, trans. Yang Hsien-yi and Gladys Yang, Beijing, 1978, Vol. 2, pp. 137–9.
7. Lytton Strachey, 'An Anthology', in *Characters and Commentaries*, 1933, pp. 148–53.
8. Lin Yutang, *My Country and My People*, 1936, p. 263.
9. Wu Ching-tzu, *The Scholars*, trans. Yang Hsien-yi and Gladys Yang, Beijing, 1957, pp. 27–8.
10. Ibid., pp. 28–9.
11. Ibid., p. 29.
12. Wong Su-ling, *Daughter of Confucius*, 1938, pp. 97–101.
13. Ibid., pp. 101–4.
14. Stephen Spender and David Hockney, *China Diary*, 1982, pp. 44–5.
15. John Webb, *Essay Towards the Primitive Language*, 1669, pp. 32–3.

16. *China As It Really Is*, by 'A Resident in Peking', 1912, pp. 154, 166.
17. Yuan Mei, 'Thoughts on Master Huang's Book Borrowing', trans. D.E. Pollard in *Renditions*, 33 and 34 (Spring and Autumn 1990), p. 193.

6. PLEASURES

1. Thomas Woodrooffe, *River of Golden Sand*, 1936, pp. 158–9.
2. Ibid., pp. 159–60.
3. W.H. Auden and Christopher Isherwood, *Journey to a War*, 1934, pp. 40–1.
4. Ibid., pp. 230–1.
5. Colin Thubron, *Behind the Wall*, 1987, pp. 190–1.
6. Peter Mundy, *The Travels of Peter Mundy in Europe and Asia*, ed. Sir Richard Temple, 1907–36, p. 190.
7. Lin Yutang, *My Country and My People*, 1936, pp. 317–18.
8. Ibid., pp. 328, 319.
9. Ibid., pp. 321–2.
10. Zhang Dai 'Six Essays', trans. D.E. Pollard and Soh Yong Kuan in *Renditions*, 33 and 34 (Spring and Autumn 1990), pp. 163–4.
11. Lin Yutang, op. cit., p. 323.
12. William Gill, *The River of Golden Sand*, 1883, pp. 47–4.
13. A.B. Freeman-Mitford, *The Attaché at Peking*, 1900, p. 272.
14. A.H. Smith, *Chinese Characteristics*, 1902, p. 187.
15. *China As It Really Is*, by 'A Resident of Peking', 1912, p. 131.
16. G.E Morrison, *An Australian in China*, 1895, pp. 46–8.
17. Freeman-Mitford, op. cit., p. 160.
18. Henry McAleavy, trans., *That Chinese Woman: The Life of Sai-chin-hua*, 1959, p. 17.
19. Mencius, 4a.26.
20. Mme Wellington Koo, *No Feast Lasts Forever*, New York, 1975, pp. 29–31.
21. Pan Ling, *Old Shanghai: Gangsters in Paradise*, Hong Kong, 1984, pp. 34–5.
22. *Marco Polo: The Description of the World*, trans. A.C. Moule and Paul Pelliot, 1938, pp. 205–6.
23. Ibid., pp. 304–5.
24. Marco Polo, *The Book of Ser Marco Polo, the Venetian*, trans. Henry Yule, 1871, Vol. 2, pp. 27–8.
25. Anon., *The Plum in the Golden Vase*, trans. David Tod Roy, Princeton, 1993, pp. 90–1.
26. Li Yü, *The Before Midnight Scholar*, trans. Richard Martin, 1963, p. 172.
27. Ibid., p. 175.
28. Marco Polo, *The Book of Ser Marco Polo, the Venetian*, Vol. 1, p. 395.
29. Thubron, op. cit., pp. 15–17.
30. Gill, op. cit., p. 7.
31. Auden and Isherwood, op. cit., p. 91.

32. Woodrooffe, op. cit., pp. 71–2.
33. Harold Acton, *Memoirs of an Aesthete*, 1948, pp. 292–4.
34. Freeman-Mitford, op. cit., pp. 101–2.
35. Auden and Isherwood, op. cit., pp. 62–4.
36. Mildred Cable and Francesca French, *The Gobi Desert*, 1942, p. 38.
37. Confucius, *The Analects (Lun yu)*, 7.14.
38. Lin Yutang, op cit., p. 307.
39. Shen Fu, *Six Records of a Floating Life (Fu sheng liu ji)*, chapter 4.

7. GODS, GHOSTS AND DEMONS

1. H.A. Giles, *The Civilisation of China*, 1911, p. 85.
2. Ibid., p. 57.
3. Liang Qichao, quoted in C.K. Yang, *Religion in Chinese Society*, 1961, p. 5.
4. Hu Shi, 'China's Sterile Inheritance', in Hu Shih and Lin Yu-tang, *China's Own Critics*, Peking, 1932, p. 66.
5. H.A. Giles, op. cit., pp. 55–6.
6. M. Simpson Culbertson, *Darkness in the Flowery Land*, 1857, pp. 123–5.
7. E.R. Huc, *The Chinese Empire*, 1855, Vol. 2, p. 198.
8. Derk Bodde, 'Dominent Ideas in the Formation of Chinese Culture' in *China*, ed. Harley F. MacNair, Berkeley, 1946, pp. 18–21.
9. Qian Duansheng, quoted in C.K. Yang, op. cit., pp. 5–6.
10. Bertrand Russell, *Autobiography*, 1969, p. 371.
11. Han Wen-kung (Han Yü), 'On a Bone from Buddha's Body', trans. H.A. Giles in *Gems of Chinese Literature*, New York, 1965, p. 127.
12. *Ennin's Diary: The Record of a Pilgrimage to China*, trans. E. Reischauer, New York, 1955, p. 340.
13. T.T. Meadows, *The Chinese and Their Rebellions*, 1856, p. 66.
14. A. Waley, *Monkey*, 1942, pp. 73–4.
15. G. Willoughby-Meade, *Chinese Ghouls and Goblins*, 1928, p. 3.
16. Kong Demao and Ke Lan, *The House of Confucius*, 1988, pp. 69–70.
17. Ibid., pp. 68–9.
18. Thomas Woodrooffe, *River of Golden Sand*, 1936, p. 72.
19. John Barrow, *Travels in China*, 1806, pp. 509–10.
20. Peter Fleming, *The Siege at Peking*, 1959, p. 40.
21. Paraphrase of H.A. Giles, *Strange Stories from a Chinese Studio*, Shanghai, 1908, pp. 448–9.
22. Liu Zongyuan, 'On the Zha Sacrifice' ('Zha shuo').
23. Xunzi, chapter 17.
24. Zhuangzi, chapter 18.
25. Ibid., chapter 32.
26. Liu Zongyuan, 'An Explanation of Heaven' ('Tian shuo').
27. *Handbook of Ritual (Yi ji)*.
28. Mozi, chapter 39.

29. Qu Yuan, *Li Sao and Other Poems of Qu Yuan*, trans. Yang Hsien-yi and Gladys Yang, Beijing, 1953, pp. 65–6.
30. Du Fu, 'The Road to Peng ya' ('Peng ya xing').
31. Wang Chong, 'On Spirits', trans. Herbert A. Giles in *Gems of Chinese Literature*, 1965, pp. 94–5.
32. Willoughby-Meade, op. cit., p. 2.
33. Osbert Sitwell, *Escape With Me!*, 1939, pp. 247–9.
34. Fleming, op. cit., p. 41.
35. L.H. Dudley Buxton, *The Eastern Road*, 1924, p. 53.
36. G.E. Morrison, *An Australian in China*, 1895, p. 5.
37. Ibid., p. 6.
38. John Francis Davies, *China during the War and since the Peace*, 1852, Vol. 2, p. 230.
39. Carl Crow, *Handbook for China*, 1933, pp. 245–7.
40. Harold Acton, *Memoirs of an Aesthete*, 1948, p. 280.
41. Ann Bridge, *Peking Picnic*, 1932, p. 98.
42. William Empson, 'The Faces of Buddha', reprinted in *The Oxford Book of Essays*, ed. J. Gross, 1991, p. 535.
43. Wu Chi-yu, 'A Study of Han-Shan', *T'oung Pao*, XLV (1957), p. 420.

8. RITES AND FESTIVALS

1. John Barrow, *Travels in China*, 1806, p. 190.
2. Confucius, *The Analects (Lun yu)*, 10.12.
3. Ibid, 10.24.
4. Barrow, op. cit., p. 198.
5. Ibid., p. 193.
6. Archie Bell, *The Spell of China*, 1917, pp. 280–1.
7. Ibid., pp. 287–8.
8. Marco Polo, *The Book of Ser Marco Polo, the Venetian*, trans. Henry Yule, 2 vols., 1871, Vol. 1, p. 343.
9. Osbert Sitwell, *Escape With Me!*, 1939, pp. 243–4.
10. Ibid., pp. 244–5.
11. Ibid., p. 244.
12. Mozi, *Mo Tzu: Basic Writings*, trans. Burton Watson, 1963, pp. 73–4.
13. Szuma Chien, *Selections from Records of the Historian*, trans. Yang Hsien-yi and Gladys Yang, Beijing, 1979, p. 186.
14. 'The Testamentary Edict of Emperor Wen', trans. Burton Watson in *Anthology of Chinese Literature*, ed. Cyril Birch, New York, 1965, pp. 86–7.
15. J.R. Chitty, *Things Seen in China*, 1912, pp. 241–6.
16. Arthur Miller, *'Salesman' in Beijing*, 1984, p. 214.
17. Bell, op. cit., pp. 243–4.
18. Mrs Arnold Foster, *In the Valley of the Yangtse*, 1899, pp. 79–81.
19. G.E. Morrison, *An Australian in China*, 1895, p. 195.

20. Huang Tingqian, 'The Clear Bright Festival' ('Qing ming'), trans. Susan Whitfield and A.C. Grayling.
21. Kong Demao and Ke Lan, *House of Confucius*, 1988, pp. 120–1.
22. Ibid., pp. 154–5.
23. Marco Polo, op. cit., Vol. 1, p. 346.
24. E.R. Huc, *Travels in Tartary, Thibet and China*, 1900, Vol. 2, pp. 19–20.
25. Sitwell, op. cit., pp. 168–9.
26. Ibid., pp. 169–71.
27. Reginald Johnston, *Lion and Dragon in Northern China*, 1910, pp. 183–4.
28. Ibid., pp. 184–5.
29. Mildred Cable and Francesca French, *The Gobi Desert*, 1942, p. 31.
30. Shen Congwen, *The Border Town and Other Stories*, Beijing, 1981, pp. 18–19.
31. E.T.C. Werner, *Myths and Legends of China*, 1922, pp. 189–90.
32. Amy Tan, *The Joy Luck Club*, 1990, pp. 68–9.
33. J. Gernet, *Daily Life in China*, trans. H.M. Wright, 1962, p. 196.
34. Li Qingzhao, 'To the Tune "Drunk Under the Shade of Flowers" ' (Zui hua yin'), trans. Susan Whitfield and A.C. Grayling.

9. SONS OF HEAVEN

1. *The Book of History* (*Shu jing*), quoted by Mencius 5a.5.
2. 'Announcement to the Duke of Shao' in *The Book of History* (*Shu jing*).
3. Confucius, *The Analects* (*Lun yu*), 12.19.
4. Mencius, 2a.1.
5. 'Biography of Lord Shang' in *Records of the Historian* (*Shi ji*).
6. Xunzi, *The Writings of Xunzi*.
7. 'Biography of Li Si' in *Records of the Historian* (*Shi ji*).
8. Xunzi, *The Writings of Xunzi*.
9. 'Biography of the First Emperor' in *Records of the Historian* (*Shi ji*).
10. Jia Yi, 'The Faults of Qin' ('Guo Qin lun').
11. Marco Polo, *The Book of Ser Marco Polo, the Venetian*, trans. Henry Yule, 1871, Vol. 1, p. 393.
12. Hugh Trevor-Roper, *The Past and The Present: History and Sociology*, 1969.
13. Archie Bell, *The Spell of China*, 1917, pp. 237–8.
14. Osbert Sitwell, *Escape With Me!*, 1939, p. 201.
15. *The Book of History*: 'The Canon of Yao' (*Shu jing*).
16. Confucius, *The Analects* (*Lun yu*), 12.7.
17. A.R. Colquhoun, *China in Transformation*, 1883, p. 296.
18. E.R. Huc, *Travels in Tartary, Thibet and China*, 1900, Vol. 1, p. 251.
19. Letter from Father Bouvet to Louis XIV, trans. Jonathan D. Spence in 'Western Perceptions of China', in *Heritage of China*, ed. Paul Ropp, Berkeley, Ca., 1990, pp. 1–14.
20. Marco Polo, op. cit., Vol. 1, p. 295.
21. John Barrow, *Travels in China*, 1806, p. 198.

22. Ibid., p. 66.
23. Willard Straight, 'An American in Asia', in *Asia*, xx. 9 (1918), pp. 864–5.
24. Reginald Johnston, *Twilight in the Forbidden City*, 1934, p. 68.
25. Lady Susan Townley, quoted ibid. p. 69.
26. Princess Der Ling, *Two Years in the Forbidden City*, 1914, pp. 356–62.
27. Ibid., p. 356.
28. Johnston, op. cit., pp. 69–70.
29. Ibid., pp. 72–3.

10. COMMUNIST CHINA

1. Mao Zedong, quoted in Stephen Spender and David Hockney, *China Diary*, 1982, p. 11.
2. Colin Thubron, *Behind the Wall*, 1987, pp. 36–7.
3. Harrison E. Salisbury, *The Long March*, 1985, p. 1.
4. Agnes Smedley, *China Correspondent*, 1984, pp. 142–3.
5. H. Forman, *Report From Red China*, 1946, pp. 154–5.
6. Ibid., p. 155.
7. Ibid., pp. 86–9.
8. John Gittings, *China Changes Face*, Oxford, 1989, p. 203.
9. B. Michael Frolic, *Mao's People*, 1980, pp. 181–3.
10. Ibid., pp. 183–4.
11. Ibid., pp. 184–5.
12. Quoted in Gittings, op. cit., p. 3.
13. Li Xiao Jun, *The Long March to the Fourth of June*, 1989, p. 65.
14. Ibid., p. 57.
15. Frolic, op. cit., pp. 72–4.
16. Ibid., pp. 170–2.
17. Chang Lin and Shu Yang, *Better to Stand and Die: The Story of Chao-I Man*, Beijing, 1960, pp. 100–1.
18. Ibid., pp. 175–6.
19. Liu Binyan, *A Higher Kind of Loyalty*, 1990, pp. 282–3.

ACKNOWLEDGEMENTS

The authors and publishers would like to thank the following for kindly
giving permission to reproduce copyright material:

Abner Stein, *The Joy Luck Club* by Amy Tan, © 1989 Amy Tan.

André Deutsch, *The Before Midnight Scholar* by Li Yu, trans. by Richard
Martin, © Grove Press 1965.

Asia Watch, *Anthems of Defeat: Crackdown in Hunan Province*, Human Rights
Watch, 1992.

Chatto & Windus, *Daughter of Shanghai* by Tsai Chin, ed. Jason Goodwin;
Peonies and Ponies by Harold Acton.

Chinese University Press, *The Literary Mind and the Carving of Dragons* by
Liu Hsieh, trans. Vincent Yu-chung Shih.

Curtis Brown Group Ltd., London, *My Country and My People* by Lin
Yutang, © Lin Yutang.

Faber and Faber Limited, *Journey to a War* by W.H. Auden and Christopher
Isherwood; *Arcadia* by Tom Stoppard.

Nicholas Fleming, *The Siege at Peking* by Peter Fleming.

Franz Steiner Verlag Weisbaden GmbH, Stuttgart, *On the Road in Twelfth
Century China* by James Hargett.

Grove/Atlantic Inc., *Anthology of Chinese Literature* ed. Cyril Birch, © 1965.

Hamish Hamilton Ltd., *Riding the Iron Rooster* by Paul Theroux, © Cape
Cod Scriveners Company, 1988.

HarperCollins Publishers Ltd., *Empire of the Sun* by J.G. Ballard; *Letter from
a Traveller* by P. Teilhard de Chardin; *Autobiography* by Bertrand Russell,
George Allen & Unwin; *China Correspondent* by Agnes Smedley, Pandora;
Monkey, trans. Arthur Waley, George Allen & Unwin; *The Secret History
of the Mongols* by Arthur Waley, George Allen & Unwin; *Getting Used
to Dying* by Zhang Xianliang.

Harvard University Press, *The Chinese Vernacular Story* by Patrick Hanan,
© 1981 The President and Fellows of Harvard College; *Mao's People* by
Michael B. Frolic, © 1980 The President and Fellows of Harvard College;
Remembrances: The Experience of the Past in Classical Chinese Literature by
Stephen Owen, © 1986 The President and Fellows of Harvard College.

Heinemann Asia, *Old Shanghai: Gangsters in Paradise* by Pan Ling.

William Heinemann Ltd., *Behind the Wall* by Colin Thubron; *On a Chinese Screen* by W. Somerset Maugham.

David Higham Associates, *Memoirs of an Aesthete* by Harold Acton; *Shanghai '37* by Vicki Baum © Lert Family Trust; *Escape With Me!* by Osbert Sitwell, © Frang Magro Esq.

Hodder & Stoughton Publishers, *The Gobi Desert* by Mildred Cable and Francesca French.

Joint Publishing (HK) Ltd., *In Search of Old Shanghai* by Pan Ling, 1982.

Jennifer Kavanagh, *The House of Confucius* by Kong Demao and Ke Lan, published by Corgi at £3.99, © in this edition (1988) by Frances Wood.

Kelly & Walsh Ltd., *Handbook for China* by Carl Crow.

Methuen London, *Autobiography* by Noël Coward (Mandarin pb); *A Higher Kind of Loyalty* by Liu Binyan; *'Salesman' in Beijing* by Arthur Miller.

Oxford University Press, *China Changes Face* by John Gittings, © John Gittings 1989.

Pan Books, *The Long March* by Harrison E. Salisbury.

Penguin Books Ltd., 'Mourning My Lot' by Qi Jian from *The Songs of the South*, trans. David Hawkes, © David Hawkes, 1985.

Peters, Fraser and Dunlop Group Ltd., *Peking Picnic* by Ann Bridge, Virago 1991.

Princeton University Press, *The Plum in the Golden Vase* trans. by David Tod Roy.

Renditions Paperbacks, 'Spring Theme: Above the Lake' by Bai Juyi, trans. A.C. Graham; 'Thoughts on Master Huang's Book Borrowing' by Yuan Mei, trans. D.E. Pollard; 'Six Essays' by Zhang Dai, trans. D.E. Pollard and Soh Yong Kuan.

Routledge and Kegan Paul, *The Eastern Road* by L.H. Dudley Buxton; *Travels in Tartary, Thibet and China* by E.R. Huc, trans. W. Hazlitt.

Thames & Hudson Ltd., *China Diary* by S. Spender and David Hockney, 1982 © Steven Spender and David Hockney.

University of California Press, *Heritage of China: Contemporary Perspectives on Chinese Civilization* by Paul Ropp (ed.), © 1990 The Regents of the University of California.

Wellsweep Press, 'Drinking by the Lake: Clear Sky at First, Then Rain' by Su Shi, trans. A.C. Graham.

INDEX